Margaret Elizabeth Sangster

A Manual of the Missions of the Reformed Dutch Church in America

Margaret Elizabeth Sangster

A Manual of the Missions of the Reformed Dutch Church in America

ISBN/EAN: 9783337296216

Printed in Europe, USA, Canada, Australia, Japan

Cover: Foto ©Lupo / pixelio.de

More available books at **www.hansebooks.com**

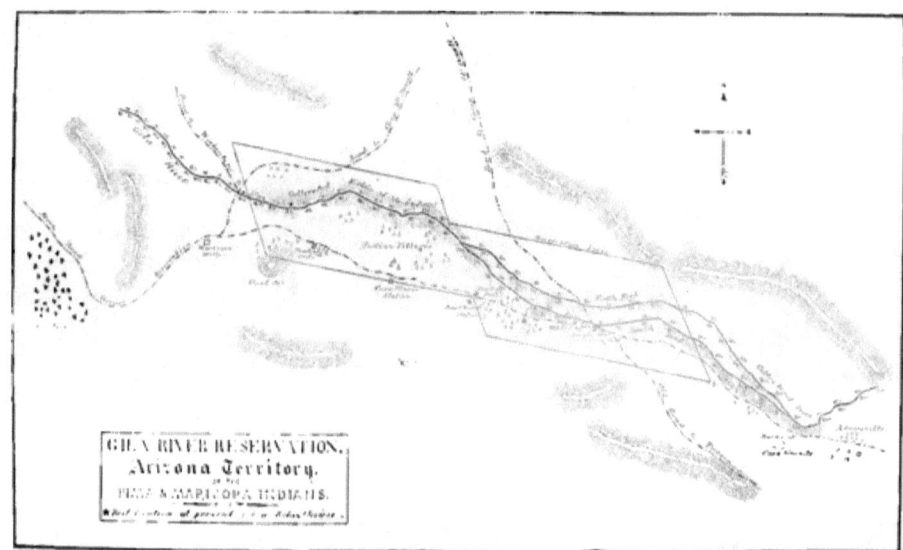

REFORMED CHURCH AND PARSONAGE AT YOKOHAMA, BAY-OF YEDO.

A MANUAL

OF THE

MISSIONS

OF THE

Reformed (Dutch) Church in America.

ISSUED BY THE

Woman's Board of Foreign Missions.

EDITED

MRS. MARGARET E. SANGSTER.

New York:
BOARD OF PUBLICATION OF THE REFORMED CHURCH IN AMERICA,
34 VESEY ST.
1877.

TABLE OF CONTENTS.

	PAGE
INTRODUCTION.	vii

INDIA.

	PAGE
HISTORICAL SKETCH OF THE ARCOT MISSION. By Rev. J. W. Scudder, M.D.	1
CHITTOOR FEMALE SEMINARY. By Mrs. J. W. Scudder	101
CASTE GIRLS' SCHOOL AT VELLORE. By Miss Josephine Chapin.	106
VILLAGE WORK. By Mrs. Ezekiel Scudder.	109
HINDU WOMEN.	115
MOST SACRED OF HINDU TEMPLES.	121
TAJ MAHAL.	129
SACRED CITY OF HINDUS.	135
GRAND MOSQUE AT DELHI.	137
FREE READING ROOMS. By Rev. Jacob Chamberlain, M.D.	139
A BRAHMIN'S TESTIMONY.	143

BORNEO MISSION.

	PAGE
By Rev. Wm. H. Steele, D.D.	150

CHINA.

AMOY MISSION.	
By Rev. Wm Rankin Duryee, D.D.	172
WOMEN IN CHINA.	
By Miss Helen M. Van Doren.	187
MISCELLANEA.	191

JAPAN.

THE LAND OF THE RISING SUN.	
By Rev. Wm. E. Griffis.	211
EXPLANATION REGARDING THE CHURCH AT YOKOHAMA.	255
DAUGHTERS OF THE ISLES.	258
FERRIS SEMINARY.	
By Mrs. Mary E. Miller.	259
CHRISTMAS FESTIVAL.	278
SUMMER EXAMINATION.	281
A VISIT TO UYEDA.	
By Rev. E. R. Miller.	292
FIRST BAPTISM IN JAPAN.	
By Rev. G. F. Verbeck, D.D.	301
NAGASAKI AND THE GIRLS SCHOOL.	310
JAPANESE EMBASSY TO AMERICA.	
By the Editor.	313
WOMEN AS MISSIONARIES.	
By Rev. Elbert S. Porter, D.D.	316

ARIZONA. 326

INTRODUCTION.

THE MISSIONS OF THE REFORMED CHURCH IN AMERICA.

MISSIONARY enterprises have achieved their greatest gains in modern times, but the missionary spirit has always been a living force in the Church of our Lord. On the day in which the cloud received Him out of the sight of His sorrowing disciples, the Master uttered as His last command, "Go ye into all the world, and preach the Gospel to every creature!" On the wonderful day of Pentecost, the baptism of fire from on high lighted a flame, which shall never go out, till it is merged in the splendor which evermore surrounds the Throne of God. The missionary spirit, in whatever way it manifests itself, is the expression in human lives, of the constraining love of Him who gave up His life that we might be redeemed. In every age, from the Apostolic to the present, there has been somewhere, working to some extent, this desire to go forth and do good; for no soul can be truly converted without longing at once to tell the glad tidings, and win others into the kingdom.

The Church of the Reformation, moved with true zeal all over Europe. Superstition and idolatry fled before it, a new civilization was born, and history took a fresh start. The Church of the Netherlands, under the Cross, was distinguished for its sufferings, no less than for its catholicity. For eighty long heroic years, it resisted grandly the cruel bigotry of Spain, and the remorseless malignity of Rome. At last a free course was secured for the Word of God; and the Republic of Holland was the offspring of Protestant truth, deeply rooted in the popular heart.

Our Dutch ancestors planted the Reformed Church in this country, at a time when all Europe was convulsed with religious wars. Directly after its independent organization here, it took measures for rearing and training a missionary ministry. The condition first of the colonies, and afterwards of the States, required such a ministry. Toward the close of the last century, the New York Missionary Society was formed; and our Pastors, with the eloquent and illustrious Dr. John Livingston at their head, joined heartily in its efforts to Christianize outlying regions. How far that pioneer, associated missionary body, contributed to awaken missionary zeal and enterprise in the American Church, it would be difficult to determine. It is very certain, however, that it originated influences which, early in the present century, resulted in the formation of the American Board.

The General Synod of the Reformed Church, at the opening of the missionary era, appointed its own committee on Foreign Missions; but soon made arrangements to carry on its work with all the Evangelical Churches, then constituting the American Board. There were at that time, wise and thoughtful men who doubted the expediency of turning over our work, as a Church, into the hands of any merely voluntary agency. Still, there was no factious opposition. At length, experience in Borneo, Arcot, and Amoy, demonstrated the duty of conducting our Foreign Missions in our own way.

Decisive action was taken in 1857; and immediately the wisdom of the measure was amply justified by the increasing liberalities of the people, by augmented efforts to strengthen missions then established, and by endeavors to inaugurate new enterprises. For twenty years the experiment has been submitted to the care of Providence, with most encouraging results.

The Woman's Board of Foreign Missions of the Reformed Church has been organized as a fit and useful, as well as needed, auxiliary to the Synod's Foreign Board. Almost at once, those who composed it, were confronted with the lack of information concerning our mission fields, and the trouble of obtaining it. If the women of our Church were to be enlisted cordially in the work, it was essential that they should know where it was, by whom carried on, what were its important features, and what the cost of various departments. They must be brought into sympathy with the men and women who had gone to distant lands to tell the old, old story of Jesus and His love. The converts must cease to present themselves as vague and unreal phantoms of the imagination, and become to them flesh and blood, human beings with like passions and a like immortality with their own.

THIS VOLUME.

This Manual of Missions is the outgrowth of necessity. We looked about us, and finding only fragmentary details in the files of our religious papers, while it was inconvenient to apply to our Secretaries for each item as we wanted it, we decided to prepare an adequate book of reference. We have had, in its compilation, the generous help of those who were best able to speak on the subjects they have undertaken. We have divided it, so far as practicable, into topical sections, properly indexed, so that information desired may be readily found. We have given it an attractive form and dress. Its beautiful illustrations, clear type, and appropriate cover, fit it to lie as an ornament on the family table, where one and another may often handle it lovingly.

A moment's attention may be claimed for the cover, since its design is emblematic. The harp, palm-branch and dove in the foreground, are introduced as the symbols of peace, promise and praise. In contrast with these, a hideous idol peers from the jungle, and one of the most ancient of Buddhist temples, the Boodh Gya in Burmah, is represented. For more than two thousand years this temple and its predecessor on the same site, with the old tree at its rear walls, have been objects of barbaric adoration and heathen rites.

Our thanks are here rendered to the Rev. Dr. Jared W. Scudder, the Rev. Dr. Wm. R. Duryee, and the Rev. Wm. E. Griffis, for the painstaking and interesting papers they have presented us on India,

China, and Japan; to the Rev. T. S. Wynkoop for his careful monograph on the Temple of Juggernaut, and to the Rev. Dr. Wm. H. Steele for his retrospective article on our abandoned mission to Borneo. We are indebted also to the artists whose skill has embellished our pages, their interest having been kind and hearty. Mr Charles E. Sickles designed the cover, and Mr. F. S. Church the small vignettes.

Nor would we forget a grateful word of appreciation to the ladies: Mrs. Mary E. Miller, Mrs. Jared W. and Mrs. Ezekiel Scudder, and Miss Helen M. Van Doren, who have told for us, in simple language, the story of their labors among heathen women. Many will be pleased to read the extracts we insert, from the letter written to one of our Secretaries, by the lamented Mrs. Doremus.

As befits a book for woman's reading, and sent forth by a Woman's Board, we have laid special emphasis on that which has been done in the cause of Female Education, in each field under our care. We think it will be plain to every observer, that the ladies, who are devoting their time and talents to the instruction of their own sex, in these darkened lands, would take high rank as instructors at home. Our own daughters are not receiving better teaching from more gifted brains and hearts, than are these girls in the far-off East, from the tender, lovely, and cultivated women, who have exiled themselves, in this cause, for Christ's sake.

Does not this fact, dear sister, carry a lesson with it? Let each press home the question, to her own soul: "How much owest thou to my Lord?"

The training of native preachers and teachers is felt to be extremely important, for obvious reasons. By attention to the reports given in this volume, by missionaries writing from their posts, it will be seen with what success this has been attempted.

One final word: The cost of this undertaking has not come from the funds of our Board. We have not felt it right thus to use the contributions of our auxiliaries, nor to divert them from their legitimate channel. Our President, Mrs. Jonathan Sturges, with rare devotion to the good cause, and genuine missionary zeal, has herself assumed the expense of publishing this Manual. The thought which inspired it, was hers. She has watched every step of its progress with maternal solicitude, and her taste has supervised it from beginning to end.

We send it to mothers and daughters. May they be stirred up, as they read its narratives, to larger efforts, to more entire consecration, and to willing self-denial, for the Kingdom and Crown of the Lord we and they love.

OUR FRONTISPIECE.

In the picture of the Reformed Church and Parsonage at Yokahama, from a photograph taken on the spot, the parsonage of the missionaries (built to accommodate two families) is seen on the left. The church edifice is 60 feet long, 40 wide, and will seat in the interior 450 persons. The property on the right is the yard of the Consulate of the United States, with our national flag at the mast-head. The avenue in front of the church leads down to the "hatoba" or landing place. Two steamers of the Pacific Mail Steamship Company lie at anchor, and in the distance are the mountains of Awa and Kadzusa. In the picture may also be noted the tiled roofs, jin-riki-sha or "man-power wagons," the gas lamp-post, the "traps" or one-horse low carriage used in Japan, and a number of natives and foreigners.

NOTE.

We acknowledge the courtesy of Messrs Harper & Brothers, who have permitted us to use several plates from "*The Mikado's Empire*," in the article on Japan. Also the cut of the Borneo Mission, taken from "*Pierson's American Missionary Memorial.*"

M. E. S.

INDIA.

MISSIONARIES RESIDENCE AT MUDNAPILLY.

THE ARCOT MISSION.

BY
REV. JARED W. SCUDDER.

THE FIELD.

THE ARCOT DISTRICT, from which our Mission takes its name, is situated on the Peninsula of India, about sixty miles from its eastern coast, and directly west from the City of Madras. Lying between the twelfth and fourteenth parallels of north latitude, and the seventy-eighth and eightieth parallels of east longitude, it covers an area of 9,093 square miles, and has a population of 3,048,980 souls. Previous to its occupation by our missionaries, a little evangelistic work had been done, and small churches gathered in Vellore and Chittoor, two of its principal towns, by agents of an English Missionary Society. A third church, also of a few members, had been organized in Chittoor, as a result of the labors of Norris Groves, Esq., an English layman of undoubted zeal and piety, but holding unique and independent doctrinal views. Beyond this, nothing had been done for the Christianization of the district; and at the time when the American Missionaries entered it, the inhabitants were, to all intents and purposes, as benighted and ignorant of the religion of Jesus, as were their ancestors a thousand years ago.

FOUNDING OF THE MISSION.

In January 1851, the Rev. Henry M. Scudder, who had already been laboring for some years in the city of Madras as a missionary of the American Board, obtained leave to seek a new and less occupied field of effort. Selecting the Arcot District, he established a medical dispensary in the large town of Wallajanugger; and, for a season, labored without coadjutors in the vast Sahara-like waste of surrounding heathenism. In 1852 he was joined by Rev. Messrs. William W. Scudder, and Joseph Scudder: and the three brothers, all still connected with the American Board, but supported by funds derived from the Reformed Dutch Church, were in 1853 constituted a new Mission, under the name of the "American Arcot Mission of the Reformed Protestant Dutch Church of America." At the date of its establishment, the entire spiritual property of the new organization, consisted of no more than "a church of eight communicants, and a small but interesting school for the children of the church members;" so much being the fruit of the preliminary work of Rev. H. M. Scudder. Such were the *little* beginnings of the Mission, which, as we shall see in the sequel, has from an almost imperceptible germ, developed into a widespreading and luxuriant tree, laden with fragrant blossoms and golden fruit.

PLAN AND METHODS OF WORK.

These are clearly and definitely foreshadowed in the Constitutional Rules adopted at the founding of the Mission. We give a brief synopsis of them:

1. Believing that the teeming populations of India, can, without any educational or other preparative human instrumentality, be readily reached and affected by the direct preaching of the Gospel in their vernacular tongues, and persuaded that the way to the triumphs of Christianity could most effectually be prepared by its public proclamation, the missionaries of the Arcot Mission resolved to make it their paramount duty to go into the streets of the towns and villages throughout the district, and persistently and patiently preach Christ and Him Crucified, as the alone hope of lost sinners.

2. The extensive distribution of Tracts and Books specially adapted to the Hindu mind and character, together with the free dissemination of the Bible in the vernaculars of the district, was recognized as a powerful auxiliary agency, only second in importance to the direct oral proclamation of the Gospel to the masses of the people; and it was determined to compose and utilize such a literature as speedily and on as large a scale as possible.

3. Appreciating the impracticability of evangelizing the millions of India through an exclusively foreign agency, as well as the importance of early transforming Christianity from an exotic into an indigenous and self-propagating institution, the Mission adopted measures for the immediate founding of educational establishments, in which native youths of both

sexes might acquire thorough equipment to serve both as aggressors on heathenism, and as conservators and cultivators of spiritual garden-spots, wherever such should be reclaimed from the dismal wastes of Paganism.

4. The necessity of instructing and spiritually training individuals and communities, who might, through the foregoing instrumentalities, be proselyted to the Christian faith, was too obvious to escape notice; and it was provided, that whenever three or more families in any one town or village should renounce heathenism, and signify their wish to be instructed, a Catechist should be placed among them, and a small, inexpensive building be erected to serve as a school-room for the children, and a place of Sabbath convocation for old and young. The worship of the true God would thus be introduced and familiarized, and, with the divine blessing, material be speedily provided for the organization of Christian churches.

5. Caste, the hoary tyrant of Hindu nationality, and Intemperance, a recently introduced but rapidly spreading vice, were distinguished as being not only formidable antagonists to the spread of Christianity, but also most potent forces working ever for the disruption and dissolution of the native Church after its establishment; and stringent rules were, therefore, framed to shut these pestilent enemies outside the precincts of the youthful Mission.

Such are the general principles, which, adopted at the founding of the Mission, have governed its policy and action to the present time; and to a faithful carrying out of these principles may, we believe, be fairly attributed much of the success that has crowned its efforts to advance Christianity in the district.

The period under review, extending from the year 1853, to the close of the year 1875, may be divided into two parts: which, for convenience, we will designate as, 1st, The Initial or Rudimental Period; and 2nd, The Village Movement, or Rapid Development Period.

I.

THE INITIAL OR RUDIMENTAL PERIOD,
EXTENDING FROM THE FOUNDATION OF THE MISSION TO THE CLOSE OF A. D. 1860.

The first Annual Report of the Arcot Mission was issued at the end of the year 1854, a little more than a twelvemonth from its organization. Tokens of a vigorous and robust youth are already perceptible. Three "Stations,"—Vellore, Chittoor, and Arnee, have been selected as convenient centres of operation, and are occupied respectively by the Rev. Messrs. Henry M., William W., and Joseph Scudder. Already, two churches, each consisting of thirteen communicants, have been organized; one in Vellore, and the other in Chittoor; and two congregations of native Christians, numbering severally about seventy souls, assemble on the Sabbath to worship their newly found Lord. An "Out-station" has been established in the City of Arcot, fourteen miles east of Vellore, and a small building of mud and thatch has been erected there to serve as a school-house and church. Four vernacular Christian schools are in operation, and a "Præparandi Class" of thirteen selected and promising lads has been formed in Vellore, which is instructed daily by the Missionary and his assistants, in the Scriptures, Systematic Theology and Heidelberg Catechism; as well as in secular studies, embracing among the rest, Sanscrit, vocal Music and Medicine. The Missionaries, accompanied sometimes by the Præparandi Class, make preaching tours in the district; and the Gospel is systematically and diligently proclaimed from street to street, in the large central cities occupied as Stations. "*Spiritual Teaching*," a tract of 96 pages, is printed and put in circulation; and a portion of the Heidelberg Catechism is in the Tamil press. In the Dispensary, kept open throughout the year, many interesting surgical operations are performed, and a vast amount of relief is afforded to the sick and suffering. Thus, within one short year of its formation, we find the Mission already fully and actively at work in all its multifarious departments. The only apparent drawback is the lack of funds to publish several tracts and treatises which are ready for the press; and to erect churches at the principal Stations. This latter need was of so pressing a nature, as to dictate the following earnest appeal to the Christian public in India:

"For church edifices, we have no appropriation. We now conduct divine worship in our private residences. Last Sabbath, at one of our Stations, the room was too strait for the people who came. We wish to build one church in Vellore, one in Chittoor, and one in Arnee. Our design is to build them in the heart of the town, in the midst of the population. Then many heathen will come in to hear the Word, as it is regularly preached. Evening meetings by lamp-light can also be held on week days, which will attract many. We need about 4,000 Rupees ($2,000) for each church edifice, making a sum of 12,000 Rupees. We do not know where we are to get this. We simply know that we *need* it. A neat, commodious, substantial building will be a perpetual declaration to the heathen, that Christians have taken possession of the land, in the name of the Lord Jesus."

The case of a young lad who joined the Mission this year, is of peculiar interest; he being its first high caste convert to Christianity in the district.

SHENGALRAYAN'S CONVERSION.

"The fact that we are about to mention will show that the preaching of the Gospel to those who attended the Dispensary has not been in vain. More than a year ago, a lad of good caste, named Shengalrayan, belonging to the town of Walkajannuger, was entered as an out-patient. He was treated for about a month and then discharged as well. He, with other patients, heard of the great Physician. He became convinced that his own religion was false, and that the Atonement of Jesus is the only hope of the soul. He applied to be received by us. We could not refuse. His father and mother visited us. They were allowed to see him whenever they pleased. Affectionate entreaty, threats, sarcasm, all were variously tried upon him, but in vain. He not only remained firm, but confounded them by the wisdom of his replies. He broke his caste of his own accord, and himself requested that the tuft of hair on his head—being a mark of Hinduism might be removed. In a few days the missionary was summoned to appear before the Magistrate with the lad. The examination was ably and carefully conducted for two days. So pertinent and firm were his replies to all questions, so consistent were his statements, so clear were his views in regard to the difference between Hinduism and Christianity, and so decided his intention to live and die a Christian, that even the head of his caste and some other influential Hindus signed a paper declaring that they considered him abundantly capable of forming an enlightened determination in regard to the subject of religion. The Magistrate decided that the lad might go where he pleased, and he is now a member of our Præparandi Class. To God alone be all the glory."

It is pleasant to complete this short history by adding that this young convert, who had forsaken home, father, mother, friends and caste for Christ's sake, proved himself to be possessed of superior natural endowments and great application.

In the following year he was baptized and admitted to the Church. After completing his course of study, he served the Mission—first as Reader, and subsequently as Catechist. He is an exceptionally good preacher, was for many years the Head Master of the Female Seminary, and is still doing excellent service in the Master's cause.

TEMPORARY SUSPENSION OF THE DISPENSARY.

The Government having made abundant provision for the sick of the district by opening a Medical Dispensary in each of the Station towns, and the missionaries feeling, that in view of the fewness of their numbers, their entire force could, at least for the time being, be most effectively utilized in purely spiritual work, the Dispensary connected with the Mission was temporarily suspended at the close of this year.

A. D., 1855.

The year 1855 opened auspiciously on the youthful Mission. The preceding twelvemonth, although it was as we have seen a period of marked general prosperity, had not passed without its trials. Ill health, and duty to a disabled father, had compelled the absence of two of three Missionaries during a part of the year, and the burden of the entire Mission had much overweighted the shoulders of the one who remained alone. Now, not only had the absent members returned with renewed health and vigor; but the arrival, in March, of Rev. Messrs. Ezekiel C. and Jared W. Scudder with their wives and a sister, doubled the strength of the Mission, and put it in its power to preach the Gospel still more extensively among the heathen. The joy occasioned by this re-union, found utterance in the following words:

"Our Mission now consists of five brothers, four of whom have companions to aid them in their duties, and the other is helped by a sister, Miss Louisa Scudder. Thus we number TEN souls of ONE NAME, ONE FAMILY, united in ONE MISSION, and serving ONE MASTER. Truly we have great cause to praise God, who, through Jesus Christ, has called so many of our family to engage in the missionary work, and has given us the privilege of being associated in one body."

Stimulated as well as strengthened by the recently arrived reinforcement, the missionaries prosecuted their Evangelistic labors with freshened ardor. The Gospel was continuously and diligently proclaimed in the streets of the Station towns, and extended tours were made among the outlying villages in the district. On these tours, the missionaries, after preaching in the streets during the morning hours, usually occupied the entire remainder of the day in receiving and instructing the crowds of heathen who resorted to their place of encampment. In the larger towns they were often engaged in this work from nine o'clock A.M. until six o'clock P.M., preaching to successive audiences, and distributing among them tracts and portions of Scripture. So large was the demand for such publications, that several editions of various works, amounting to no less than 1,760,000 pages were printed during the year.

Pastoral, educational, and other miscellaneous work within the Stations was also assiduously attended to. Two services on the Sabbath; daily exposition of the Scriptures; a class for the instruction of communicants and catechumens on Wednesday, and several prayer-meetings during the week;—these, with daily street-preaching to the heathen, amply filled the time and taxed the industry of the Missionaries and their native assistants.

These multiform and abundant efforts were not barren of results. No large ingathering of converts was, it is true, made from among the heathen;—a result, indeed, hardly to be expected so soon,—yet the close of the year exhibits a notable advance on its beginning. The aggregate of native Christians has swelled from 150 to 350; two new schools have been opened; a Church has been organized at Arnee; and the communicants number 75 against 26 in 1864. A part of this increase was owing to accessions from the congregations of the Gospel Propagation Society, and of Mr. Groves, who, on withdrawing from the district, transferred their adherents to the spiritual guardianship of the Arcot Mission.

We extract from the Report of this year, several interesting sketches, showing that the Gospel leaven was doing its silent but effectual work in the lump of heathenism.

A HINDU DEFENDING CHRISTIANITY.

"As I was one morning speaking to a company of Hindus, some one in the crowd came forward to oppose me. A fine looking native in the assembly took the defence out of my mouth, and very cleverly and forcibly discomfited my antagonist. This man afterwards came to see me; and I found, to my astonishment, that he had possessed a Tamil Bible for many years; that he knew it well, and could quote it readily; that he did not worship idols; that he was in the habit of daily meditating on God's Word and praying; that he everywhere openly declared Jesus to be the only Saviour; and yet, that he remained in connection with the heathen. He lives in Vellore. I frequently see him. He tells me frankly that an opposing wife, caste, and the shame of the Cross, kept him from being baptized. I have reason to believe that a man professing to be a Christian, conversed several years ago with this Hindu; and instead of enforcing upon him Christ's command to come out from the heathen and be baptized, left him to infer that, in his opinion, he would get to heaven in his present course. I have often clearly showed this Hindu, out of the Scriptures, that he has not a saving faith, and that he has no prospect of heaven, inasmuch as he lives in the perpetual violation of that command. Will not each one who reads this account lift up a prayer to the Father of Lights for this interesting man, who stands so near the gateway of Jesus' kingdom, and yet does not enter in."

DANIEL; A TROPHY OF GRACE.

"Our new graveyard contains a single mound, near which I must linger to drop a tear; not through grief for him whose dust is gathered there, but for my own loss in his departure. My sorrow, however, is mingled with a greater joy. Although the thought is a mournful one,—that I shall never see again upon earth his intelligent, happy face, and that I shall not hear again his gentle persuasive voice setting forth to his countrymen the good tidings of salvation,—yet how can I do otherwise than rejoice in the assurance that he is now in his Father's house. Surely tears must here give way to smiles, and lamentations be changed to thanksgivings. It is the grave of Daniel, once a Pagan, dwelling in heathen darkness and worshipping idols; but now, a redeemed soul in heaven. More than eight years ago he renounced Hinduism. He gave most satisfactory evidence that he had become a new creature in Christ Jesus. I baptized him. Some years after his conversion, I asked him to come to Arcot, and assist me in preaching to the heathen. This he did. He was a faithful follower of the Lord Jesus. His friends cast him out; his wife forsook him; but he had found the pearl of great price, and nothing could induce him to barter that away. He lived a holy life. He died a happy death, falling sweetly asleep in Jesus. We can never forget him; we remember him as a trophy of grace; a monument of what the Lord can do for a Hindu, an earnest of what He *will do* in cases without number, as the Sun of Righteousness diffuses His rays through every part of this land."

THE POWER OF TWO OLD TRACTS.

"Some time since, a man of high caste called to see me. He brought with him two old tracts, carefully folded in a handkerchief. One was, the 'Jewel Mine of Salvation' in Telugre. It was much worn, and partly destroyed by constant use. He said he had long been wishing to procure perfect copies of these tracts, and, hearing in the bazaar of a Missionary's presence in Chittoor, he came immediately to secure the prize. He listened with eager interest to the Gospel, and seemed greatly rejoiced to receive the tracts. I have seen him several times since. His history is very interesting. Many years ago, as a regiment was passing, some one dropped a book by the side of a well. It contained the Gospels of Mark and Luke, and some of the Epistles. A Reddy (a native landholder of high caste) found the book; but as he could not read Tamil, gave it to an old man, the father of my visitor. The father, on looking at it, said: 'This is a book for sages, not for an ignorant man like me.' His wife, thinking that it might hereafter prove useful, put it carefully away in an earthen pot. There it remained four or five years. The old man died. The son was asked to take charge of a school. He did so, and thinking that this long neglected book might assist him, he took it out and read it. He did not at first understand its contents. Again and again he read it, and light began to dawn upon his dark mind. He soon became convinced that Hinduism was false, and that this book contained the only true way of salvation. His views of Scripture truth, and especially of the plan of salvation, were surprisingly clear. When particular doctrines were referred to, he would at once show his knowledge of them by apt quotations from Scripture. He derived all his knowledge from the portions of the Bible and Tracts he had read, never having been instructed by missionaries. I believe the man is sincerely desirous to become a Christian. Though of high caste, he on several occasions ate food in the catechist's house, thus showing that he had no regard for this feature of heathenism. He seemed very near the kingdom of heaven. He was repeatedly urged to take a stand at once, to renounce heathenism, and openly profess his faith in Jesus. He acknowledged this to be his duty; but, dreading the persecution which would ensue, concluded to put it off for a season."

A WANDERER IN SEARCH OF TRUTH.

"The case of an old man living near Arnee is of unusual interest. During his younger years he was a heathen after the strictest sect. To quiet the cravings of the immortal soul, he had travelled far and wide; performed all manner of rites and ceremonies, tortured his body, and spent his little fortune in almsgiving. All this was done to obtain forgiveness of sins and hopes of heaven, but it only left his soul in greater anguish. In his journeying he met a touring missionary. He received from him a portion of the Old Testament, in which he found the Ten Commandments. He determined to obey them to the letter. He soon found this was impossible; and that, do what he could, he was constantly breaking one or another of God's commands. He sought more light, and obtained a New Testament. His eyes fell on the compendium of the Decalogue. 'Ah!' said he, 'this is just what I want; this can be obeyed with greater ease. I can certainly love God with all my heart, and my neighbor as myself?' With renewed courage he set himself to the task, but was soon convinced of his inability to accomplish it. He was now led to study more carefully the sacred volume and the simple plan of salvation. He found there that the Saviour, by His obedience and death, had fulfilled the law in man's behalf. He renounced idolatry, of his own free will, even before coming to the missionary; he broke caste—which was in his case very high—and began to worship the God of the Bible. He repeated to the missionary a form of prayer, composed by himself, which he was in the habit of using daily. It evinced a thorough knowledge of Scripture, a simple child-like faith, and an entire dependence on the merits of Christ. He is in the habit of preaching the Gospel to his fellow villagers; but they call him mad. His reply, in one instance, was: 'I learn from the Scriptures, that he who would be wise, must first become a fool. As I am striving for heavenly wisdom, I may be, in this sense, mad as you say.' His family, in consequence of his having broken caste, will not permit him to eat with them. They cook his food and place it outside the door for him. When urged by the missionary to come out from the world and make a public profession of Christ, he replied, 'Not now; I will go home; and if I hear Jesus say that it is my duty to forsake my kindred and tribe, which I must necessarily do if I join your Church, I will cheerfully obey. At present, I cannot make up my mind that it is essential for my salvation.' We cannot but hope that this old man, though still living outside of external religious influences, has been savingly impressed by the Holy Spirit, and that he will yet be brought into the church of Christ. When he left the missionary, he requested an interest in his prayers. This request the writer has never heard an inquiring Hindu make before."

The want of church edifices and of buildings for the accommodation of the two Seminaries was still pressingly felt, and the missionaries reiterated with urgency, their appeal of the preceding year, for funds wherewith to supply the defect. In closing the Report, they express deep obligation to R. M. Binning, Esq., of the Madras Civil Service, for the present of a complete and costly set of tents. This was a most useful and welcome gift; as the missionaries, during their tours, had frequently been obliged to pass the day with no shelter from the burning sun but a green tree, and with no accommodation better than the bare and parched ground.

REFORMED CHURCH AT VELLORE.

A. D., 1856.

A peculiar interest ever attaches to the early, formative period of a great enterprise; and we have, therefore, given, at some length, the record of the first two years of the Mission's existence. Our space, however, does not provide for for such continued details; and we must pass the remaining portions of this Initial Period under more rapid review, touching only salient points of interest.

The year 1856 was marked by the following events:

The publication of "*Sweet Savours of Divine Truth,*" a comprehensive Catechism in Tamil, which has been of great service in the native congregations; the organization of two new churches, one in Arcot and the other in Coonoor; the completion and dedication of a neat and commodious church edifice in Vellore; the foundation and partial erection of similar buildings in Chittoor and Arnee, and the adoption of Coonoor as an additional station. All of which events are good evidence of healthy growth and vigorous expansion.

This adoption as a Mission Station of a place situated at a considerable remove from the Arcot District, though under ordinary circumstances it might have seemed undesirable, was clearly indicated by the leadings of Providence. The health of the Rev. Joseph Scudder, never very robust, had become so seriously impaired as to forbid his laboring any longer on the heated Indian plains; and his return to America appeared imperative. Just at this juncture, a native Christian congregation, which had been gathered by the efforts of two English gentlemen in Coonoor, a town situated on the heights of the

Neilgherries, and bathed in a charmingly salubrious atmosphere, was offered to the Arcot Mission. The timely offer was gladly accepted; and the invalid missionary was appointed to occupy the place, and make it the centre of his pastoral and evangelical labors.

The force of foreign missionaries in the Arcot District proper, already reduced by this removal of the Rev. Joseph Scudder to Coonoor, was still further weakened by the departure of the Rev. W. W. Scudder on furlough to America. Yet, by the Divine blessing, the prosperity of the Mission does not appear to have suffered any abatement; for we find that the aggregate of its Christian adherents had increased during the year from 350 to 459, and of the communicants from 75 to 126.

We make room here for the case of a man whose conversion, occuring at this period, proved, in the sequel, of much moment to the interests of the Mission:

DANIEL'S CONVERSION.

"About four months ago, a man called at my house, and requested an interview with me. On my enquiring his errand, he related the following facts about himself: For many years a member of the Roman Catholic Church in this place, (Arnee) he had been employed by that body as an itinerant proselyting agent; that is to say, his office was to travel from village to village, and induce as many heathen as he could, to place themselves under the dominion of Popery. Acting in this capacity, he had been the means of bringing numerous persons over to that faith. The manner of his becoming a Roman Catholic, was this. While he was yet a heathen, his mind moved as we believe, by the Spirit of God, became dissatisfied with the faith of his ancestors. The rites and ceremonies of Paganism brought no peace to his troubled conscience, and he longed for some one to teach him a better way. While in this state of mind, he met a Roman priest, whose representations persuaded him to seek salvation in the bosom of that Church. For a time, he found a species of relief by faithfully observing the round of duties and penances imposed by his new spiritual guide. But this state of things did not long continue. The closer his acquaintance with Antichrist, the more was he persuaded that the cravings of his immortal spirit could never be satisfied with a humanly-appointed ritual. Fastings, penances, and saint-worship were all faithfully tested, and all alike failed of the desired end. Without were doubts, within were fears. Thus tossed upon the sea of uncertainty, and longing for a peaceful haven, he conceived the idea of separating himself from the Roman Catholic Church, and going into the far interior of the country. There, removed from priestly supervision, he hoped to establish a religion less incongruous with his views of true worship. This plan, chimerical indeed, but illustrative of his deep feeling and anxiety, he was, in various ways, prevented from carrying into effect. After a time, coming into communication with some of our Christians, he learned the differences between Protestantism and Popery. Light broke in upon his soul. The long desired knowledge was at last gained; and, like Bunyan's Pilgrim hastening towards the wicket, he entered, trembling yet rejoicing, into the way of life. His first step was to renounce Papacy with all its forms. This he did in the face of a most bitter opposition. So threatening and watchful were his enemies, that he was compelled to remove his family by night, and take refuge on the mission premises. Even after he had cast off his shackles, every possible effort was made to fasten them on him anew. Emissaries were sent among us to represent him as unworthy of the least confidence. We were told that his sole object in joining us was to get money, and the like. But God turned these weapons against their framers, and they finally retired discomfitted and confused. On further acquaintance, we learned that he had never been the possessor of a Bible; and it would be difficult to portray the satisfaction which beamed in his face when the Word of God was first placed in his hands. Although he had, for six or eight years, been a member of the Papal church, he knew almost nothing of the essential doctrines of Christianity. No sooner, however, had he freed himself from that communion, than he gave all diligence to the study of the Bible; and most rapidly has he derived truth from its sacred pages. May the entrance of the Word give light to his soul! Since joining us, he has manifested an earnest desire for the enlightenment of his relatives and friends. Being a man of extensive connections, and not without influence among them, it is hoped that through his agency, accompanied by the Divine blessing, many may be induced to cast off the bonds of Popery and Paganism, and seek light and life at their fountain head. It may be that, through his instrumentality, 'a great door and effectual will be opened unto us,' as unto Paul in Ephesus."

The sequel of the story appears in the report of the succeeding year:—

"Some of our readers will remember the account given in our last report of a man who had renounced Romanism, and placed himself under instruction at this Station. The hope was then expressed that not only would he and his family become sincere believers, but that, through their instrumentality, many others might be induced to listen to the truth. We rejoice to say that this hope has not been entirely disappointed. About six months ago, the missionary had the pleasure of baptizing the whole family, and of admitting the parents to the communion of the Church. In December last, their eldest daughter who had endeared herself to our hearts by the gentleness of her disposition, fell asleep, uttering with her last breath, the name of Jesus. Daniel, for such is now the father's name, has, from the first, manifested a tender solicitude for the conversion of his numerous connections, who live in villages not far away. Visiting them from time to time, he has proclaimed the Gospel, and urged them to accept it. Influenced by his representations, six families have already promised to renounce heathenism, and bear the Christian name; and thus, a new door of usefulness seems to be opening before us.

"To complete the history, we will add that Daniel was the means a few years later of greatly stimulating and forwarding the village movement, to be noticed farther on; and that after serving the mission actively for nearly twenty years, he is now an old man, awaiting his transfer to a better world."

A.D., 1857.

The year 1857 was to the Mission, one of mingled clouds and sunshine. Among the circumstances depressive and faith-trying were the sad defections of certain church members; and the unexpected departure of the Rev. H. M. Scudder to America, caused by the sudden and complete prostration of his health. To these may be added the Sepoy Mutiny, which, sweeping like a fiery tidal-wave, carried desolation and death over the northern half of the continent, and threatened continually to overflow and devastate its southern latitudes as well. But God's protecting hand was about His servants in

Arcot, shielding them from peril and disaster. While missionaries in other parts of the land fell a prey to the sword of the Infidel, these here were permitted to pursue their labors, not without some anxiety it is true, but still uninterrupted and undisturbed. Although their number was reduced once more to only three, the Lord's hand was not shortened thereby. Indeed, the events of the year, as a whole, were of a nature to give them much cause for thankfulness and encouragement. They were permitted to rejoice in a considerable augmentation, both of adherents and communicants. The congregation at the new station of Coonoor was nearly doubled. Six heathen families, all residents of a single village, indicated their intention to forsake Paganism and bear the Christian name; a very cheering fact, as being the first token manifested in the district, of a movement in masses towards Christianity. After long waiting and hoping, the Church edifice in Chittoor, a beautiful and spacious building, occupying a prominent and most eligible position on the principal street in the town, reached completion; and with services both in English and Tamil was, on the 14th of January, 1858, solemnly and exultantly dedicated to the Triune Jehovah.

And lastly, the "Reformed Church of America," convinced that the best interests of her foreign work and of all concerned in it, would be more effectually advanced by "separate action," did, at the meeting of General Synod, in June of this year, 1857, resolve to annul her compact with the American Board, and to assume the immediate care and conduct of her own Missions. This was a measure peculiarly grateful and encouraging to her missionaries in India; for

REFORMED CHURCH IN CHITTOOR.

while their relations with the American Board had, with a single exception, been eminently cordial and satisfactory; they, nevertheless, now experienced new thrillings of emotion, as they found themselves pressed directly to the breast of their own mother, and felt the full, warm pulsations of her great heart rhythmically responding to and sympathetically blending with their own. And so the year went out in a bright sunset, which, while it bathed their landscape in light, served also to illumine and embellish the very clouds, whose shadows had cast somewhat of gloom over their spirits.

A. D., 1858.

We pass this year with only a brief reference. It was a period, in some respects, of much trial and discouragement. To supervise four widely separated Stations and meet their multiform requirements, there remained now in the Arcot District, only the two younger members of the missionary force: and even these were much hampered and embarrassed by serious and continued illness in their families. Under these adverse circumstances the Mission, while on the one hand it does not appear to have suffered any notable deterioration, did, on the other, unquestionably feel the absence of that expansive elasticity and cheering success which had marked the preceding periods of its history.

A. D., 1859.

The arrival in the early part of 1859 of the Rev. W. W. Scudder, accompanied by a new missionary, the Rev. J. Mayon, infused new strength and courage into overburdened and somewhat dejected hearts. This accession of force led to the occupation of the new Station of Palamanair, a town of about seven thousand inhabitants, situated on the borders of the Telugu country, twenty-six miles west of Chittoor, and forming the centre of a populous district thickly studded with villages, —thus presenting an excellent field for evangelistic labors.

The native congregations in Arnee and Coonoor, who had hitherto been, much to their regret, without houses of worship, took possession this year with happy and thankful hearts, of their completed and dedicated Church edifices. A sweet-toned bell,* the gift of the "Scudder Missionary Society of the Third Reformed Church of Philadelphia," hung in the tower of the Arnee building, and uttered its silvery notes of invitation to the dwellers around, heathen and Christian alike. The dedication services in Coonoor, attracted large audiences of both Europeans and natives, the latter of whom freely expressed their interest and joy at exchanging the straitened and inadequate limits of a small school-house for their well-appointed and comfortable church.

Perhaps the most important and, to the missionaries especially, deeply interesting event of the year, was the ordination of their first native pastor, the Rev. Andrew Sawyer. The services were held in the Church at Chittoor, in which town the candidate, an old and tried servant of the Lord, had labored as catechist and lay-preacher for many years; and had secured the respect and love of all who, through the long

---

* It may not be amiss to state here that other Churches and Sunday-schools have presented bells to the Arcot Mission; notably the Sunday-school of West Troy, which has, I believe, four bells ringing out there.

period of his probation, had witnessed his blameless life, and profited by his eloquent and forceful preaching. In the large audience, which crowded the building, were many heathen, attracted by the novelty of a ceremonial, altogether without precedent in their idolatrous town. The newly ordained minister was soon after installed pastor of the native Church in Arcot.

It was in this year, also, that the "Arcot Seminary,"—hitherto known as the "Præparandi Class,"—sent forth its first graduates into the Lord's vineyard. Three young men who had gone through the prescribed course of six years instruction and training, were appointed to labor as readers and schoolmasters in the Mission. The number of students in the institution at this time was twenty.

In summing up the results of the year, the Annual Report says :—

"Though we have no remarkable accessions to record, we have every ground for encouragement in our work. There has been a steady increase in our numbers and strength since the publication of our last report. Our Stations have never been in a more flourishing condition; our churches have never been better attended; and a pleasing spirit of more earnestness and prayer pervading the body of our native Christians, leads us to hope for richer and more abundant blessings."

The statistics of this year are somewhat defective; but approximately, the congregations may be recorded as numbering in the aggregate, 579, and the communicants, 149.

The year, auspicious in its beginning, and prosperous in

its continuance, did not, however, end without its trial. The complete prostration of the Rev. Joseph Scudder's health, and the long continued and apparently hopeless illness of Mrs. J. W. Scudder, imperatively demanded a change of climate; and the working force of the mission was once more reduced to three, by the embarkation in December of two families for America. Vellore and Coonoor were left vacant by the withdrawal of strength; and the ship which bore the missionaries away, both carried and left behind her disappointment and sincere regret. The Rev. Joseph Scudder, after his arrival at home, kept his relation to the mission unsevered for many years, always hoping to return to his work in India; but his shattered frame never recovered sufficiently to warrant the step, and the remainder of his life was passed laboring for the Master in the United States. His term of foreign service was seven years. He died at Upper Red Hook, N. Y., Nov. 21st, 1876, and now sleeps in Greenwood Cemetery, beside his brother Samuel, who, though consecrated to the missionary work, was taken away while preparing to engage in it.

A. D. 1860.

We must content ourselves with a bare resumé of the events of this year. The Rev. H. M. Scudder returned, but with still imperfect health, to the mission. Two new missionaries, the Rev. J. Chamberlain, and S. D. Scudder, M. D., arrived; the former in April, and the latter in December. A small church was organized in Palamanair with encouraging prospects of success and enlargement. Marked indications of the presence of God's Spirit in both Seminaries, resulted in the conversion and admission to the Church of two lads in the one, and five girls in the other. Several, more than ordinarily interesting, instances of conversion, from among the Roman Catholics are found in the Report of this year. We give one of these in the words of the young man who was himself the subject of his relation:—

"When the Rev. H. M. Scudder resided in Arcot, he often instructed me in the truths of the Bible; but God did not then open the eyes of my understanding fully to apprehend the truth. Still, the doctrine taught was not in vain. Like an insect gnawing at my heart, it troubled me day and night. When Rev. Andrew Sawyer came here, he also faithfully continued these instructions; and God eventually opened the eyes of my mind to see that the religion according to which I had been walking was a false one, the creation of the man of sin. According to the advice of the Apostle in 1 Thess. v: 21, 'to prove all things and hold fast that which is good,' I carefully examined the whole subject, and determined to leave the temple of idols, and enter the temple of the Lord. The world, the flesh, and the devil combined to hinder me, and the troubles they caused me were not few. Space will not permit me to recount all these troubles; but I will briefly refer to a few of them. My mother, incited by Satan, did all in her power to prevent my attending church, and to make me forsake the truth I had embraced, to deny my Saviour, and to despise His salvation. She followed me to the church, and taking her position at the entrance, uttered all manner of abuse, blaspheming God and His truth. She also influenced the minds of my wife and children to act in the same way. I was, however, encouraged by the words of the Lord, 'If any man will come after Me, let him deny himself and take up his cross and follow Me.' My mother, wife and friends determining to make me forsake the truth, did all in their power to bind me again with that chain of superstition from which Christ had released me; thus proving the truth of the scripture that 'a man's foes shall be they of his own household.' Failing in these efforts, my mother went weeping to the priest, and engaged his services to draw me back into error. I consulted with my pastor, and he repeated many texts of scripture to encourage and comfort me. Strengthened by these, I did all in my power to bear witness to the truth in presence of these enemies of my soul. Remembering also the words of the Lord, 'Fear not them which kill the body, but are not able to kill the soul, but rather fear Him who is able to destroy both soul and body in hell,' I was encouraged to withstand all efforts to entice me away from the truth.

"These evil-minded persons appointed a day to discuss the differences between us; but when we met them, instead of speaking concerning the truth, they began to abuse me in every possible way, and tried to frighten me into a compliance with their wishes. Finding that I withstood all these attacks, the priest, at last, came in great anger and questioned me as follows: 'Who is the head of your Church?' I answered, 'Christ.' 'Who forgives your sins?' I said, 'Christ only. There is no one else empowered to forgive sins.' 'Do you mean to make disturbances in my church?' I answered, 'Not I, but Christ.' At this he became very angry and commenced beating me. Afterwards, on three succeeding Sabbaths, he cursed me before his whole congregation. These are some of the trials I have been called to endure, but the Lord has delivered me out of them all."

The mother and the family of this young man subsequently renounced Romanism, and joined the congregation at Arcot.

This brings us to the termination of our "Initial Period."

The annexed comparative table, exhibits the progress made and the results attained during the seven years of its continuance. The first column shows the statistics of the year 1854, and the second those of 1860.

ITEMS.	1854.	1860.
Stations.	3	6
Out-Stations.	1	0
Missionaries.	3	8
Native Ministers.	0	1
Catechists.	3	4
Readers.	0	2
Schoolmasters.	5	5
Colporteurs.	0	1
Churches.	2	6
Communicants.	26	154
Baptized Children.		220
Total of Adherents.	170	612
Pupils in Arcot Seminary.	13	20
Pupils in Female Seminary.	0	14
Number of Day-Schools.	4	5

II.

THE VILLAGE MOVEMENT, OR RAPID DEVELOPMENT PERIOD.
EXTENDING FROM THE YEAR 1861 TO THE YEAR 1875, INCLUSIVE.

We have now reached the beginning of our second Period, designated, "The Village Movement, or Rapid Development Period," because of the features which most conspicuously marked its history. Its almost uninterrupted prosperity and unbounding successes, justly entitle it to the distinction of being called the palmy period of the Mission. The introductory pages of the "Eighth Annual Report" so well describe its auspicious commencement, that we cannot do better than transcribe a part of the record:

"This Mission, which, by the culture of the great Husbandman, is becoming a tree with boughs and flowers and fruits, sprang from a slender shoot. In January 1851, a missionary pitched his tabernacle in the North Arcot district, and worked, for a season, alone in a wide and weary waste of heathenism. Afterwards another laborer came. Then still another arrived, and the three were constituted a Mission in 1853. A church of thirteen members was organized. Three small congregations, previously existing in the district, were given over to us. In 1855, after four years of labor, and this accession, our congregation contained three hundred and fifty souls, of whom seventy-five were communicants; and now, this day, we number nine Missionaries, one Native Pastor, six Churches, six Catechists, four Readers, six Teachers and seven hundred and ninety-six nominal Christians, of whom two hundred and thirty-two are Communicants. See what the Lord has wrought! We gaze upon His stately steppings,

THE ARCOT MISSION.

MISSION CHURCH AT M^cDNAPILLY, WITH HOUSES OF NATIVE HELPERS.

and wonder and adore. He has transcended all our expectations. By His grace, our work has not been like the duckweed that floats upon stagnant tanks. Nay, it has proved to be a germ planted by Him in His own garden. He has nurtured it, and truly it has become a spreading tree. The dew is on its roots. The glow of the sunbeam is on the ripening fruit; and we, a cheerful band of brethren and sisters, gather under its pleasant shade, and sing the Lord's song in a strange land. Our mouth is filled with laughter, and our tongue with singing: for He hath done great things for us, whereof we are glad."

Limited space forbids any further attempt at a detailed tracing of the Mission History from year to year, for such a record would take the dimensions of a large volume. We must content ourselves, therefore, with brief and only partial sketches formed from an analysis and classification of the work and successes of the Period under review. Let our first subject be that of the Village Movement throughout the district.

THE VILLAGE MOVEMENT.

We have already noticed the earliest token of this movement in the intention expressed in 1857, by six heathen families, all residing in a single village, to renounce heathenism and embrace Christianity. But much time elapsed before the promise became an actuality; for not until the year 1861, does Sattanbady, the name of the first Christian village, appear on the records of the mission.

The accession of this community was the primal ingathering of a harvest, the antecedents of which had been—arduous labors, long waiting, and earnest continued prayer. More than six hundred persons had, indeed, previously been gathered into the Christian fold; but the increase had hitherto been chiefly by individual conversions; and the missionaries were longing for the larger and more comprehensive movement of masses of people towards Christianity. The veritable initiation of such a movement, therefore, became naturally enough, the occasion to them of great joy and hearty thanksgiving to God. We will let them utter their emotions for themselves:—

"Where our churches exist, believers have light in their dwellings; but in the territory of heathenism around us, there is darkness which may be felt. Year by year, entering these domains of Night and Death, we have preached Him who is the Light and the Life. We have prayed for the day-star and the dawn. Now we begin to see some lines of light on the distant sky. Twenty-two miles from Arnee in a village called Sattanbady, fifty-three persons have formally renounced Roman Catholicism, and have joined us. We have received them, and placed over them a catechist and a schoolmaster. We cannot describe our joy in welcoming this our first Christian village. Long have we asked and looked for such a result. Pray with us, dear friends, for those who have come under our teaching and care, that they may not only endure such persecution as may come upon them, but that they may be strengthened and blessed thereby. Pray also that in this dismal midnight region of idolatry, Christian villages may everywhere spring up as centres of light and fountains of life. Pray that the vast superstructures of superstition which frown upon us in every quarter, may become as handfuls of cotton before the prairie fire.

"Still farther south of Arnee, towards Gingee, several families have made known their desire to join our mission. The prospect is inviting. Our eyes glance wistfully over that moral desert, and we know not yet whether this promise of good may turn out to be a treacherous mirage, or a real lake on whose banks we may be permitted to cultivate gardens for our Lord. Praying that it may be the latter, we grasp the plough and the seed basket, and go forth."

A catechist was immediately placed in charge of the new Christian community, and a school of twenty-five scholars was established in the village. The children, not one of whom knew so much as a letter at its opening, were reading nicely in less than a year, and recited their catechism and Scripture texts with no little pride and ardor. The marvellous improvement of these young savages, and the generally satisfactory conduct of the adult villagers gave much gratification and encouragement to the superintending missionary. Ere long, other families united with the congregation; and the advancement of the people in knowledge and good conduct was so rapid, as to warrant the organization among them of a Christian Church as early as 1863.

Thus was most happily inaugurated the Village Movement which spread gradually and steadily over the greater part of the mission field. The progress of this encouraging success will appear from the following Summary:—Adherents were gained in three villages, in 1863; in three more, in 1864; in eight, in 1866; in three, in 1867; in thirteen, in 1868; in three, in 1869; in four, in 1870; in four, in 1871; in thirteen in 1872; and in two, in 1873. In this Village Movement, which continued about twelve years, Christianity gained a foot-hold in no less than fifty-seven different localities; and the number of Christian adherents increased from 612 to 2,725; giving a net gain of 2,113, and an average annual gain of 176. In a few of these localities, adverse circumstances prevented the permanent establishment of the faith: but notwithstanding all drawbacks, we find the agents of the mission, at the close of the year 1873, ministering to Christian congregations in fifty widely scattered out-stations,—as these rural villages are called,—in addition to the eight Stations, or principal centres, located in the largest cities and towns of the district.

A brief sketch of the plan ordinarily pursued in this special work, may prove interesting to the reader. Whenever several heads of families in a village signify a determination to become Christians, two or more native catechists of approved judgment and experience, are immediately sent to confer with them; ascertain their motives; candidly warn them of the trials and persecutions they must inevitably encounter, and acquaint them with certain rules and requirements; promised compliance with which, on their part, is an indispensable condition of their reception as catechumens. If, after such conference, their motives seem sincere, and their resolution remains unshaken, they are probationally received as Christian adherents of the mission: they, on their part, signing a solemn pledge to renounce heathenism with all its distinguishing insignia, and practices; to avoid intoxicating drinks and substances; to send their children to school; to keep the Sabbath; to attend divine service regularly, and to use all diligence in gaining acquaintance with the Scriptures and their requirements. This compact having been made, they receive an early visit from the missionary, who has perhaps hitherto, from prudential considerations, kept in the background. Should his personal inspection confirm the favorable judgment arrived at by the native agent, a catechist is sent to reside in the village; conduct divine worship on the Sabbath and through the week; and, with the assistance of a schoolmaster, or of his own wife as schoolmistress, to instruct the old and the young, making it his chief duty to render them familiar with Christian law and doctrine. Finally, the village is visited as often as possible by the missionary himself to examine the school, note the moral progress of the adherents, encourage their efforts to disenthrall themselves from obnoxious prejudices and usages, and stimulate them to a diligent cultivation of new and estimable habits of thought and conduct.

It is surprising how rapidly illiterate and degraded people often improve under this system, faithfully and perseveringly applied. A marked and pleasing change is soon noticeable in in their appearance and demeanor. Rough uncouthness gradually wears away. Well-kept hair and clean clothing, tell of a newly acquired self-respect. The features become serener, and expressive of inward restraint. Quarrelling and base language are, by degrees, discontinued; and, in many cases, there is satisfactory evidence of a heart-work, which can be causatively traced to environing accidents; but only to the internal operation of the Almighty Spirit, transforming, regenerating, creating anew in Christ Jesus. And thus the great end the missionary has in view, is, by God's blessing, achieved in these subjects of Divine grace; and he gathers them with abounding joy about the table of the Lord. Numerous interesting illustrations might be recounted; we content ourselves with citing a single case typical of many:

"This Church (Kandiputtur) has met with a great loss this year, in the death of Aaron, one of its oldest members. A few years ago he was a heathen, but through God's marvelous grace, he was called into the kingdom and grace of His Son. His growth as a Christian was marked and rapid. Throughout his long and trying illness, he manifested, at all times, a sweet spirit of resignation to the Lord's will, and often expressed his cheerful readiness to commit himself and all his interests to His gracious disposal. He rested in the assurance—an assurance of which he often spoke—that if called away from the body, he would ever be present with the Lord. The Catechist has furnished the following short biographical notice of him:

"'By the grace of the Lord Jesus Christ, Aaron, a member of the American Mission Church in Kandiputtur, fell asleep in the Lord, August 23d, 1869. When he first became a Christian, he was exposed to many trials and persecutions on the part of the inhabitants of his village. Relying, however, upon the aid of the Lord, he was enabled to triumph over them all; and became an efficient instrument for the extension of the Christian religion in our midst. Though he was uneducated, and unable to read any language, he was not idle. In whatever place he might be, and wherever he went, he constantly spoke with others of Christ Jesus, the life-imparting germ, and of His priceless redemption. At the same time, to the extent of his ability, he pointed out and refuted the errors of heathenism.

"'He had a remarkably firm faith in Christ. Moreover, he treasured in his mind many precious passages of Scripture; and in his great afflictions, these constituted the supporting staff upon which he safely leaned. Last May, when he was attacked by disease, he attributed his sufferings to no other cause than his own ill desert. Feeling that the Lord was chastening him for his sins, he manifested great sorrow on account of them; and sought and found comfort only in the Word of God, and in earnest prayer. He requested me to have daily prayers in his house, and to read the Bible to him. Though weak in body, he, too, in true faith, would call upon God in prayer. He told me, if the Lord would forgive his sins, and restore him to health, he would devote the rest of his life entirely to His service; that wishing for no recompense, he would go with me from village to village, laboring to the extent of his ability for Christ. He, moreover, cherished the design of building a belfry to the church in which it was his custom to worship.

"'When, however, he learned that he must die, he seemed to lose all interest in earthly things. He manifested no anxiety about his wife and children, his lands and possessions; but, with unwavering confidence in his Lord, he committed all his cares to Him. Thus, with a true faith and assured hope, in perfect comfort and peace, he fell asleep in Jesus. Though after the flesh we sorrow over his departure, yet we greatly rejoice, because of his triumphant death. 'And I heard a voice from heaven saying unto me, Write, Blessed are the dead which die in the Lord from henceforth; yea, saith the Spirit, that they may rest from their labors, and their works do follow them.'"

Churches have been organized in eleven of these outlying villages; and the communicants generally lead consistent lives.

When we remember, that only a few short years ago there was not a single native Christian outside of the principal Stations, how much reason is there for rejoicing over the redemption from the encompassing wilderness of these charming garden-spots—verdant, blooming, and redolent with the fragrance of thanks-givings to Him, who, by His blessings, has made them to rejoice and blossom as the rose!

The sincerity, fortitude, and perseverance of these village Christians have been, in almost every instance, put to the test of persecution. Avowal of their new convictions places them, almost invariably and immediately, in a very trying position; and for a long period, they suffer many annoyances and hardships. Relatives disown and shun them, as if they had the plague. Life-long friendships are severed as with the blow of an axe. The village washerman and barber refuse their services. They are cut off from the privileges of fire and water. Neighbors, hitherto helpful, now scornfully and with bitter tauntings, refuse assistance in times of misfortune or embarrasment. Heathen masters eject them from employment, reducing them often to actual want. Old, hereditary debts, long forgotten or overlooked, are raked up, and settlement is peremptorily demanded. False suits are instituted, and triumphantly carried through the courts by unblushing perjury. Brahmin and other high caste officials stretch their authority to annoy, harass and pauperize them. The Monigars, or Headsmen of the communities, cut off the perquisites they have been accustomed to receive as village-watchmen and servants; forbid bazaarmen and moneylenders giving them credit; debar them from renting land to cultivate on shares, and oppress them in many other ways. All parties, high and low, harmonize and co-operate in heaping disabilities with curses and maledictions upon them. Not unfrequently, they are maltreated, beaten and even threatened with death. In some cases, their houses are burnt over their heads. Such are among the trials they are called to endure. Yet, with here and there an exception, they have manfully and uncompromisingly breasted the waves of surging persecution. The vast majority have passed unshaken through searching and protracted trial; and in most of the older villages have, with the assistance of the missionaries, succeeded in living down, or at least greatly mitigating the malignant opposition and cruelty of their heathen neighbors. But we may not dwell longer on this part of our subject.

EVANGELISTIC WORK AMONG THE HEATHEN.

Christ's last command to His church: "Preach the Gospel to every creature," has ever been the motto on the banner of the Arcot Mission. We have seen that among its fundamental rules, is one requiring its missionaries to make the oral proclamation of the truth to the masses of the people, their primary and most important work. In some missions, notably in those of the Scotch, the "Educational Method," as it is termed, in contradistinction to the "Preaching or Itinerant Method," has been employed, to the total or almost total exclusion of the latter; and at times, a good deal of sharp controversy has arisen as to the relative merits and efficacy of the two plans. Without entering into the discussion, for which there is no room here, suffice it to say that the missionaries of our Church in India, while not repudiating the Educational, have yet regarded the Preaching Method as the more scriptural, apostolic, Christlike; a method, the adoption and pursuance of which lead most closely in the footsteps of the divine Master, and His inspired followers. In harmony with this view, we find them giving paramount significance to this department of labor, devoting to it as much time as possible, prosecuting studies specifically adapted to its requirements, and shaping all their plans with an eye to its efficient performance. To traverse the district in its length and breadth; to enter every town, village and hamlet, calling upon men to repent and believe on the Lord Jesus; and to place in as many hands as possible, religious books and portions of Scripture to be read and pondered at leisure; these were the purposes contemplated.

The field of operation covers an extent of country about 250 miles long, by 50 miles broad; containing, in addition to the larger cities of 10,000 inhabitants and upwards, thousands of smaller towns and villages; the latter grouped at convenient distances around the former in concentric circles, and occupied chiefly by an agricultural population.

The method which has, in experience, proved most effective, may be briefly sketched as follows: One or more missionaries and a few native assistants make their preparations to leave home and spend several consecutive weeks, or months it may be, in itinerating the district. Tents, provisions, and books for distribution are sent in advance. A favorable spot is chosen as a centre, and the camp is established in the shade —if it can be found—of some umbrageous grove. Every morning, before the dawn lightens the east, the missionaries with their native attendants, sally forth; and, leaving the nearer villages for evening work, go out to a distance of three or four miles from the encampment. Here they separate into couples, composed usually of one missionary and one catechist. Each party enters a village; and, a favorable position having been secured, a passage of Scripture is read, or a lyric in the vernacular is sung in a loud tone, with the view of collecting the inhabitants. In general the visitors are almost immediately environed by a crowd of dusky auditors, who ordinarily listen with respectful attention to the message of truth. Opportunity is given for asking questions, and amicable discussion is not discouraged. At the close of the interview, books and tracts are distributed among those who can read; and the visitors, after inviting the people to seek further instruction at their tent, pass on to another street or to a neighboring village, where the same process is repeated. Thus, four or five places are reached by each party every morning; and in the evening, one or two more within easier distance of the centre. When the circle is completed, and every inhabited spot within its circumference has heard the voice of the preacher, the tents are moved to a new locality; and so the work goes on, until circumstances compel a return to the home Station. By this plan, systematically and perseveringly followed up year after year, the entire district, large as it is, has been toured over repeatedly; until, it is safe to say, there is no town or village in it, which has not become more or less familiar with the teachings of Christianity. Three millions of people have, by this agency, been brought within Gospel influences: and the diligent sowing among them of the good seed has ever been associated with earnest prayer that, watered by heavenly dews and warmed by celestial sunshine, it might germinate and mature and fructify abundantly to the glory of God.

Nearly allied to this itinerant labor is the evangelistic work done by the missionaries and native helpers in the immediate vicinity of the Stations and Out-stations. This is steadily prosecuted, Sundays excepted, every day throughout the year. The streets of the cities, and the outlying villages within a radius of five miles from each centre, are systematically and as frequently as possible visited and preached in. In this way, vast numbers of heathen hear the Gospel not once, but repeatedly every year; and the claims of Christianity are kept before them more continuously and persistently than before the inhabitants of remoter places, who can be reached only at longer intervals of time. This particular species of effort is therefore regarded, and justly, as being the most important and effectual of any put forth by the Mission. At the close of this section will be found a tabular statement showing,—so far as the statistics are available to the writer— the extent of the evangelistic work in both its branches.

As to the results of this vast and laborious system of aggressive evangelistic effort, they are to be seen partly, and most conspicuously, in the actual conversion of many individuals, and of entire communities as well, to the Christian faith. The history of this success has already been given in the preceding section, and need not be repeated here. It is enough to say that all accessions to the mission from among the heathen are directly traceable to the faithful and assiduous proclamation of the truth in the district. The divine blessing has uniformly and manifestly accompanied this specific form of effort; and the largest increments of Christian adherents have always been synchronous with its most energetic periods. We give some extracts showing the estimation in which, after extended experience, it is held by the missionaries; and, at the same time, illustrative of another phase of its success, which, while it is somewhat occult and indeterminable, is not on these accounts any the less real and important. We refer to the general beneficial effects which the persistent preaching of the Word has indubitably produced upon the consciousness of the entire mass of the heathen throughout the district.

FROM REPORT OF 1865.—" Great numbers of people have repeatedly heard the Gospel through this agency. Though no large results appear, we see clear evidence that the foundation stones of Hinduism are receiving heavy and crumbling blows, shaking the edifice throughout all its massive extension; and promising, sooner or later, to bring the vast structure to the ground—a broken, shapeless, irretrievable ruin."

FROM REPORT OF 1866.—After giving the statistics of evangelistic labor for the year:—

" Thus do we strive to make known the truth of the Gospel. We sow the seed in faith, beseeching the Lord to own and bless our labors. He has blessed them; and we feel confident that He will continue to bless them more and more abundantly. His Word is becoming known throughout our district. The Gospel is placed in the hands of many who, we are led to believe, read and ponder its truths. We could point to many places where the people are considering the subject of coming out on the Lord's side. We hope to welcome many during the coming year."

FROM REPORT OF 1867.—" Our experiences assure us that Christianity is assuming a high position in the land. It is gradually gaining for itself a respectability and force, in testimony of its divine origin and importance. The heathen, though they still stand aloof, acknowledge its superiority and power, and treat its adherents with less antipathy and scorn than in times past."

FROM REPORT OF 1868.—" The proclamation of the Gospel to the adult population of our district, is the chief object of our mission, and to it we devote our best energies. We have no reason to regret the time and strength bestowed upon it. A marked and cheering change has been noticed by us, as to the manner in which the people listen to the Gospel message. The story of Jesus' love was formerly heard with indifference, or with undissembled scorn. Now, it often secures the subdued and earnest attention of those whom we address. Almost all violent opposition has passed away. A spirit of serious inquiry as to the claims of Christianity seems to be rapidly pervading the district; and quite a number of village communities have placed themselves under our care and instruction during the past year. These effects of the simple preaching of the Gospel greatly encourage us. A vast preparatory work is being done. When it pleases the Lord to follow these labors with a copious outpouring of His Spirit, a great and saving change will take place among the people. Let our daily and importunate prayer ascend to Him for that Spirit."

FROM REPORT OF 1869.—" This mission has, from the first, held the principle that preaching the Gospel to the masses is the divinely appointed agency for evangelizing the heathen; and has required its missionaries to regard this as their primary and most important work. Without wishing to be dogmatic, or to call in question the efficiency of other modes of labor, we may be permitted to say, that the experience of fifteen years has abundantly confirmed the view we have adopted. Our conviction is established that, for this district at least, there is no superior or more promising instrumentality. God has here put upon it the seal of success. It is the simple proclamation of the Gospel in the towns and villages of our mission-field that has, with the divine blessing, brought in more than two thousand adherents to Christianity, and established fifteen churches within our bounds. It is the simple proclamation of the Gospel that has diffused a knowledge of Christ and His religion throughout large sections of North and South Arcot. To hundreds of thousands of their inhabitants, Christianity is no longer a thing 'new and strange;' but a common and familiar topic of talk and discussion. The missionary is not met so often as formerly with a stare of blank amazement or of idle curiosity. Intelligent questions about the leading doctrines of the Gospel, prove that his message has been pondered and canvassed by thinking minds. Confidence in pagan myths and hoary superstitions is manifestly shaken. Open opposition has signally decreased; and when offered, as it still sometimes is, takes the form more of an attack upon Christianity, than of a defence of heathenism. In many places leading men, though yet unprepared to break the shackles of caste and immemorial usage, do not hesitate publicly to avow their conviction that the Puranas are false and the Bible true. Some even venture to affirm that Jesus, must eventually, displace Vishnu and Siva. With these *facts* before us, we are encouraged to persevere in the method selected. The leaven has entered the mass of the people, and we are content to watch and aid its working, confident that it will go on until, in God's own time, the whole lump shall be leavened.

"We not unfrequently see or hear the remark, that the 'Preaching Method,' though well adapted to the lower classes, does not and cannot reach the higher, and fails altogether in reaching the female population. From this, we dissent. It is conceded that in large cities, the proud and wealthy may keep aloof from the preaching missionary, and that the ladies of the Zenana are beyond the range of his direct efforts. But our experience denies that he fails to reach the higher classes generally, whether male or female. Throughout this district, the Vellala and the Reddi, the Chetty and the Mudaliar, listen as readily as the Pariah and the Chuckler. Even the secluded Brahmin is sought and preached to in his sequestered Agraharam. As for the women, they seldom fail to compose a part of our audiences. Standing in the doorways and on the outskirts of the crowd, they listen as attentively as the men. In many Telugu villages, the weaker sex cluster about the preacher, while their less courageous husbands and brothers listen at a greater distance."

"We shall not attempt to give the results of this branch of our work, for many of them are not such as to be thrown into statistical tables. But they are none the less real. Knowledge has been increased; interest has been excited; the Gospel message has been discussed in many a locality; thousands, though still determined not to embrace it, yet begin to admit its truth, and several more villages are expressing a wish to adopt Christianity as their religion. Four men of good caste have joined us during the year, and are receiving instruction as candidates for baptism. We firmly believe that this work is gradually but surely dislodging heathenism, and preparing the way for the general acceptance of the true faith. It may be that many years, perhaps generations, must pass before our hopes, founded on the promises of the God of Truth, will be realized. But this is not our concern. Sooner or later, the predicted end will surely come, and we labor on happy in the confidence that God will, by accomplishing his purposes, vindicate the infallible certainty of His given word."

We close this topic with a few exceptionally interesting cases of individual conversion, resulting directly from evangelistic work.

ABRAHAM REDDI.

" One of the Adults who has received baptism in the past year, demands a brief notice as a case of peculiar interest. He is a young man of the Reddi caste, who, some time since heard the Gospel preached in the streets of Chittoor. His attention was at once arrested, and he determined to examine the claims of Christianity. He came to Vellore for further instruction, and soon became convinced that Jesus is the only Saviour of mankind. Of his own accord he broke his caste, and threw in his lot with the people of God. His friends have recently been here, and did all in their power to persuade him to return to his village. He has, however, resisted their efforts, fearing lest he should fall into the snare of the devil and make shipwreck of his faith. He has been with us about nine months, and his whole conduct has manifested a steadfastness and earnestness which lead us to believe that he is indeed one of the Lord's chosen people."

We add, with much gratification, that Abraham Reddi has served the Master with exceptional piety and zeal ever since his conversion. His remarkable sweetness and equanimity of temper, combined with uncompromising firmness in all matters of duty and devotion to his Lord, have made him a great favorite, as well as an eminently useful man, among both Christians and heathen. The miraculous transformation

ABRAHAM AND FAMILY.

of a degraded pagan into a trophy of grace so lustrous and symmetrical, is worth ten times all the money expended on the Arcot Mission.

ANOTHER REDDI CONVERTED.

Several missionaries on a tour, visited the village of Kotta Kotai, about twelve miles north of Chittoor. They met in its street with a young Reddi, concerning whom one of them writes as follows:—

"This young man, there first heard of the new and living way, and resolved to walk in it. He visited us at the bungalow; expressed his determination, and, though faithfully informed of the difficulties that awaited him, and of the trials he might be called on to encounter, he shrank not; but voluntarily renounced caste; abandoned all; and for fear of detection and its inevitable consequence, immediately went to a catechist's house in Chittoor. There he remained for some days learning more of the truth, and evincing most resolutely his abhorrence of idolatry. Though his subsequent conduct has not been, in all respects, so satisfactory as could be desired, he has shown no inclination to return to his former practices; and we trust that more intimate acquaintance with Christian truth may develop his character, and strengthen him in the faith."

A BRAHMIN CONVERTED.

"A young Brahmin joined us at Mudnapilly, at which place we spent a few days while touring in that region. We had preached several times in the town and surrounding villages, and had noticed this young man in his visit to our tent for the purpose of procuring books; but we had no intimation of any wish on his part to embrace Christianity until the day of our departure, when he came and asked permission to accompany us. He left, unknown to his friends; divested himself of his sacred thread and tuft of hair, two decided marks of heathenism; broke caste, by eating with our Christian boys; attended us during the remainder of the tour, going with us into the streets to preach; and gave us every reason to be satisfied with his sincerity and earnestness. He has now been with us nearly six months. About three months ago he was, at his own request, baptized."

A PERSECUTED CONVERT.

"On our last tour, we found a lad whom we had lost sight of for nearly a year. He joined us from heathenism about two years ago. A short time afterwards, a desire to see his friends so overcame him, that he ran away from the Seminary into which he had been admitted. He, however, gladly returned with two native Christians whom we sent in search of him. When the next vacation occurred, I gave him leave to go home for two weeks. He went, but did not return. Nearly a year passed, when one of our preaching tours brought us near his native village. He made his appearance at our tent, and declared that he had been prevented from returning to us by his relations. It seems that they did everything in their power to induce him to apostatize from the faith, and relapse into heathenism. Failing in every other attempt, they thought to secure him by forcing him into the marriage relation. A girl was brought and placed at his side, and the nuptial ceremony was performed. As he refused to tie on the *tali*,* his friends caught his hands and forced him to do it. As soon as he was released, he tore the *tali* from the neck of the girl, protested against the violent proceedings and left the house. Not only did he resist every attempt to make him worship idols, but he went from place to place reading religious tracts to the people, and telling them of the Saviour. When he heard of our arrival, he hastened to our tent, and declared his determination never again to leave us. I could scarcely credit this account which the lad gave of himself, until his heathen relatives came and confirmed every word of it. When I asked them whether he had refused to worship idols,

---

* The tali is the Hindu marriage token corresponding to our wedding ring. In the nuptial ceremony, the bridegroom ties it around the bride's neck.

they answered most bitterly: 'Yes, and he has done nothing for the last eleven months but preach Christianity.' They did all in their power to induce him to return home with them. He, however, resisted their entreaties, and is now pursuing his studies again in the Seminary."

CONVERTED FROM IDOLATRY BY AN IDOL.

"Another lad joined us a few months since. He was attending the annual festival at a celebrated temple, when the huge idol-car came to a sullen stop, and could not be moved on by the united efforts of the multitude. It remained out all night, and persons were stationed about the idol to guard its jewels from robbery. As the young man witnessed this scene, he became convinced that an idol which cannot help its own car and guard its own jewels is not a god. This conviction was strengthened by a tract which was handed to him during the festival. Shortly after, he wandered up to Arcot. Weary and faint, he sat down on the steps of our church. Soon the wife of the native pastor came to the church, and seeing the lad, spoke to him of the Saviour, who said: 'Come unto me all ye that labor and are heavy laden and I will give you rest.' He entered the church, listened to the sermon, and afterwards held a long conversation with the native pastor. As the result of this, he determined to become a Christian. He was sent to Vellore, and has been under instruction ever since."

A DETERMINED BRAHMIN.

"A Brahmin came to us a few months since, and besought us to receive him to the Christian religion. As we had known nothing of him previously, and as his knowledge of the Bible was limited, we put him off. We, however, instructed him, and supplied him with religious reading. He is still urging us most earnestly to receive him, though we have told him of the fearful sacrifice he must make in becoming a Christian. He declares that it is the Spirit of the Lord who has brought him to his present state of mind; that he simply throws himself at Jesus' feet, and that he is prepared to meet all the trials which may follow his change of faith. We have seen nothing in his conduct to cause us to doubt his sincerity, and shall probably soon comply with his urgent request to be received."

Such instances might be cited *ad libitum*, but the above will suffice for illustrative purposes.

TABLE SHOWING EVANGELICAL WORK DURING TWELVE YEARS.

ANNO DOMINI.	NUMBER OF ADDRESSES.	NUMBER OF AUDIENCES.	NUMBER OF BOOKS DISTRIBUTED.
1864	3,113	93,824	8,481
1865	2,976	82,337	5,022
1866	3,978	79,939	5,461
1867	2,901	91,470	4,479
1868	6,679	202,283	8,949
1869	10,171	235,392	8,945
1870	13,875	337,385	11,500
1871	13,927	330,814	11,698
1872	11,819	344,397	8,379
1873	11,974	338,399	5,336
1874	12,548	359,804	6,390
1875	10,513	297,132	6,254
12 YEARS	104,474	2,793,176	90,894

There is no statistical record of the evangelistic work done during the first eleven years of the mission's existence. It should be remarked, that in the above table, the statistics of the four years,—1864 to 1867, inclusive, are incomplete; returns having been made by only a part of those engaged in the work. From 1868, onward, the record was fully and accurately kept, and may therefore be relied on, as giving a correct view of the work done during that period.

FREE READING ROOMS.

As an additional means of instruction and evangelization, Free Reading Rooms have been opened in the business streets of several of the larger Stations. These rooms are supplied with religious and secular magazines, periodicals and newspapers for general reading. Bibles, tracts and miscellaneous books are also kept for sale, and one or two catechists attend several hours daily, to preach and to converse with visitors, who often assemble in large numbers. At one of these Reading Rooms, the Gospel was preached in a single year 268 times, to 12,860 heathen, and 299 religious and educational works were sold.

EDUCATIONAL DEPARTMENT.

THE ARCOT SEMINARY.

The prime necessity of securing an efficient staff of Native Assistants, was, as we have before mentioned, fully appreciated by the Mission at the earliest period of its existence. The difficulty of procuring and transporting foreign laborers to the field—to say nothing of the comparatively large expenses unavoidably connected with their maintenance there, renders it sufficiently obvious, that as much as possible of the work of evangelization should be devolved upon qualified natives, whose services can be at once more easily procured and far more economically continued. Add to this, the fact that the self-sustentation of the native Christian church, independently of foreign aid,—a consummation in the last degree desirable, is conditioned by an adequate supply of indigenous pastors and teachers, and the further fact that only such pastors and teachers can eventually meet the social and sympathetic exigencies of the native churches; and we need say no more as to the eminent suitableness of making the education and training of such men, one of the capital aims of thought and effort.

Moreover, experience has amply proved that in India, at the present stage, at least, of Christian development, each mission can secure a serviceable corps of native helpers only by its own prevision and effort to that end; and that missions which depend on a supply, from sources however good, external to themselves, are invariably hampered and embarrassed by both the paucity and incompetence of their native coadjutors.

Moved by these considerations, the Arcot Mission has always desired and sought to make its Male Seminary, a first-class educational establishment; and to approximate its constitution and scholarship, as closely as the nature of things would allow, to those of colleges and seminaries in more favored lands.

The effort has proved, partially, a success. We say partially, because adverse circumstances, which, on a retrospective view, are the more to be regretted as they seem not to have been altogether unavoidable, have certainly postponed, not to say prevented, the full attainment of what has continually been desired and aimed at. The unanimous sense of the mission has always demanded that at least one missionary, relieved of other duties, should devote his whole time and effort to the Institution; and that the expenditure of money needed for its vigorous maintenance, ought to be limited only by a judicious economy. But, in point of fact, neither of these desiderata has been compassed. The first has even been thwarted by the small number of missionaries, laboring under too great tension; and the second by a pecuniary condition, always restricted and incommensurate to the demands of the institution. The consequence is that, while moderately good results have been unquestionably reached, and a fairly useful body of native assistants have been trained and inducted into offices suited to their acquirements and abilities, the primary and paramount aim of the Seminary, viz., the supplying of ordained pastors to the native churches, has not been accomplished. Its graduates are, in the main, excellent men, well qualified to be teachers and catechists; and many of them have proved signally useful in those capacities. Yet the fact remains that, owing chiefly to a partial lack in them of self-reliant judgment and of original. independent energy, neither the Classis nor the missionaries have ever yet deemed it best to ordain any one of them as a minister of the Gospel. We believe that this defect in character is traceable mainly to the privation of a constantly formative and stimulating personal influence which cannot be had in India, apart from the foreign agency. Had the lads, while in the Seminary, been uniformly in direct disciplinary contact with a missionary devoted especially to its superintendence, we doubt not that the infirmity alluded to, would have been, in a large measure, corrected if not thoroughly cured; and that a sufficient number of the graduates would have been found qualified, in this respect as they already are in others, for the highest office in the Church. We have dwelt somewhat at length and emphatically on this point, because now more than ever it is important that native pastors should be provided for the native churches. Yet, notwithstanding that urgent appeals have been made, there seems little immediate prospect that the difficulty will be remedied. Unquestionably a missionary ought to be specially appointed to this department, and that without delay; else must much of the fruit, acquired by long years of patient toil, be either lost or suffer sad deterioration.

We pass to a brief descriptive and historical sketch of the Seminary:—

The students at the Institution are all boarders, and—a few weeks excepted,—spend the entire year within its walls. Thus they are kept—as is very necessary in India—under constant supervision and training. In fact, they are regarded as children of the mission, and every effort possible, with the means in hand, is made to equip them physically, mentally, and spiritually for the work to which they are prospectively destined. The curriculum is arranged to continue six years, and is as liberal as circumstances will allow. It embraces:—

IN THE ACADEMIC DEPARTMENT:

Geography; Grammar and Readings in four languages, Tamil, Telugu, Sanscrit, and Greek; Mathematics, including Arithmetic, Algebra, and Euclid; History, universal and particular; Natural History; Astronomy; Anatomy; Moral Science, and Anthology in four languages.

IN THE THEOLOGICAL DEPARTMENT:

Exegesis of the Old and New Testaments with Commentaries and Analytical text-books; Harmony of the Gospels; Shorter, and Heidelberg Catechisms, with Commentaries and proof-texts. Exposition of Prophecy; Sacred Geography; Church History; Lectures on Theology, Didactic, Polemic, Pastoral, &c.; Whateley's, and Rhenius' Evidences of Christianity; Rhenius' Body of Divinity; Test of Religions; Butler's Sermons; Beschis' Instructions to Catechists; Pilgrim's Progress; Claude's Essay, with practical sermonizing, &c., &c. The pupils are also experimentally trained for evangelistic labor by occasionally accompanying the missionaries on their itinerating tours, and by weekly excursions with the teachers to neighboring heathen villages; in the latter of which, the boys themselves have been known to preach to more than 16,000 people in a single year.

The classes are examined every week, by the missionaries in charge; and annually by a committee of the Mission, and also by the Government Inspector of schools separately. We would gladly quote some of the reports of the examiners, but space forbids; and we must content ourselves with the remark that those reports are, in general, eulogistic of the institution and its students; and that the Government emphasizes its approbation by making an annual award of several hundred Rupees to meet in part the salaries of the native teachers.

Habits of cleanliness are inculcated and enforced; and industry, as well as health, is promoted by requiring a measure of physical labor on the arable land adjoining the building. The spiritual interests of the pupils are looked after with prayerful diligence, and, we rejoice to add, with the happiest results; as is evinced by the pleasing fact, that almost all the graduates are now leading consistent and useful lives as servants of Christ and agents of the Mission. The expense of board, clothing, and books for each student, averages $40 per annum.

There is room barely to epitomize the history of the Seminary during the period under review. In the year 1861, there were only twenty boarders. The quick development of the village movement, which began in 1864, surprised the mission with but a small and, relatively to the rapidly expanding work, an utterly insufficient staff of assistants; and the embarrassment resulting therefrom, induced a correspondingly rapid annual enlargement of the Institution until it reached its highest number of fifty-two students in 1869. The supply of native helpers having, in time, overtaken the demand, the list of pupils has, since then, gradually narrowed down to the figure of twenty-nine in 1876.

The large increase of boarders in 1865 and 1866 necessitated what had previously been desirable, viz., the erection of a building for the institution. Up to that time the students had occupied s null, ill-ventilated out-houses, situated on ground so low that " water stood six inches deep in the rooms whenever it rained heavily." The increase of occupants augmented, by over-crowding, the already sufficiently obvious unfitness of the damp and unhealthy premises. Cases of dysentery, fever and congestion of the lungs, became alarmingly frequent; and it was feared that the constitutions of several of the sufferers were permanently shattered. Urgent appeals, enforced by these painful arguments were made, and resulted in securing, in the year 1867, an appropriation of $9,000. Eligible grounds, on which already stood a house suitable for the residence of the missionary and his family, were immediately purchased, and the Seminary building soon began to rise from the earth. It was completed in due time, and on the 23d December, 1868, was occupied by the school, after its solemn dedication with interesting exercises, to the service of God. It is a handsome and substantial brick edifice, with ample accommodation for eighty or more boarders. See Illustration on page 62.

The great drawback to the complete success of this Institution, has, from the first, been the want of the continued and exclusive services of a competent Head. Desirable as it was that two missionaries, one of them devoted to the Seminary, should reside at Vellore; the claims of other sections of the field upon the limited foreign force were always too pressing to admit of such an arrangement. Consequently, the time and efforts of the one missionary stationed at Vellore, being of necessity distributed among a multiplicity of cases and duties, it was simply impossible for him, without neglecting equally pressing interests, to give the Seminary the attention

ARCOT SEMINARY, VELLORE.

which its importance merited. Repeated, but always unsuccessful attempts were made to engage a European master. And so the Mission was reluctantly compelled to content itself with the possibilities of the situation. All that could be done with the best native teachers procurable, was done; their instructions being supplemented, so far as other engagements would allow, by those of the missionaries and missionary ladies residing at the Station. As already stated, the results, while they have been by no means a failure, have yet fallen short of the chief aim of the school, viz: providing native pastors for the native churches.

We close this sketch with one or two pertinent extracts from the latest Mission Reports:

"We cannot leave this subject without urging upon the Board the necessity of sending a man out specially for this Institution. The indispensableness of this action is felt every day. The fact that good native teachers have been secured, does not affect the question. It still needs the impress of a western mind, western discipline, and a western code of morality to make the boys strong and efficient; and not till these are secured, will they go forth thoroughly armed as far as human training goes."

Again: "There is, however, an indispensable condition to the efficiency and success of this Institution in the future, and that is a proper master. Each year convinces us more and more of this. If we want efficient men who, in addition to a thorough educational training, shall carry with them a moral force that shall make itself felt, they must come in contact more intimately and more continuously with a well-trained western mind. This can only be effected by a missionary giving his *whole time* to the interests of the school, and spending the greater part of each day with the lads. However well-trained and educated a native may be, he does not possess the power and tact of successfully training other minds; and the experience of other and older Missions has led them to supply their higher institutions with trained European teachers. The result is that men going out of institutions so furnished are at a premium, men capable of meeting responsibility and inspiring confidence."

"This is no new question with us. We have thought and talked much about it privately, and at our Mission conferences, and have again and again proposed to the Board to send out either a minister or layman to take charge of the Seminary and devote his whole time to its interests. Financial embarrassment and other causes, however, prevented. Still, so fully were we impressed with the necessity and importance of this measure that we resolved at our annual meeting in 1874 to try and secure the services of a teacher from Germany, and meet his salary, for a time, from such donations as we could obtain from friends in India. This project, however, failed. Our work has now reached a stage in which the services of such a master have become more than ever necessary, even indispensable to our efficiency and success. Though men who go out from the Seminary are many of them good men with fair attainments and good purposes, they yet lack some of the traits of habit and thought which are essential to complete success; and which the miscellaneous character of our present efforts, however useful, can never secure to them. Nothing short of a well-qualified foreign master who will make it his *business* to train these young men, will meet the case. The subject is of the utmost importance; for the future of our mission depends very much on the character of the agents we employ. A missionary could not devote his powers to a better purpose, and we earnestly hope the Board will give the subject immediate and serious consideration, and send us a man as early as possible."

FEMALE SEMINARY AT CHITTOOR.

The women of India have for ages been rigidly debarred from all educational privileges. The laws of the sacred Sastras, equally with the hereditary and inveterate prejudices of the people, are inexorably hostile to the intellectual culture of the female sex. None but courtesans learn to read and write; and, if by any possibility, a respectable woman should become possessed of even these elementary acquirements, the fact would, unless carefully concealed, brand her with indelible shame. Missionaries have from the first, appreciated the importance of rebuking this barbarous and abhorrent usage, and of demonstrating to the Hindu by the actual education and elevation of members of the sex, the possibility and feasibility of blending moral excellence and purity with intellectual culture, in the *tout ensemble* of woman's character. Influenced by these considerations, as well as by a wish to confer the priceless gift of science upon the defrauded moiety of India's people, and pressed, furthermore, by the conspicuous suitableness of providing intelligent and companionable wives for their native assistants, the Arcot Mission gave timely attention and prominence to the subject of Female Education. Girls' schools were opened immediately on its establishment, and so early as the year 1855, we find this record: "Three orphan girls have been taken into the Missionary's house as boarders, who, with three other large girls, are instructed daily. These will probably form the germ of a Girls' Boarding School.

We would be glad to increase the number, but have not the means for their support. Those already received are maintained by private charity." Two years later the number of boarders was seven, and in 1860, had increased to fourteen. At this period, we find the "Female Seminary" among the permanently established institutions of the Mission: still small from the lack of funds, but prosperous and full of hope for the future.

MANAGEMENT AND AIMS.

The Seminary has always been under the superintendance of the missionary-lady, resident at Chittoor, assisted by an excellent matron and one or two native teachers. Its design is not so much brilliant scholarship and striking results, as it is the qualifying its pupils to perform in a womanly and efficient way, the duties of the station in life, which as the wives of native helpers or teachers in primary schools, the greater part of them are expected to occupy. To raise them above their prospective condition, would be tantamount to making them disappointed and discontented, not to say unhappy women, for the greater part of their lives. The aim therefore, is not to anglicize, but conversely, to keep them simple-minded Hindu girls; retaining all such native customs as are innocent, and suited to their particular sphere in life. A plain but thorough education in Tamil, Telugu and English, together with proficiency in needlework, cooking and general domestic economy, is the result kept in view. Cleanliness and thrifty diligence are prescribed and insisted on. The pupils make their own clothes, do the cooking and all other household work connected with the institution, and are required to keep their persons as well as the building, scrupulously neat and orderly. While on the one hand no pains are spared to extirpate fatuous and irrational prejudices, and to break up pernicious habits, on the other, every effort is made to imbue the pupils with right principles of thought and action; and, above all else, to lead them to a whole-hearted consecration of themselves to the Saviour. A large proportion of their time every day is given to the study of the Bible, and they are early made conversant with the Heidelberg and other Catechisms. It is not saying too much to add, that consequently their acquaintance with sacred history and biblical doctrine is larger and more thorough than that of most girls of their ages in Christian lands.

The rapid development of the Mission in the years 1863 and 1864, rendered necessary a corresponding enlargement of the corps of native helpers, and in 1865 it was decided to increase the number of scholars in each Seminary to fifty. This action made the erection of adequate quarters for the teachers and pupils an urgent necessity. The missionary in charge of the Female Seminary had already, in 1863, written as follows:

"It is very desirable that a suitable building should be provided for this institution. The boarders, averaging twenty-five souls, are crowded into two small godowns,* adjoining the Mission-house. These are open to the observation of every passer-by. This compels an amount of vigilance and anxiety

---

* Small outhouses or offices, measuring ten by twelve feet.

which is very trying. All acquainted with the dangers attending female boarding-schools in India, will at once apprehend the needfulness of affording proper accommodation and seclusion to the girls. This we cannot do, from want of funds. The missionary will be glad to receive donations for this purpose."

Again, in 1864, he writes:—" In the report of last year, I represented the desirableness of providing a suitable building for the accommodation of the Seminary. I am now compelled to speak of it as an absolute necessity. Health, cleanliness, and morality, all demand that the scholars shall no longer be kept in the small, crowded and uncomfortable rooms which they have hitherto occupied in one of the Station outhouses. The mission has long felt the need of a change, and has authorized me to put up a proper building, provided I can raise the needed funds. I am sorry to say that my appeal last year proved almost fruitless. About 400 Rupees were all the moneys donated in response, whereas 2,500 Rupees, at the smallest calculation, is the sum required."

Once more in 1865, after recounting the cheering prosperity of the school during the previous year, he adds:—

"I am sorry, however, that I am still forced to complain. The Seminary is utterly without proper accommodations. Nearly thirty girls are yet crowded into two small, low godowns, contracted and without ventilation. Health, cleanliness and morals are all at stake. For two years I have made loud appeals for relief. But there has been no adequate response. During the last twelve months about one thousand Rupees were subscribed towards erecting a suitable house; and, with the approbation of the Mission, I began and have carried the work up to that amount of expenditure. At least 2000 Rupees more, are necessary to complete the edifice.

I can only call out again, hoping and praying that, by the blessing of God, the call may prove loud and effective enough to enter Christian hearts, and cause them to well forth benevolence in furtherance of this most worthy enterprise. Christian mothers, think of the comforts and privileges and blessings with which a bountiful Providence surrounds your highly favored daughters; and in gratitude to the Giver, send your gifts and offerings to release their humble sisters from discomfort and danger. Every Rupee you give for this object will, I feel assured, be returned with large interest into the treasury of your prosperity. 'There is that scattereth, and yet increaseth' 'The liberal soul shall be made fat, and he that watereth shall be watered also himself' Good security, surely, for all who will send contributions to this work!"

Up to this point, the Missionary's tune is decidedly in the key minor, despondent; but just here we find a sudden and enlivening transition to the key major, triumphant. In 1866, he writes:

"It gives me great pleasure to say that the building begun in 1865 is now almost completed. It is a spacious and commodious edifice; and will conduce largely to the comfort and health of its inmates. Thus, a great source of anxiety and vexation is dried up."

And in 1867:—

"This Institution furnishes the brightest coloring in the picture of our work for the year. The removal of the pupils from two small, unventilated godowns into a large and airy building has proved in every way beneficial. The transfer has been strikingly productive of improvement, physical, mental and moral. The girls are firmer in health, immensely more cheerful in disposition, brighter in intellect, and, on the whole, much better behaved than in former years. The only wonder is that, in their old quarters, they did not degenerate into living mummies. We, as well as the inmates of the new building, revel in plenty of room, plenty of air, and plenty of resulting comfort, all of which are found in our recently completed seminary building. We are very thankful for it, and its conveniences."

It is but justice to state that, of the money expended in the erection of this building, the greater part, $2,000, was given by Mrs. Susan Gridley, a noble Christian lady of Utica, N. Y.

Possessed now of ample accommodation, the Seminary rapidly increased the number of its pupils from thirty to fifty-five; this last being the highest figure ever reached. The services of a competent principal were secured; the course of study was enlarged and systematized; more effective methods of teaching and discipline were introduced, and the Institution was placed on altogether a better footing. The pupils, besides undergoing a weekly examination by the lady in charge, were subjected once a year to a thorough testing of their acquirements and progress by a committee of the Mission. The reports of the committees have been uniformly favorable, and in many instances highly commendatory. We give a single extract :—

"The Female Seminary Committee beg leave to report that they have thoroughly examined all the classes in the studies of the year; and are happy to say that the examination has been very creditably sustained, showing both diligent application on the part of the students and persevering drilling on the part of the teachers. The classes showed also a very pleasing proficiency in music by singing christian lyrics in chorus both in Tamil and Telugu, which were rendered in perfect harmony and rhythm, with distinct pronunciation, and in a sweet tone of voice. The committee went over the spacious building lately erected, and inspected the sleeping, eating, cooking, bathing, and other rooms, and found them all clean and neat. They furthermore partook of the mid-day meal of curry and rice prepared by the girls themselves, and found their housewifery unexceptional."

In addition to the examination by the Mission Committee, the pupils have, of late years, been subjected to a distinct examination by officials of the Government. E. C. Caldwell, Esq., the Government Inspector of Schools, in his report of 1874 to the Director of Public Instruction, says:—

"*Sir:* I have the honor in forwarding the accompanying certifying memorial of the American Mission Girls' Boarding School at Chittoor, to report that the school is held in a large and commodious building, built expressly for the purpose, and that it is more than ordinarily well and efficiently managed. The number of pupils on the roll was fifty-four, of whom fifty were present for examination. Their attendance, owing doubtless in part to the pupils being boarded in the establishment, was remarkably good. Their answering too was particularly good, with the exception in arithmetic of a few girls whose progress in that branch was not in keeping with their standard on other subjects. In sewing, as in the case of the schools of the same mission in Vellore, the girls were generally far in advance of the standards required of them."

A grant to the Seminary of Rupees 688, was awarded by Government as the "result" of this examination. The crochet and other fancy work done by the girls is sold from time to time, and has of late realized from Rupees 200 to 250 a year. The proceeds of the sales added to the annual grants of Government under the "result system" materially assist in the maintenance of the institution.

The religious complexion of the Seminary has been singularly bright and cheering. From its origin almost, the blessing of God in the operation of His Spirit has conspicuously attended the efforts made to lead the pupils to a personal surrender to Christ. There have been periods of exceptional interest in spiritual things. The observance of the "week of prayer" in January, 1860, was followed by a manifest tenderness of feeling. Voluntary prayer meetings were held, and five out of the fourteen boarders were received to the communion of the church. In 1863 six girls were brought to the Saviour; and the religious interest pervading the school had its exponent in the observance of three meetings for prayer spontaneously held by the pupils every day throughout the year. The report of the same period contains the following noteworthy statement:—

"We record with delighted gratitude the fact that all the girls who from the first have been graduated from this Seminary, either went out of it professing Christians, or became such shortly after their separation. The most of them are partners of our own native helpers; and, so far as we know, all of them without exception have, up to this time, lived consistently as disciples of Jesus. How precious and encouraging is this evidence that the blessing of Jehovah is upon our Female Seminary."

Similar records embellish the reports of 1868, 1872, 1874 and 1876, in which years respectively eight, eighteen, seven and nine girls avowed themselves the handmaidens of the Saviour. In all sixty-four pupils have been gathered into the church; and twenty-six of the forty-three girls now in the institution are communicants. Verily the record is one calculated to stimulate the zeal and beneficence of all who have been in any way conducive to such felicitous results.

The systematic benevolence of the scholars, exercised at the cost of veritable self-denial, must not be omitted from our picture. Many of them orphans, and all from poor families, they are without "spending money" and other potential sources of school-girl charity. Yet, in recent years, we find these humble Hindu girls contributing to religious and charitable enterprises an annual average of ninety Rupees—a very large sum relatively to their circumstances. It should interest American Christians, and pique their generous impulses, to know that the pupils of the Chittoor Female Seminary amass this sum by voluntarily and cheerfully denying themselves a portion of their allotted food every day through the year. Benevolence which goes partially hungry, that it may relieve the gnawing necessities of others is as indubitably genuine as it is charmingly beautiful.

Death has seldom visited the Seminary. One little girl nine years old, died in November, 1866. During the early stages of her illness she spoke sweetly of her Saviour, testifying delightfully to her faith in His blood. Subsequently she was seized with convulsions and remained unconscious to the end. Jessie, aged fourteen, died in April, 1869. She suffered much for several months previous to her decease; but her trials were borne with meekness and submission. Her pastor saw her frequently, and was much cheered by the spirit she manifested. Full of confidence in her Redeemer, she repeatedly and emphatically expressed the wish to be released from her pains and find rest with Jesus. Her end was perfect peace. Two more girls, one of whom was a communicant, were taken off by typhoid fever in 1872. Continued delirium prevented any intelligent manifestation of religious consciousness; but it is hoped that both are in a happier world. A fifth, concerning whom no special record is found, died a year or two ago. These are all the deaths which have occurred in a period of more than twenty years.

The annexed table gives the statistics of the institution from its inception to the present time.

STATISTICS OF THE FEMALE SEMINARY, FROM 1855 TO 1876.

	1855	1856	1857	1859	1860	1861	1862	1863	1864	1865	1866	1867	1868	1869	1870	1871	1872	1873	1874	1875	1876
Total number of boarders	3	4	7	11	14	13	12	20	25	30	34	46	46	53	55	55	48	54	54	53	43
Admitted to ch'h					5			6			4	2	8	5			18		7		9
Married						1	1	3	3			2	2	4	1	7		4		9	8
Died										1				1			2			1	

OTHER EDUCATIONAL AGENCIES OF THE MISSION.

I.—THE PRÆPARANDI SCHOOL.

This is an institution founded in the year 1863 as a refuge for young men and boys rendered homeless and friendless by their renunciation of Hinduism and adoption of Christianity Quite a number of such persons join the Mission almost every year. Many of them are from the higher castes, and some are members of wealthy heathen families. These converts, are, as a matter of course in every instance, renounced and left helpless and destitute by their relatives and friends. In the earlier periods of the Mission they were received directly into the Arcot Seminary; but this policy having proved disadvantageous in some regards, a separate school was established for their education and training. Into this they are admitted on probation; and after passing through a preparatory course, are, if found worthy, subsequently transferred to the higher institution with a view to their becoming agents of the Mission. The original number, six, had increased to forty-three in 1870. Sixty-six of the students have been, at various times, baptized, and eighteen admitted to the Church. "Some bright lights have gone forth from this institution, and are doing good service for the Master." Were there space, cases of great interest might be related here.

II.—CASTE GIRLS' SCHOOLS.

Misses Martha Mandeville and Josephine Chapin joined the mission in 1870. After devoting some time to the study of the language—both ladies assisting meanwhile in the instruction of classes in the Arcot Seminary—they, in 1872, opened in Vellore, two schools designed exclusively for the daughters of the higher classes of Hindus. These schools met almost immediately with a degree of success quite unexpected, in view of the hereditary national prejudices against female education. A third school was established in 1873; and an aggregate attendance of from 160 to 180 scholars was secured. The Bible has been used as a text-book, and religious instruction given with little or no opposition on the part of the parents. The pupils were examined in 1874 and 1875 by E. C. Caldwell, Esq., the Government Inspector of Schools. In the former year fifty-five and in the latter fifty girls passed successfully, and received the hearty commendation of the inspector. As a result of the examinations, the schools are awarded about $300 annually; which sum nearly covers the expense of their maintenance.

The following extracts from late reports are of interest:—

"Sewing is still an important feature in these schools. Many of the girls in the advanced classes are able to cut and make their own garments. In this, we are already reaping some of the fruits of our labors. A few months ago one of the older girls in Sullivanspettah school begged to be allowed to teach a small class in sewing. She proved herself so capable, that, for the present, she has charge of all the sewing classes in that school. A more dignified and womanly character can scarcely be found in one of her years and stature. She seems especially fitted to fill a responsible position."

"The Scriptures are taught daily, and a great change is manifest both in children and parents in regard to this branch of study. The people protested strongly at first against the introduction of Christian instruction; and the children seemed to have imbibed the prejudices of their parents. Now, they drink in Bible truths almost eagerly; and not only carry their Catechisms and Bible portions to their homes, but are permitted to read and study them there aloud without interruption."

"The secular instruction is thorough and efficient, and the Scripture lessons are learned with great interest by the little girls, and with little or no opposition from their parents. The anniversary recently held was attended by a large and interested audience of native gentlemen who expressed great pleasure on witnessing the proficiency of the little girls in their lessons. Their sewing was also greatly admired and commended. There seems no reason why the schools should not go on increasing in numbers and influence, and gaining the favor of the people, if they could only have proper superintendence."

"These schools have been continued during the year, 1876, with increased prosperity. The number of scholars has increased, so that there are now 220 names on the roll. Both schools have been examined by the Deputy Inspector and a grant of nearly 800 Rupees awarded. Besides secular studies, the girls are instructed in needlework and in lessons from the Bible. The latter seem to be especially interesting to them, and they never tire of listening to stories from the Old and New Testaments. We feel confident that the seeds of divine truth sown in these youthful minds will bear fruit in the future."

Miss Chapin was compelled by the failure of her health to return to America in 1874, and in the following year Miss Mandeville was appointed to take temporary charge of the

Female Seminary in Chittoor. Mrs. E. C. Scudder, and after her departure, Mrs. John Scudder, have done all they could, consistently with other duties, to supply the place of the young ladies. But the schools have suffered, and are still suffering from the lack of adequate superintendence. It is extremely desirable that such superintendence should be supplied without delay.

III.—PRIMARY SCHOOLS.

Of these little need be said. Established in every Station and Out-station of the Mission, they are conducted at trifling expense; are taught by graduates of the Seminaries, male and female, and serve as feeders to the higher institutions. Their function is humble, but necessary and useful.

MEDICAL DEPARTMENT.

ARCOT DISPENSARY.

Mr. S. D. Scudder, M. D., was commissioned by the Board a medical missionary in 1860, and arrived at Madras in December of that year. It was expected that he would as soon as possible establish a Mission hospital and dispensary, and after having studied the language for a time, he was directed to do so. A suitable building was selected and engaged in Vellore, and the institution was just about to be opened, when his plans were suddenly frustrated by the embarrassment of the treasury, occasioned by the American war. Debarred temporarily from his specialty, he was ordained by the Classis of

Arcot to the gospel ministry, and in 1862, he was placed in spiritual charge of the Arcot Station. Unable, however, to suppress professional instincts, and unwilling to abandon the medical work, he, with the consent of the Mission, opened in that place a dispensary on a very small scale. The exigencies of the Mission caused his removal in the following year to Palamanair. Here, again, his renewed hopes and efforts were defeated by the want of an appropriation, and we find him balked, yet not despairing, venting his disappointment thus:

"I stated in my last report that I intended opening a dispensary at Palamanair. Though the Lord has not yet permitted me to fulfill that statement, I reiterate it, and still believe that the way will be opened. During the past year, I have been permitted to aid both medically and surgically, a large number of persons. But how many have I, in sorrow, to refuse! I have no money, no place in which to receive patients, no apothecary and no medicine. Not one Christian friend has, during the year, sent me pecuniary aid. I do not write, however, as one despairing. The Lord will not permit me to abandon this most important work. My heart is in it; my most earnest desire is to carry it on. I spent many long, hard-working years, and visited many lands in pursuit of medical knowledge. The knowledge obtained, shall through no lack on my part go to naught. I mean to have a dispensary, and I call upon the Lord's people to aid me in carrying out my intention."

This discouraging state of affairs continued until near the close of the year 1865, when the Foreign Board, though still carrying the debt incurred during the war, and having no funds collected for the special purpose, determined, in view of the great desirability of establishing a medical branch of this work in Arcot, to sanction the immediate opening of a dispensary and hospital, and directed the Mission to start the enterprise without delay. The joy occasioned by this action, found utterance in the following hopeful and glowing words:

"God has at length answered our prayers. After five long years of hope deferred and earnest efforts discouraged, when it appeared indeed, imperative to abandon the object, the small cloud betokening the ardently longed for rain arose; our Secretary wrote that we might hope anew for the dispensary. And we now know that it has been allowed by the Executive Committee. In the joy of our hearts, most truly can we exclaim: 'Bless the Lord, O my soul; and all that is within me, bless His holy name.' We hope very soon to commence operations. This action of the Committee in sanctioning a dispensary, under very adverse circumstances, is certainly one of great faith and true Christian nobility."

The hospital was opened in the city of Arcot, March 17, 1866. It met with considerable opposition at the outset. There was already in the place a small civil dispensary under charge of an East Indian apothecary; and this man, jealous of the new rival enterprise, exerted all his power to crush it in its incipiency. This he did, chiefly by spreading false reports to the effect that the missionary's object in establishing his dispensary, was to force Christianity upon the people; that to accomplish this he would stick at nothing; that by mixing unclean water with the medicines, and by keeping low caste servants to wait on the patients, he would destroy their caste;

that he was an intruder, and the Government would be angry with all who resorted to him for medical aid, &c., &c. These reports, while they did not materially influence the respectable and more intelligent natives, undoubtedly deterred the mass of the people—whose timidity, born of ignorance, is ever sensitive to such representations—from coming to the hospital; and after several months' trial, it seemed as if the undertaking must fail for lack of patients. It was at length determined to address the authorities, proposing that inasmuch as one efficiently conducted infirmary would meet the wants of the district, the Government should remove its dispensary with the attending apothecary, and give exclusive possession to the American establishment. This proposition, though adversely reported on by the English Collector of the district, was not only acceded to by the Government; but an order, the terms of which were extremely complimentary to the Mission, was immediately issued directing that the civil dispensary building together with its furniture and stock be turned over to Doctor Scudder for his institution; "which," the minister said, "the Government would desire to see started under as favorable auspices as possible." More than this, the Collector was ordered to pay to Doctor Scudder "one half of the annual amount hitherto devoted to the maintenance of the dispensary;" the Government requiring only "that he should submit an annual report on the working of his Arcot Dispensary."

Thus opportunely released, under a good Providence, from embarrassment, the institution sprang, almost instantaneously, into full and successful operation. The thickly populated district, and three large cities of from thirty to fifty thousand inhabitants each, all lying within two miles of the hospital, began at once to pour in their crowds of sick and suffering people; and the missionary doctor soon had his hands more than full of work. From the start, the gospel was regularly preached every morning to the assembled patients; and religious tracts and books were freely distributed among them without offence.

The native gentry and aristocracy showed themselves quite as ready as did the masses, to profit by the skill of the newly arrived physician. A lady-relative of the once famous and powerful Nawab of the Carnatic, was medically attended in her royal abode; the foreign doctor being admitted, contrary to all conventionalities, into the inner apartments of the palace. Mahommedan women of rank, who had perhaps never before emerged from their residences, were brought in closely covered conveyances to the hospital; and, tightly veiled, privately sought advice in the female ward. Brahmins and other high caste gentlemen visited the institution daily, many of them manifesting an enlightened interest in its economy and operation; and it became no strange sight to see several of them at a time occupying the benches on the verandah, and reading, as is their custom, aloud from the Scriptures, "the Bazaar Book," "Spiritual Teaching," or some other religious work. High and low, all came freely to the dispensary. The records show that members of no less than thirty-nine different castes continually resort to it for medical aid.

Various means were used to make the institution spiritually, as well as physically, a remedial agency. In addition to the daily preaching and distribution of tracts, already mentioned, Bibles and religious books—too large to be gratuitously bestowed, were kept for perusal on the premises; and even the admission tickets, one of which is given to each patient on his first presenting himself for treatment, were pressed into the service of truth, by printing texts of Scripture on one of their faces. A female Bible reader was employed in the woman's ward; and prayer meetings were held in the building for the in-patients, who, contrary to what was expected, offered no objections and seldom refused the altogether voluntary attendance solicited. The means were promptly blessed of God. We cannot withhold the account of the first two conversions which occurred within a few months of the opening of the dispensary.

CONVERSION OF A MOODELLIAR.

"God has blessed our dispensary. There have been two cases of, we trust, *true* conversion within its walls. Both cases are most interesting. We can give only a brief account of each. The first is that of a high caste man, (Moodelliar caste.) He applied to be received as an in-patient in May last. He was a mere wreck; his whole constitution was shattered by one of the worst of diseases. There seemed no hope of his recovery; but as he had come from a distant place he could not be refused, lest, turned out, he should die in the street. For two months he lived, as it were, upon a moiety of hope; his lower limbs paralyzed, and he in appearance a living skeleton. But it was not God's will that he should die. Our exertions were finally crowned with partial success. He is now able to walk about a little, and is slowly improving. He has renounced heathenism, broken his caste, and for some months declared most firmly and constantly his determination to love and serve the true God. He earnestly requests baptism."

"The other case is that of a Pariah woman, who was received as an in-patient in September last. She was exceedingly ill for some time, but finally recovered so far as to take her discharge from the hospital. When she was taken in, she was in extreme danger of death. She was plainly told her condition, and urged to turn her attention to spiritual matters, to endeavor to make that preparation for eternity which she so greatly needed. One must see to appreciate the fearful carelessness, callousness, and almost utter indifference with which most Hindus meet death: but very much to our surprise and gratification, this poor woman at once manifested a remarkable anxiety, a sincere desire to know what she must do, and begged most ardently to be instructed in the truth; declaring that she really wished to become a Christian, and knew that she must believe in Jesus alone, in order to be saved. She seemed to improve slowly from that time, and when she was discharged, that she might return to her work and support her two daughters, she declared with much firmness, as well as humbleness, that she would, with the help of the Lord, walk as a Christian. Unfortunately, she attempted too much, and by over-exerting herself had a relapse; her old disease, dysentery, attacking her with even greater malignancy than before; and very soon proving fatal, although every exertion was made and every care taken of her. A short time before she died she begged to be baptized. As she was failing very fast, the holy rite was administered,—the dresser and two or three of our church members being present. It was a solemn and impressive scene, one which the walls of that hospital probably never before witnessed. The poor woman became speechless almost immediately; but her satisfaction, her overflowing joy were most manifest on her happy, radiant countenance. Though suffering acutely, she died with a smile of peace on her lips, her hands clasped and raised toward heaven. When, just at the last, she was asked if she fully, truly, trusted in the Lord Jesus Christ, firmly believed Him to be her Rock and her Salvation, her only stay and comfort in the hour of death, her face lighted up with the joy of her soul, and her signs of assent were given with that faith the true believer alone can possess and exhibit. She was a poor widow, with two daughters, one almost an infant, the other a girl of perhaps thirteen years. These orphans are thus thrown on our hands, and we must take care of them. When their mother first understood that she must die, she begged us most earnestly to promise never to desert her little ones; to provide for and train them up in the fear of the Lord. Her mind could not be at ease, until we assured her that they should be cared for and religiously brought up. We cannot send them out into the cold wicked world, for they are utterly unfit to care for themselves. They are Christian children now, children of the covenant, and we must support them. Thus has our mighty God brought back to Himself, as we truly hope, through this institution, four of the lost, wandering sheep and lambs of His precious fold. One He has sealed to all eternity; she, is safe forever. The others we have the joy of spiritually caring for, praying for, and endeavoring to confirm in the faith. He who hath begun the good work, is able to finish it; to keep them all unto the end, and make them bright jewels in His own crown of glory."

We regret our inability to follow the history from year to year of this institution; certainly one of the most important among the agencies employed for the evangelization of the district. A thoroughly readable, not to say fascinating, account might easily be compiled from the detailed records before us; but we have space for little more than a concise and very general epitome of its operations and results.

Once fairly afloat, the institution enjoyed uninterrupted prosperity and success. Its curative and sanitary efficacy, too obvious to escape the attention even of the most stupid and prejudiced, soon became widely known through the district. In the year 1867, the second of its existence, 15,507 patients were treated; and in the following year, 1868, more than double that number—33,170—received advice and medicine within its walls. The attendance steadily increased until, in 1870, it reached its climax of 53,963. In each of the two succeeding years there were about 43,000 patients, and thence the number diminished gradually to 33,945 in 1875. This falling off must not be attributed to any declination of efficiency in the hospital, or diminution of confidence on the part of the people. It is sufficiently accounted for by the facts: First, that medical treatment, continued through several successive years, had not only cleared away accumulations of chronic disease, but had furthermore considerably ameliorated the general public health; and second, that the Government having, in the meantime, opened new dispensaries and strengthened old ones in various parts of the district, the inhabitants, naturally enough, resorted to the nearer rather than the more remote sources of relief.

The estimation in which the hospital was held by the Government authorities will best appear by a few extracts taken from their own records:

"The Collector of North Arcot wrote to the Chief Secretary of Government on the 24th of April, 1867, as follows: 'I have the honor to submit the annual report on the civil dispensary at Ranipet, now in medical charge of Dr. Scudder. So far, the results of the amalgamation are, in my opinion, exceedingly satisfactory. Comparing the returns, I find that the number of in-patients and out-patients admitted to the dispensary during the five months it was under charge of a paid apothecary was 41 and 1,233 respectively; whereas during the four and a half months it has been in Dr. Scudder's hands, the figures are 96 and 1,652. These latter results, it is also to be borne in mind, would have probably been much larger, had the full Government allowance been at Dr. Scudder's disposal. The figures should, I think, be accepted as conclusive on the two principal points, viz., that Dr. Scudder has the confidence of the people as a medical man, as a professional man; and that the principles on which the institution is being conducted have not given offence to the religious scruples of the native community.'"

On the 16th of May, the following order was passed:

"The Governor in Council has perused with much satisfaction, the very favorable report submitted in the foregoing letter on the civil dispensary at Ranipet under the management of Dr. Scudder."

Immediately after issuing this order, the Government donated rupees 1,000 to the hospital, and doubled its annual allowance.

In May, 1869, the dispensary was honored with a visit from His Excellency, Lord Napier, Governor of Madras, who, accompanied by his staff, carefully inspected the institution.

The following minute was read by His Excellency in Council, on the 3d of July succeeding:

"During my recent tour in North Arcot, I had occasion to visit the dispensary and hospital at Ranipet, in charge of the Rev. Silas Scudder of the American Mission. It is not necessary for me to enlarge upon the excellence and usefulness of this institution. It holds the position of a Government dispensary. By placing a Government building and a portion of the revenues of a charitable foundation at the disposal of Dr. Scudder, the Government manifested their entire confidence in his character and his discretion, as well as in his professional attainments; for some considerations of a delicate nature were involved in the surrender of a State Establishment to a foreign missionary. That confidence has been entirely justified by experience. The number of patients, as set forth in the accompanying annual reports, proves that the minister does not impair the physician, and that the heathen are not kept away by the temperate and conciliatory form in which the truths of Christianity are presented to their attention. On the other hand, it is unquestionable that the great experience which Dr. Scudder possesses of the country, and his accurate knowledge of the language, render him peculiarly fitted for the office of a propagandist of European science in an Indian community. I can bear testimony to the solicitude with which the in-patients are treated, and to the general efficiency of the material arrangements. Some defects in the accommodation, furniture and distribution, are explained by want of funds and by the character of the building. Dr. Scudder has brought to my notice several particulars in which the Government might still contribute to the improvement of the establishment."

After allusion to needed alterations, which he recommends to be made at the public expense, His Excellency remarks:

"In conclusion, I beg to call the attention of Government to the good service which the American Mission is rendering to humanity and enlightenment, by the education of native medical students, and by the translation of medical works into the vernacular of the country.

(signed) 'NAPIER.'"

On the 17th of July, a Government order was issued, authorizing the improvements suggested by Lord Napier, and concluding with these complimentary words:

"The Government avail themselves of this opportunity of recording their appreciation of the great benefits which the American Mission has rendered, and continues to render, to humanity and enlightenment, by its operations in connection with the Ranipet dispensary and kindred institutions."

THREATENED DESTRUCTION AVERTED.

In the year 1871, an official letter from the Board of Foreign Missions communicated the startling order, that the Treasury being $50.000 in debt, it had become impossible to sustain the present outlay of the Mission; and that, therefore, its work must be curtailed to the amount of $5.000. The Mission had no alternative but to comply, and after many days of careful and anxious conference, most reluctantly adopted, among other baleful but inevitable resolutions, the following:

"1st. To abandon our medical work, close the dispensary, inform the Government that we can no longer sustain it, and request them to take charge of everything belonging to them."

"2d. To send the Rev. S. D. Scudder, M. D., home, in view of the fact that his special work has ceased."

The Government, on learning this decision, resolved to save the institution if possible, and immediately made an additional grant of Rupees 1.500 to its funds. This sum, with the usual Government allowance, being sufficient to maintain the dispensary, though on a somewhat narrower scale than before, it was, notwithstanding the departure of Dr. Silas Scudder, continued under the charge of the Rev. John Scudder, M. D., who added its care to his other duties, until the arrival, in 1874, of H. M. Scudder, Jr., M. D. The expenses of the Establishment have, ever since 1871, been met entirely by Government, the Mission contributing nothing beyond the services of the physician in charge.

LYING-IN HOSPITAL.

Among the almost numberless trials of India's women, perhaps none is more distressing than the treatment they are subjected to in childbirth, and especially in cases of difficult labor. The functions of the midwife are performed always by superannuated females, whose temerity and cruelty are as reckless as their ignorance is dense and absolute. Their system—if system it may be called—of operative midwifery is marvellously barbarous; and the frightful tortures inflicted upon women in complicated labor, are too revolting to be described. Missionaries are not unfrequently called—often, alas, too late to rescue miserable dying victims from the grim consequences of the ordeal, as fruitless as it was shocking, through which they have passed. The subject is one which conventional decorum, very properly, forbids us to open out in this place. It is sufficient to mention the *fact* that cases are, from time to time brought to the hospital, of poor sufferers who have been enduring not only natural agonies for five, seven, and even ten days; but have in addition, undergone every barbarity which ignorance, stimulated by perplexed fear, could suggest. We need hardly add, that, in the majority of these deplorable cases, human art can do little more than palliate tortures which have only too surely effected their fatal work.

The subject was brought, by Dr. S. D. Scudder, to the notice of Government, in the year 1870; and the authorities were urged to send to every large dispensary, an educated nurse or midwife, not merely to attend lying-in-women, which would of course be her duty, but also to instruct and train other females in this particular department. Such skilled women, it was argued, would at once be employed by the higher native families; and the custom once established among the better classes, would soon work its way among the lower and more ignorant. The Government gave a favoring response to this appeal, and authorized the additional expense of a lying-in-ward at the Arcot dispensary; but owing to some red tape technicality, the money was not forthcoming for several years. We are happy to say, that this urgently needed department is now in full and successful operation.

The latest Report of the Mission says :—

"The success of the Lying-in-Hospital has exceeded our most sanguine expectations. Its popularity continues to increase, and its benefits are appreciated more and more by the people. The number of patients for the past year was eighty-five, and the number of operations six.

"Should this beneficent movement, suggested and initiated by the Arcot Mission, of establishing Lying-in-Hospitals throughout the rural districts be carried out, as is probable, by Government, it will prove an incalculable advantage to thousands who are now exposed to insufferable torments, resulting from the want of a little enlightened skill and attention."

NATIVE MEDICAL STUDENTS.

Soon after the opening of the dispensary a class of native Christian young men was, under the ruling of the Mission, formed, to be instructed in medicine and surgery, with the view of fitting them for medical missionary work in remote stations and districts where the advice of physicians is not obtainable. On this topic we must limit ourselves to the single remark—that several of these young men, after completing their course of study, have practiced successfully in various parts of the mission field, some of them reporting from seven to eight hundred patients a year; and that their services have proved very acceptable to the native community. We give a single extract, illustrative of their skill and usefulness:—

"Several months since the magistrate of Kalastri, in great haste, sent word to our Head Assistant Collector, that a most serious attempt had been made by a ryot of that place to exterminate a whole family—that the victims were lying at death's door, bleeding profusely, and urging that a dresser might be sent at once to their aid. On application by Mr. Wilkinson, I despatched Solomon [one of the medical students,] with the necessary medicines and surgical instruments, promising to come myself as soon as possible. The next day, in company with Mr. Wilkinson, I visited the place. The despatch of the medical assistance, had been providential indeed. The history of the case was briefly as follows: A well-to-do man of the Komiti caste, one of the highest in India, harboring an old enmity against a family related to him, determined to kill them all. Purchasing a large heavy scimitar he engaged a pensioned native officer to instruct him thoroughly in sword exercise. For eight months he thus daily drilled; when, after carefully arranging his affairs, he sold his property and bestowed the proceeds upon his village temple with the exception of a small sum. This he placed in the hands of a friend with the request that should any fatal accident befall himself, it should be used in decently burning his body with the usual funeral rites; that, as he intended to give himself to constant meditation and prayer, he wished to dismiss all subjects of a mundane character. Choosing his opportunity when the men of the house were in the street, he attacked first one and then another, cutting and slashing them in the most frightful manner, and leaving them for dead. The old mother hearing the cries of her sons, ran out of the house to their rescue, but only to meet with the same fate. The murderer then went to a well near by, into which he threw himself, and from which he was taken out dead the next morning. It is scarcely possible to describe the character of the wounds received by his victims. One man had the entire top of the scalp cut off, and long gashes through the ribs, so that the air escaped through them from his lungs at every breath, with other dangerous wounds. The old woman, seventy years of age, was cut down through the collar-bone and shoulder-blade, through the head of the bone of the upper arm, three-fourths of the hand of the same side cut away, the thumb and forefinger alone being left, and her body fearfully gashed in various places. I found that

Solomon had done almost all that was possible under the circumstances. He had taken up and ligatured the severed and bleeding arteries, brought together and stitched the wounds neatly, administered the necessary medicines and made the needed applications. I certainly felt proud of the young man. He had done us great credit. As the relatives earnestly begged that he might remain, I consented. He is there still, although more than three months have elapsed, and without doubt has saved the lives of these people. When I left them, I thought their case hopeless. Through God's mercy they have been spared, and are now out of danger. I relate this incident not only to show what the young men of our medical class can do, but to point out one of the many ways in which the Lord permits us to do good among this people. During these three months Solomon has been engaged not only in caring for these patients, but in general medical work; and, above all, in daily preaching the Gospel in that far-off heathen village. The magistrate has, on several occasions, sent me the best accounts of his behavior, and added that he has gained the good will of the people generally."

"Another incident is worth recording. The young man was called on to go out to a village four miles from Kalastri to see a woman who had been in labor for nearly five days. On examination he found what is commonly termed a '*cross birth*.' The child, to be delivered, must be turned. This is no easy operation. He had, however, been present at several such operations at the hospital, and assisted us in them. His own story is, that while he fully appreciated his responsible position, he determined, after a prayer to the Lord for help, to attempt it. He succeeded in safely delivering the suffering woman. She is living and doing well. The joyful lad wrote me at once, declaring it was only through the Lord Jesus he had succeeded. Will any one say this young man is not competent to go out and begin the medical missionary work?"

MISCELLANIA.

BENEVOLENCE OF THE NATIVE CHRISTIANS.

The Hindu classics abound in pithy and elegant aphorisms eulogistic of benevolence. Witness the following, whose beauty of form only, but not of sentiment, is marred in the translation:

"Benevolence seeks no return. What gives the world back to the gushing clouds?"

"To exercise benevolence towards the worthy, is the whole design of labor and the acquisition of property."

"The wealth of a wise benevolent man is like the full waters of a public tank. All may come and freely draw from it."

"The wealth of the liberal man is like the ripening of a fruitful tree in the centre of a town."

"If loss will result from benevolence, such loss is worth procuring by the sale of one's self."

"Griping avarice is not to be reckoned among other faults. It stands alone, greater than all."

Our native Christians are free to give according to their ability. The most of them are extremely poor, the average earnings of each one not exceeding six cents a day. Yet many cheerfully and regularly contribute one-tenth of their income; an offering which cannot be made without veritable self-denial, as it must be deducted not from affluence, but from pinching poverty. The women, in some places, daily, before cooking, dip a handful out of the often scanty provision of family rice, and set it apart for the Lord. Our seminary girls have, for years, voluntarily denied themselves a fixed proportion of their daily food, that they might have something to help others with. The catechists and teachers, whose average income may be set at eight dollars a month, have organized themselves into the "Sahodara Sangam," or Society of Brothers, through which they every year assist their needy fellow. Christians, with sums by no means inconsiderable in the aggregate. Calls for special contributions, meet almost invariably with a hearty response; in evidence of which, we quote a notable and praiseworthy instance:

"The Rev. Dr. Jared W. Scudder went to America, two years ago, on account of the severe illness of his wife. Her health is restored, and they are now ready to return. Our committee is pecuniarily disabled, and cannot send them. When our native churches learned this, they resolved upon a united effort to raise money enough for the Rev. Dr. Scudder's passage to India. Their action was spontaneous, cheerful and prompt. They organized committees, drew up subscription papers, and thoroughly canvassed the congregations. They have pledged themselves as follows:

	Rs.	A.	P.
The Arcot Church, for	142	5	0
The Arnee Church, for	75	0	0
The Chittoor Church, for	146	14	0
The Coonoor Church, for	225	0	0
The Palamanair Church, for	75	0	0
The Vellore Church, for	315	2	0
Total	978	5	0

It must be remembered that these sums are entirely independent of what the missionaries contribute. This result has amazed us. Great personal sacrifices have been made. Most of our church members are poor; many, are very poor. Yet has their deep poverty abounded unto the riches of their liberality; for to their power we bear record, yea, and beyond their power they were willing of themselves. If Christians in America were to exhibit a tithe of the beneficence shown by these poor native Christians, we should be obliged without delay to summon a meeting of the Mission to decide as to what could be done with superfluous thousands of rupees. As each missionary has given rupees one hundred or more to the same object, a sum has been sent to America sufficient to bring back our brother and his family."

PUBLICATIONS.

The following are works, which have been prepared and issued by the Mission:

"Spiritual Teaching,"	In Tamil.
do. do.	In Telugu.
do. do.	In English.
"Jewel Mine of Salvation,"	In Tamil.
do. do. do.	In Telugu.
"Sweet Savours of Divine Truth,"	In Tamil.
do. do. do. do. do.	In Telugu.
"Bazaar Book,"	In Tamil.
do. do.	In English.
"Heidelberg Catechism."	In Tamil.
"The Liturgy of the Reformed Church,"	In Tamil.

All these are works of considerable size, containing from 90 to 400 pages each. Besides them, several editions of the Scriptures in Tamil and Telugu have been printed for the

Mission by the Madras Bible Society. Small tracts, for distribution, are purchased from the Madras Tract Society.

There are very few towns or villages in the Arcot District, in which to-day, portions of the Bible and Christian publications cannot be found. The free dissemination of this religious literature has undoubtedly been, next to the preaching of the Gospel, the most effective means of sapping the foundations of Hinduism, and preparing material for the building of the Lord's Temple in the land.

PERSONNEL OF THE MISSION.

NAMES OF MISSIONARIES.	DATE OF JOINING THE MISSION.	PERIOD OF LABOR.	DATE OF RETIREMENT.
Rev. H. M. Scudder, D.D., M.D.	1853	11 years.	1864
Rev. W. W. Scudder, D.D.	1853	20 "	1872
Rev. Joseph Scudder, D.D.	1853	7 "	1859
Rev. E. C. Scudder, M.D.	1855	22 "	1875
Rev. J. W. Scudder, M.D.	1855	22 "	
Rev. J. Mayou.	1859	10 "	1869
Rev. J. Chamberlain, M.D.	1860	17 "	
Rev. S. D. Scudder, M.D.	1861	11 "	1875
Rev. John Scudder, M.D.	1861	16 "	
Rev. E. J. Heeren.	1872	5 "	
Rev. J. H. Wyckoff.	1874	3 "	
H. M. Scudder, Jr., M.D.	1874	3 "	
Miss Martha Mandeville	1870	7 "	
Miss Josephine Chapin	1870	4	1874

THE ARCOT MISSION.

The Rev. Messrs H. M. and W. W. Scudder labored in India several years before the organization of the Arcot Mission. Their entire terms of missionary labor were respectively twenty, and twenty-five years.

COMPARATIVE TABLE SHOWING THE RELATIVE STATISTICS OF THE ARCOT MISSION IN THE YEARS 1854, 1860, &c., TO 1876.

STATISTICS.	1854.	1860.	1876.
Stations.	3	6	9
Out-stations.	1	0	40
Male Missionaries.	3	8	6
Female Missionaries.	3	9	8
Native Ministers.	0	1	2
Catechists.	3	4	22
Readers.	0	2	26
School Teachers.	5	5	49
Colporteurs.	0	1	4
Churches.	2	6	20
Communicants.	26	154	778
Baptized adults not Communicants.			232
Baptized Children.		220	938
Total of Christian Adherents.	170	612	2574
Arcot Seminary Pupils.	13	20	30
Female Seminary Pupils.	0	14	43
Day Schools.	4	5	49
Caste Girls' Schools.	0	0	2

CHITTOOR SEMINARY.

THE CHITTOOR FEMALE SEMINARY.

BY

Mrs. JARED W. SCUDDER.

In the year 1855, three orphan girls occupied a small room in the house of the resident missionary in the town of Chittoor. This was the beginning of the now prosperous "Chittoor Female Seminary." For a number of years we had no regular school-house, and the children were crowded into two small rooms in an out-building of the mission house. It became painfully evident that it was injurious to both health and morals to have from twenty-five to thirty persons living in two apartments, and loud appeals were made for relief About one thousand rupees were subscribed, not even a third of the desired sum, and the Mission authorized the erection of a building, the cost of which should not exceed the amount subscribed. It was begun, and we laid its foundations with the hope and belief that further means would be provided to make the edifice suitable and complete. Nor were we disappointed, for the Lord raised up a kind and generous friend in Mrs. Susan Gridley, of Utica, who gave us the greater part of the necessary funds. We have now

A LARGE AND COMMODIOUS EDIFICE,

consisting of a court surrounded by verandahs, giving access to ten comfortable dormitories, a large school room, apartments for the matron, who is a faithful East Indian widow, and a kitchen, store-room and bath-room, the last furnished with three large tubs. Soon after taking possession of these apartments another great want began to make itself felt, and that was

A PLACE FOR THE GIRLS TO PLAY

and take exercise in. So urgent did this need become that we determined to make another appeal to the ladies of America and this appeal was promptly and generously responded to by

MRS. R. J. BROWN OF NEW YORK CITY.

who sent us money for the purpose. A brick wall was thrown around a large piece of adjoining ground. This forms a spacious enclosure, which can be entered directly from the school building, and has proved of the greatest value, affording increased health, happiness and brightness to every member of the institution.

THE OBJECT OF THE SCHOOL.

The course of study in the school has been from year to year gradually enlarged and systematized, and the pupils make very commendable progress both in the vernaculars and in English. The latter is an accomplishment which has been introduced only within the past five years, and has proved a great gratification to both scholars and parents. The great object of the school is to train up a class of girls, who shall be fitted to teach in the primary schools of our Christian villages, and to become good and faithful wives to our native helpers. We therefore strive to teach them such things, as will, in our opinion, best qualify them for the position they are expected to occupy. They learn to cook, to sew, and to do all kinds of housework. They also become adepts at crochet and tatting. For several successive years, I sold their work, for nearly one hundred dollars; and was enabled in this way to give them more comforts, and better clothing than I could otherwise have afforded.

ROUTINE OF THE DAY.

The usual routine of the day is as follows: Rising at half-past five o'clock, some of the girls set themselves to the thorough cleansing of the building, while the others draw water, for culinary and bathing purposes, from two deep wells, which are situated within the courts of the edifice. After all is made neat and tidy, every girl takes a bath, and dresses for school. At eight o'clock the bell summons all to assemble in the school-room for prayers, after which come the lessons, consisting of History, Dictation, Geography, Grammar, Arithmetic, Bible verses and catechism in the Tamil language. At twelve, the session ends and they prepare for dinner. From half-past one to three P. M., the time is spent in studying Telugu and English; and then follows a short recess, after which the girls assemble on the verandah of the missionary house, to sew or do fancy work until half-past four, when they are at liberty to go to the play-ground, or otherwise amuse themselves until dark. The natives of India are fond of music, and catch our tunes very readily. These children already sing in two parts quite well, and if any one would be kind enough to present them with an instrument, it would not, I think, be very long before there would be creditable performers among them.

MARRIAGES.

Twice, during the time we lived in Chittoor, my husband had the pleasure of marrying nine of these young ladies to as many young gentlemen of the Vellore Seminary, making eighteen persons standing up at once, to be united in matrimony. It was a pleasing and interesting sight, and I would have been glad to have had it witnessed by the patrons of the school here in America, for I know how much they would have enjoyed the occasion. Most of these marriages turn out well.

CONVERSIONS.

I am happy also to be able to state that very few of the girls leave the Seminary without becoming professed followers of the Lord Jesus, and very many give pleasing evidence of a thorough change of heart. They are all self-denying, and like to be charitable, as the following fact will show. Each of the scholars is entitled to two rice-cakes in the morning, which is the only food they have until noon. And yet they all give up one cake every day, and keep the money thus saved to put in the collections at church. Which of our American sisters, large or small, would be willing to go without half of her breakfast, every day, that she might present it to the Lord? Another thing which has struck me is the reverential manner in which they ask a blessing before they partake of their food. Although they have fasted long, there is no undue haste. Each girl stands in her place before the heaping dish of curry and rice, and all is silent as one of the older ones steps out into the court and repeats a prayer, to which the others listen with bowed heads. Many in Christian lands would do well to follow their example.

NUMBERS.

In the last year of my stay in India, there were fifty-five boarders in the Seminary; but some of these have since been married, and gone to reside in other places, and two have died. The number of pupils is, at present, forty-four. We would have no difficulty in adding to the names on our school list, if it were advisable. The Board, however, find it so hard to keep us supplied with funds, and counsel retrenchment so strongly, that the enlargement of the school must reluctantly be postponed until brighter days come.

A PLEA FOR ASSISTANCE.

This seems a fitting place for me to ask our sisters in this land to aid us. Why will not some of you who love to work for the Master, take this matter in hand, and provide a support for part, if not all of these girls, many of whom are orphans?

ANNUAL COST OF EACH CHILD.

The expense is about $30.00 a year for each child, including education, clothing and board. How small a sum when compared with the good it may do! Many of the pupils are not only elevated and refined by their stay in this Seminary, but are brought into the Kingdom of God.

THE CASTE GIRLS' SCHOOLS
AT VELLORE.

BY

Miss Josephine Chapin.

The Caste Girls' Schools, at Vellore, India, were established by Misses Mandeville and Chapin in 1871.

The first school was opened with eighteen pupils, and it now numbers nearly one hundred and fifty. The second school has seventy pupils on record. A third was established and successfully carried on for a time, but the prevalance of malarial fever in the district where it was located, obliged us to give it up.

The aim of these schools is to carry the word of God to the daughters and families of the better classes of Hindus, whose caste, a social and religious distinction, makes them almost inaccessible to missionary effort. While we instruct them in secular studies and in needle-work, the one object for which the schools were founded, is made paramount to every other. All of the children who are old enough to read, are studying the Bible daily, and learning the way of salvation through Christ. The examinations which many of them pass, show that they have a good knowledge of the gospels. A large number of the pupils are now reading the Bible in their homes to their fathers and mothers, brothers and sisters.

These schools are by means of a "Grant in Aid," obtained from the British Government, in a measure self-supporting. The amount now drawn by the largest school defrays its expenses. The pupils are examined annually by an inspector appointed by the Government, and a fixed sum is drawn for each one who reaches a prescribed standard.

FIRST STANDARD.

The first standard comprises Reading in the First Reader, Dictation in the same, Arithmetic, Addition and the Multiplication Table as far as five times five, sewing, hemming and stitching on coarse work.

SECOND STANDARD.

Twenty-five lessons in the Second Reader, Dictation in the same. Addition, Subtraction, Multiplication, with the table to twelve times twelve, and Division, sewing, plain hemming, felling and stitching.

THIRD STANDARD.

The Second, and a part of the Third Reader, Dictation, Arithmetic through Reduction, Fractions and Proportions, and some knowledge of Grammar, Geography and sewing. The pupil is now required to cut and make a woman's jacket, in the presence of the Inspector. Some of our pupils have passed this standard at the age of fourteen. Teachers for our sewing classes have been trained in the school.

PREMIUMS FOR PROFICIENCY.

After the annual examination our anniversary is held, and prizes are awarded to each pupil who has successfully passed. Extra prizes for good conduct, and the best examination in New Testament history are also given. These meetings are very popular, and our rooms are crowded by native gentlemen, who take a wonderful interest in our work. One or two of those present favor us with interesting and appropriate addresses.

THE COST ANNUALLY.

The annual cost of these schools is comparatively small. Fifty dollars, supplemented by a Grant from the Government, will defray the expenses of a school for twenty-five or thirty girls.

The illustration on page 106, represents an Indian devotee, engaged in his superstitious worship.

VILLAGE WORK IN THE ARCOT MISSION.

BY

Mrs. Ezekiel Scudder.

In the numerous villages surrounding our principal stations are gathered, here and there, little Christian congregations which form a very important and interesting department of our work. The villagers are a very simple unlearned class of people—mostly cultivators of the soil. They have grown up as heathen, but hearing the glad tidings of salvation through Christ, preached in their streets, some of them have desired to know more of these things, and have come to us for instruction. They promise to abstain from certain heathenish practices, to rest on the Sabbath, and to observe Christian duties, as far as they understand them.

We then send a catechist or Bible reader to live among and instruct them. He gathers them together daily for prayer and study of the Bible, teaches them the Lord's Prayer, the commandments, the Apostles' Creed, and a simple catechism. All, old and young, learn these things. It is sometimes surprising to see how much of Bible history and Bible doctrine, they learn in this way, while unable to read a word of it for themselves; with the simple undoubting faith of children, they receive the great essential truths of the Gospel, that Jesus

Christ, the Son of God, loves them; that He died to save them, and that their sins may be forgiven for His sake.

For all this we thank God and take courage, believing that this faith will in due time bring forth its appropriate

AN IDOL WHICH HAD BEEN WORSHIPPED FOR 1,000 YEARS.

fruits,—holiness of heart and life, and good works which others may see, and learn to glorify our Heavenly Father. But at present, it must be confessed, we have often to mourn the fact that our Christians are not always models of Christian propriety in their conduct. Their old habits will cling to them, and the evil influences about them are very hard to resist.

One of our best and most consistent men once said to me:

"Something of the old heathen nature will always cling to us older people, but *our children* will grow up better Christians than we are. Until I was twenty years old I never knew that it was wrong to tell a lie. Now, my little child is taught to speak the truth, and she will never know the temptations that I have to struggle against."

We can all see that this is true, and accordingly we find much of our most interesting and hopeful work among the young of our flock.

SCHOOLS.

Schools are established in all these Christian villages, and every effort is made to bring the children of the congregation together for systematic instruction. The education given, it must be confessed, is very elementary; and the methods of study and of teaching, would doubtless seem very peculiar to those familiar only with the costly and well-ordered school system of our own favored land. But they are suited to the habits and present necessities of the people, and are doing a good work.

It would be difficult to convey to the uninitiated, an idea of the extreme simplicity and economy of all the arrangements in this village work. The school-house, which in many cases serves also the purposes of a church edifice, is formed by four low mud walls, with a thatched roof and a mud floor. Small openings in the walls admit light and air. The furniture consists of a plain table and chair, or bench, for the use of the teacher, with perhaps a small box to contain the books and slates which we furnish for the use of the children. In the larger and more flourishing schools, a blackboard and a map of the world are also allowed; and in these they take great pride and delight. The children are seated cross-legged on the mud floor. Of their costume it is scarcely worth while to speak, there is so very little to speak of! A strip of cloth, often a very small one, around the loins, completes the toilets of most of them; though the catechist's children, and a few others, usually wear also a simple calico jacket, and the girls a little petticoat.

They study in loud inharmonious concert, each one trying to make more noise than his neighbor. The din seems to us intolerable, and we wonder whether anything can be learned in such a bedlam. But presently the classes are called up, and we are surprised to see how fluently and well they recite.

Much time is given to religious instruction. A simple catechism is taught orally to the youngest scholars, a larger one to the older ones, with Scripture texts and stories from Bible history. They learn also the simple rules of arithmetic, and elementary geography and grammar. A child who can pass examination in these, with reading and writing, may, if desirous of farther education, obtain admission to the Seminaries at Vellore or at Chittoor.

Many of these village children have proved excellent scholars, and some are now occupying positions of great usefulness in the Mission work. Those who remain in the villages and grow up as tillers of the ground, as their fathers have been, are forming an intelligent, respected and influential class of Christian men and women.

TRIALS AND DISCOURAGEMENTS.

We are not without some trials and discouragements in this good work. Most of the people are very poor, and they better understand the ills of hunger than those of ignorance; and appreciate more highly the merits of a good dinner, than of a good education. A child who is old enough to frighten away the crows from a field of grain, or to lead a cow or a goat out to graze, has a pecuniary value in the family; and so, too often, he is taken from the school, just as he is beginning to learn, and is sent to earn his living in the fields. Thus, our schools have sometimes seemed in danger of degenerating into classes of infants, too young to be really benefitted by them.

To meet this difficulty, the teachers have undertaken to hold

EVENING SESSIONS,

and this plan has happily proved a great success. Not only the Christian children, but many heathen boys, and some grown men, busy all day in the fields, come into the school at night and study bravely, often till a late hour. Not content with this, in one place, they begged the privilege of coming together for an hour before daylight each morning, and then took their books and slates with them to the fields, that their leisure moments during the day, might be improved in learning. Of course, students so enthusiastic could not fail to make good progress, and I have seldom been more gratified than I was in meeting and examining this school, shortly before I left India.

I was in camp with my husband, about two miles from the village, and as there was only a foot-path between the places, I could not venture to traverse it in the heat of the day; so the school came to me. For once the children were released from their accustomed work, and the little army came trooping to our tent, nearly fifty of them, with such bright faces, and bringing with them, their books, slates, maps and blackboards. We spent several hours together most pleasantly, they proud and happy, to show me how much they had learned, and I, quite as happy to see such a sight in a place where a few years before, ignorance and superstition had reigned undisturbed.

NUMBER OF CHILDREN UNDER INSTRUCTION.

Sixteen years ago we rejoiced over the small beginnings of this village work. Now, there are more than forty of these little congregations, whose members are gradually growing in intelligence and Christian character, and in their schools 800 children, Christian and heathen, are daily taught the blessed truths of the Gospel.

We commend this unassuming work among the poorest and humblest class of our people, to the sympathies and earnest prayers of our Christian friends.

The picture at the beginning of this sketch, represents an idol, which had been worshipped for 1,000 years. It was given up when the whole village of Nalaporapilly, India, became Christian in 1872. It is simply a dark, unsightly mass of stone, with no beauty or comeliness, yet generations of men, women and children, gave it honor and praise. Thank God that they now have learned the better way of His love.

HINDU WOMEN

It must be remembered that so early as twenty years ago, to ask a Hindu lady whether she could read and write, was to offer her the vilest possible insult. Women, fortunate enough to have acquired any education, were careful to hide the fact from all but their immediate relatives. The only class among females who received instruction were the dancing girls of the temples, whose position was parallel with that of the ancient vestal virgins. They lived a life of open shame; yet families of the highest rank were willing and even anxious to consecrate one daughter to this service, thus obtaining the favor of the gods.

How weary and tedious must have been the hours spent by listless unoccupied women, within the walls of the zenanas! Their sole employment, the preparation of food for their husbands, and the light tasks of their housekeeping; their minds inactive, or filled with childish jealousies, it was small wonder that some of them clung to idolatry as their only refuge. In heathen, as in Christian lands, women are more religious than men, and more assiduously seek the protection of the being whom they regard as their friend and helper. To propitiate the kind gods and ward off the designs of the cruel, are to Hindu women sacred duties. Very early in life the mother leads her little son, with garlands over his arms, and hands filled with fruit and flowers, to the shrine of some neighboring idol. If he is frightened at its horrid aspect, for there is no beauty or tenderness in the forms or faces of these gods which men have made, she coaxes him with fond caresses, or compels him by force to approach and offer his gifts. As anxiously and faithfully as the Christian mother teaches her precious ones to lisp the name of Jesus, and kneel to Him in prayer, so the heathen instructs hers concerning Siva and Brahma and Vishnu.

TREATMENT OF WIVES.

Unwelcome at her birth, and regarded as a curse, the little daughter in India, is never the cherished darling of the house as she is with us. So soon as she reaches the verge of womanhood, a husband is found for her, and she is married. Frequently the betrothal ceremony has taken place long before, so that a girl of six or eight may have been given away by her parents to a man of sixty or seventy. Should the prospective husband die before his child-bride grows old enough to become his wife, she is condemned for life to the position of a widow. Widowhood, is by custom, a life of enforced seclusion; and, while the widow may continue to reside with her own or her husband's relatives, she must always wear coarse clothing, and jewels and embroidery are rigidly forbidden her.

"When a father wishes to get his daughter married, he sends for a *ghottok*, or go-between. This man generally belongs to the lowest class of Brahmins, and his business is to introduce the father of a young man who wishes his son to be married, to the father of one who wishes to find a bride-groom for his daughter. If the fathers are mutually satisfied with the connection, the marriage takes place, and the *ghottok* receives a handsome present in money from both families."— From "*Faith and Victory,*" by the late Mrs. Mullens, English Missionary to Calcutta.

When the important day arrives, the bridegroom repairs to the house of his father-in-law. The women's apartments are full of visitors, engaged in merry-making. The bride is covered with jewels, gold and silver; her hair is braided and adorned with flowers, and she now, for the first time, meets the man who is for the future, to be, in the most literal sense, her lord and master. The priest, standing without the door, presents offerings of rice, flowers, Ganges water and sandalwood; recites prayers and texts, and finally pronounces the ceremony concluded. The bride is soon after lifted into a covered palanquin, and conveyed to her husband's home. This is frequently the home, too, of his parents; and, as it is customary for all the sons to remain at home with their wives, the wife now becomes a member of a little community, over which the mother-in-law exercises a very despotic control.

The Rev. Jacob Chamberlain, of the Arcot Mission, has kindly permitted us to make the following extracts from his lecture on "The Curious Things of India:"

"Women are looked upon as a necessary article of household furniture, to be tolerated accordingly; but the men treat them often worse than they treat their cows and oxen. The wife walks always some paces behind her husband, who is not ashamed to ride, though he be strong and well, while she, pale and delicate, drags herself along a journey of miles, leading her little child by the hand, or carrying a burden. She cooks his food, but must wait patiently till he has finished his repast, before she can eat a morsel. Then she feasts on what he may have left. Here is a quotation from an ancient and venerable law which relates to the sex :

"'Manu. ch. v. 146-8. Hear now the laws *concerning women !*

"'Nothing must be done by a girl, by a damsel or by a woman, even in her own dwelling according to her mere pleasure. In childhood must a female be dependent on her father, in youth on her husband, her lord being dead, on her sons; if she have no sons, on the near kinsmen of her husband. If he left no kinsmen, on those of her father. If she have no paternal kinsmen, on the sovereign. *A woman must never seek independence.*'"

For a husband to whip his wife is a common thing. When I remonstrated with a Hindu neighbor, and told him it was wrong for a husband to whip his wife, he looked up in unmitigated astonishment, saying : "Why how in the world can we make them behave, if we don't whip them ?"

But women have one means of retaliation. The immovable customs of the country, do not allow a Hindu to eat in any other house than his own. He cannot go to his brother's or his friend's house to take a meal. There are no restaurants. He is dependent on his wife's thrift and skill for neat and palatable food, prepared as he likes it. If she be driven to exasperation, she can cook his rice, and set it before him, but just as he is about to partake, she may pour ashes over the mass, and utterly spoil it. Or she may mix his curry, so hot, that his throat and palate will be nearly scarified. If these attempts fail in reducing him to submission, or in insuring her better treatment, she has a last resource. She can run away to her father's house. Once there, it is an asylum where she is privileged to remain, till the husband comes in person, with promises of kindness, and the present of a new dress, to solicit her return.

If an educated man find himself left alone, and consequently very uncomfortable, he probably shrugs his shoulders, and hums over to himself the old *Sanscrit* proverb:

"The flowers of the fig-tree, (which has no apparent blossom) a white crow, a fish's foot in the water, one may see, but not what is in a woman's mind!"

If he be too submissive, and the wife gets the upper hand, so that he becomes what we call a hen-pecked husband, his neighbors will quote the *Telugu* proverb:

"She grinds pepper on her husband's head."

Marriage is almost obligatory. The Hindus regard bachelors with great disfavor. Again, they have a proverb to this effect:

"Get a good wife if you can; if not, get a bad one. Marry you must!"

NATIVE CHRISTIANS.

One of the most gratifying results of conversion among the Hindus, is the very different manner in which husbands treat their wives and daughters. They sit together at the table; side by side, they walk to Church, the father carrying his little girl as proudly as if he was carrying his son; and the love of a common Saviour, unites them in a home.

THE MOST SACRED OF HINDU TEMPLES.

BY THE
Rev. T. S. Wynkoop.

The great temple of Juggernaut, (more properly written Juganât,) is situated on the sea-coast of the Bay of Bengal, in the province of Orissa, 300 miles to the south-west of Calcutta. It is one of the most celebrated places in India, and for many hundreds of years has been annually visited by millions of Hindus. All the land within twenty miles of the shrine is considered holy; but the most sacred spot is enclosed within a stone wall from twenty to thirty feet high, and forms nearly a square, the enclosure being six hundred and seventy feet in length, and six hundred and forty feet in breadth. Within this area are about fifty temples, dedicated to various idols. The temple, however, to which all the others are subordinate, is that of Juganât, one of the forms assumed by Vishnu.

THE IDOL.

The image of Juganât is probably the coarsest in India. The figure does not extend below the loins, and it has no hands, but two stumps in lieu of arms; on which occasionally, the priests fasten hands of gold. This deformity is accounted for by a strange legendary tale. Some thousands of years ago in the Satya Yuga or Hindu Age of Gold, the Maharaja Indradyumna, of Oojein, in Malwa, applied to a celebrated manufacturer of gods to make a new idol of Juganât. The request was granted, on condition that the Prince should be patient, and not interrupt nor examine the work on any pretence whatever, as it never could be completed if any attempt were made to see the process. This caution was not duly attended to. The Prince, unable to restrain his curiosity, insisted, after a time, upon seeing what progress had been made. From that moment, no further work could be done, and he was obliged to be content with the imperfect image.

ANTIQUITY OF THE TEMPLE.

In the year 1131, of the Christian era, the Kesari Vansa or Lion Kings of Orissa, who had occupied the throne for nearly seven hundred years, were set aside by another dynasty known as the Ganga Vansa, or Sons of the Ganges. The Lion Kings were worshippers of Siva. The new dynasty were devoted followers of Vishnu, and set to work at once to signalize their triumph by erecting a temple to Juganât. The date of its completion is given variously, as 1174 or 1198, A. D. The main temple measures eighty feet across the centre, and its great pyramidal dome rises to a height of one hundred and ninety-two feet. Directly connected with it, is an ante-chamber, and the two together are one hundred and fifty-five feet in length. Two other chambers or porches were added afterward, the Dancing Hall and Hall of Feasting, making the whole length of the temple about three hundred feet.

NUMBER OF PRIESTS EMPLOYED.

It may be easily supposed that a large establishment of priests and others is attached to such a temple. A writer in the *Asiatic Journal* was informed by one of the head men that the number consisted then of 3,000 families, including 400 families of cooks to prepare the holy food. The provisions furnished daily for the idol and his attendants were 220 pounds of rice, 120 pounds of pulse, 188 of clarified butter, 80 of sugar, 32 of vegetables, 10 of coagulated milk, 20 of salt, with lesser amounts of various spices, and 22 pounds of oil, for the lamps at night. This holy food is presented to the idol three times a day. During the thirteen festivals held each year, a considerable quantity of extra food is required. In addition to this is the food cooked and sold to the pilgrims, the temple of Juganât being the only place in India where the rules of caste are so far relaxed as to allow all classes of Hindus to eat together, without defilement in the sacred presence of the Lord of the World. For days, before the great Car Festival, food is cooked within the court of the temple for at least 100,000 pilgrims, and on these occasions the 400 families of cooks have full employment.

THRONGS OF PILGRIMS.

It would be difficult to estimate exactly the number of visitors to the temple, as it varies greatly from year to year, according to the healthiness or otherwise of the season, the degree of general prosperity throughout the country, and the greater or less sanctity and importance of the particular year.

But probably in no ordinary year would the number fall short of half a million, while frequently as many as two or three millions of persons attend in the course of a year.

Until very recently the pilgrimage to Juganât was accompanied with a deplorable amount of distress and suffering. Fifty years ago, when the East India Company was still throwing obstacles in the way of mission work and deriving a revenue from the pilgrim tax, a British military officer wrote the following:

"The loss of life by this deplorable superstition probably exceeds that of any other. The aged, the weak, the sick are persuaded to attempt this pilgrimage, as a remedy for all evils. The number of women and children, also, is very great. The pilgrims leave their families and occupations, to travel an immense distance, with the delusive hope of obtaining eternal bliss. Their means of subsistence on the road are scanty; and their light clothing and little bodily strength are ill calculated to encounter the inclemency of the weather. When they reach the district of Cuttack, they cease to experience that hospitality shown elsewhere to pilgrims; it is a burden which the inhabitants could not sustain, and they prefer availing themselves of the increased demand for provisions to augment the price. This difficulty is more severely felt as they approach the temple, till they find scarcely enough left to pay the tax to government, and to satisfy the rapacious Brahmins. The pilgrim, on leaving Juganât, has still a long journey before him; and his means of support are often almost, if not quite, exhausted. The work of death then becomes rapid, and the route of the pilgrims may be traced by the bones left by jackals and vultures. The country near the temple seems suddenly to have been visited by pestilence and famine. Dead bodies are seen in every direction. Pariah dogs, jackals and vultures, are observed watching the last moments of the dying pilgrim, and not unfrequently hastening his fate."

ASIATIC CHOLERA AND ITS RAVAGES.

Fearful outbreaks of cholera have sometimes occurred in connection with the pilgrimage. The following description was written by a missionary of the Car Festival in June, of the year 1825:

"The mortality did not much appear before the 18th; on the 19th it was exceedingly bad, for the day before the rain began to fall, and more came on the 19th and 20th; and for the next three days it fell in torrents. At this time the scene had reached its height, and was truly shocking on every hand. In every street, corner and open space, in fact,—wherever you turned your eyes, the dead and dying met your sight. On the evening of the 19th, I counted upwards of sixty dead and dying, from the temple down to the bottom end of the hospital, (about half a mile) leaving out the sick that had not much life! At the corner opposite the hospital, on a spot of ground twelve feet square, I counted ten dead and five sick! This was the case, while there were several sets of men in active employ burying the dead! You will perhaps think, if the streets were thus crowded, what must be the various Golgothas? I visited but one, and that was between the town and the principal entrance, and I saw sights I shall never forget. The small river there, was quite glutted with dead bodies. The wind had drifted them together, and they were a complete mass of putrifying flesh! They also lay upon the ground in heaps, and the dogs and birds were able to do but little towards devouring them."

The number of pilgrims present on that occasion was estimated at 225,000, and the mortality among them could not have been less than 20,000. They carried the disease with them from Juganât, and whole provinces were soon ravaged by it.

SUICIDE OF PILGRIMS NO LONGER PERMITTED.

In view of such wholesale destruction of life, we almost forget those who have prostrated themselves under the idol car. From time immemorial this mode of death has been thought to be peculiarly meritorious. At other sacred places in India the same thing occurs under different forms; as at Allababad, where, formerly, it was not unusual for pilgrims to drown themselves, according to a prescribed ritual, at the place of meeting of the holy streams, and where, now that this is prevented by the police, suicide is accomplished by cutting the throat in the river. For many years, however, the British government in India has done all that could be done to prevent and alleviate the cruelties of Hinduism. Widows are no longer burnt on the funeral pile, infants are no longer thrown into the Ganges at Sangor Island; pilgrims are not permitted to cast themselves under the wheels of Juganât. At all the festivals, there and elsewhere, on British territory, a strong police force is stationed under European supervision. Hospitals are established, with skilled attendants, and supplies of medicine, free of charge. Thus, the worst scenes of Juganât's temple are witnessed no more.

THE FALL OF THE FIRST STONE.

The most significant event of recent years, in connection with the temple, remains to be mentioned—in closing this account. About a year ago, in 1876, just after the three gods, who occupy the inner shrine (Juganât, his brother, Bulbhadrâ, and their sister, Soobhadrâ,) had been removed from their dais or throne, to take their annual excursion, drawn in the famous car, some great stones from the roof fell in, and would have killed the attendants, and smashed the gods, had they not fortunately all been absent. If a star had visibly fallen from the heaven, there could hardly have been greater consternation throughout Orissa, where for a long time a prophecy has been current among the people, that "when the first stone should be unfastened, the temple should not stand." It must be remembered that since the temple was completed, nearly 700 years ago, not a trowel has been laid upon it by way of repair. The immense blocks of stone, of which the magnificent dome is composed, are not kept together by cement or mortar of any kind, but are made fast by an elaborate process of dovetailing; the slabs being arranged in horizontal layers, narrowing towards the end, which is covered by a huge headpiece, carved and ornamented. One of the stones that fell, measures ten feet in length, by five in breadth, and four in thickness. As the damage is imperceptible to the eye, owing to the intense darkness in the interior of the edifice, it is impossible to say what is the condition of the remainder of the inner roof or cornice. It is thought that the repairs will take at least fourteen years, and during all this time no public worship or festival can be held. It is not unlikely that the prophecy may be fulfilled, and the deserted temple given over to decay.

But, however this may be, it is certain that the vast structure of India's idolatry, which has stood so long, and caused such misery and woe to that fair land, is doomed. The fall of the stone in Juganât's temple, like the handwriting on the wall of Babylon, is a symbol of the hand of God upon it, and is so regarded in India. That impending destruction may be, for a time, retarded, but cannot be long prevented. God speed the downfall of it, and build, full soon, in living stones, the new temple, to the praise of the glory of His grace, through Jesus Christ our Lord.

>
> Come swiftly joyful day,
>   When Christ the Lord shall reign
> His gentle royal sway
>   O'er all the world maintain!
>
> The darkling shadows lift,
>   The golden dawn appears,
> The mists of error drift
>   Before the brightening years!
>
> The Prince of Peace will bring
>   His ransomed captives home,
> And men and angels loud shall sing,
>   The King of Life has come!

THE TAJ MAHAL.

From Rousselet's magnificent work on "India and Her Native Princes," we extract the interesting description of this splendid work of Oriental art. We have inserted the picture, that those of our readers who are not familiar with the subject, may gain some idea of the wealth, splendor and taste of the great empire which we are trying to win for the kingdom of our Lord and Master.

"The Taj was built by the Emperor Shah Johan, as a mausoleum for the **Empress** Mumtazi Mahal, or Taj-Bibi, who died in giving birth to the Princess Johanera. This woman, celebrated alike for her talents and her beauty, inspired the prince with such love and admiration, that he resolved to raise to her memory the most beautiful monument that had ever been constructed by man. After a grand consultation of all the architects in the east, the plan of Isa Mahomed was adopted. The mausoleum was commenced in the year 1630, and not completed until 1647; and during those seventeen years, 2,000 workmen were employed. 140,000 car loads of pink sandstone and of marble were used in this great work, and each province of the empire contributed precious stones for its adornment. The jasper came from the Punjaub, the carnelian from Broach, the turquoise from Thibet, the agates from Temen, the lapis-lazuli from Ceylon, the coral from Arabia, the garnets from Bundlecund, the diamonds from Punnah, the mountain rock-crystal from Malwa, the onyx from Persia, the chalcedonies from Asia Minor, the sapphire from Colombo,

THE TAJ MAHAL, AT AGRA, INDIA.

and conglomerates from Jopulmore, Gualin and Sephia. Notwithstanding these contributions, and the forced labor of the workmen, the total cost of this gigantic work was about $2,000,000.

The Taj is situated on the banks of the Jumna, its golden crescent rising 270 feet above the level of the river. The garden in front of it is surrounded by high embattled walls with a pavillion at each corner. The principal entrance is a monumental pointed arch, containing seven apartments, and crowned with a row of kiosks; the exterior is of red sandstone, relieved with bands of white marble, and the tympanum of the centre arch, are ornamented with mosaics of agate and onyx. A caravanserai for travellers extends around the entrance court.

On entering this gate, we suddenly found ourselves in front of the Taj, which appeared in all its dazzling whiteness at the end of a wide paved avenue, bordered on each side with tall cypress trees. The first view of the Taj is most striking. Like a mountain of white marble, it rises mysteriously above the sombre and luxuriant vegetation of the garden.

The terrace of pink sandstone on which the Taj stands, is 960 feet in length, and 330 in width; and one end of it is bathed by the Jumna, while the other is only a few feet above the level of the garden. A magnificent platform of white marble is erected in the centre of this terrace, measuring fifteen feet in height, and 285 feet on every side, which forms a pedestal for the mausoleum; and at each corner of the platform is a marble minaret, upon which rests a light cupola 150 feet from the ground.

The mausoleum itself is constructed like an irregular octagon, the longest side of which measures 120 feet; and it has a terraced roof with four pavillions placed at the corners, and a magnificent dome in the center.

Each façade is pierced with a high Saracenic gate, flanked on either side by two rows of niches. Such are the proportions and the plan of the Taj; and they may be equally applied, though on a smaller scale, to other Indian monuments; but every line has been calculated with such consummate art, that not a flaw can be detected. The entire edifice, from the base to the summit, is built of white marble, overlaid with mosaics, forming inscriptions, arabesques, and other decorations. Every part of the exterior, with the single exception of the dome itself, is covered with these marvellous mosaics. Bishop Heber remarked, with truth, that the Taj had been designed by Titans, and finished by jewelers."

Bayard Taylor, in writing on the same theme, says:

"I ascended to the base of the building, a gleaming marble platform, almost on a level with the tops of the trees in the garden. Before entering the central hall, I descended to the vault where the beautiful Noor-Jehan is buried. A sloping passage, the walls and floor of which have been so polished by the hands and feet of thousands, that you must walk carefully to avoid sliding down, conducts to a spacious chamber. There is no light but what enters the door, and this falls directly upon the tomb of the Queen in the centre. Shah-Jehan, whose ashes are covered by a simpler cenotaph, sleeps by her side. The vault was filled with the odors of rose, jasmine and sandal-wood, the precious attars of which are sprinkled on the tomb. Wreaths of beautiful flowers lay upon it, or withered around its base.

These were the true tombs; the monuments for display being placed in the grand hall above, which is a lofty rotunda, lighted both from above and below, by screens of marble wrought in filagree. It is paved with blocks of white marble and jasper, and ornamented with a wainscoting of sculptured tablets, representing flowers. The tombs are sarcophagi of the purest marble, exquisitely inlaid with blood-stone, agate, carnelian, lapis-lazuli and other precious stones; and surrounded with an octagonal screen six feet high, in the open tracery of which, lilies, roses and other flowers are interwrought with the most intricate and ornamental designs.

THE ECHO.

The Dome of the Taj contains an echo more sweet, pure and prolonged than that in the Baptistry of Pisa, which is the finest in Europe. A single musical tone uttered by the voice, floats and soars overhead, in a long delicious undulation; fainting away so slowly that you hear it after it is silent, as you see, or seem to see, a lark you have been watching, after it is swallowed up in the blue of heaven.

The concurrent testimony of travellers, concerning this wonderful poem in marble is the same. It has a grave serenity of atmosphere, and its size, finish, environment, and occasion alike impress the beholder's mind. One Pilgrim tells us that—on the tomb of the lively Empress lies, as its central ornament, a tablet; and on that of her husband, a pen, indicating the Hindu belief, that the mind of women is a page, on which the man writes what he pleases. Even in this transcendent memorial of love, the thought of man's superiority was thus embalmed. Yet, if love was strong enough in Heathenism, to build a fane, beautiful and glorious as this, over its lost idol, what may it not do, in living stones and Christian homes, when the women of India, shall be brought to adore at the feet of Jesus, and their husbands and children with them, acknowledge Him as supreme?

THE SACRED CITY OF THE HINDUS.

THE SACRED CITY OF THE HINDUS.

The Hindus consider the city of Benares to be placed in the centre of the earth, and to be the most sacred city in the world.

There are no less than eighty thousand Brahmins or "holy caste" Hindus residing here, and the city also abounds with the so-called "sacred bulls" and "sacred monkeys." There are more than a thousand temples, and over five hundred thousand enshrined deities.

More than one hundred thousand pilgrims visit Benares annually; twenty thousand of whom may be seen rushing at one time into the river Ganges, at a given signal, that they may bathe at the proper moment. The river is reached by flights of broad steps, and on these the Hindus pass the busiest hours of the day, bathing, dressing, and saying their prayers, lounging and gossiping.

Benares is believed by some to be eighty thousand steps nearer heaven than any other part of the world. Ten miles around Benares is said to be such holy ground, that whoever dies within this area is sure of going to heaven, however great a sinner he may have been.

THE GRAND MOSQUE AT DELHI.

THE GRAND MOSQUE OF DELHI.

Delhi is a city of venerable memories. During many centuries, she was to Asia, what Rome, at her period of greatest splendor, was to Europe. In the early dawn of Aryan history, Indrapêchtra rose on the site, which in the year 57, B. C., became the beginning of Delhi. Allusions are made in the old epic poem of the Mahabharata to heroes, who flourished here hundreds of years before the Christian era.

The Plain of Delhi is a vast archæological museum. Successive dynasties removed the city from one place to another, and the ruins which remain, display every period of Hindu architecture, from the time they first used cut stone to the present day.

The Grand Mosque, of which we have thought well to insert a picture, that our readers may gain some idea of the richness of Moslem art, is regarded by the followers of Mohammed with particular reverence.

It is built of red sandstone. It stands upon an immense terrace, to the summit of which, three magnificent staircases lead, each of which terminates in a monumental doorway. These open into a spacious paved court, ornamented with a fountain. At the end of this, extends the broad façade of the Mosque. "It is composed," says a French traveller, "of a long row of narrow arches, on each side of a lofty doorway, in the form of a pointed arched niche; three white marble domes crown the edifice, which is flanked by two minarets, striped longitudinally with white and pink, and elevating a delicate cupola of white marble, in the air, to a great height.

. The effect of the vivid, though severe, colors, which clothe every part of the building, is, when touched by the glorious sun of India, incomparable. The dark red of the galleries, the black and white marble of the façade, the white domes, the golden pinnacles, and the rose-colored minarets, stand out against the blue background of the sky, not crudely, but with a severe harmony."

The interior, long jealously closed against Europeans, is now open to all. It is luxurious and beautiful.

In contrast with these massive monuments of Hindu, or of Musselman art, what are we showing to India? The plain little house of prayer, the sanctuary with its bell in the spire, to summon the worshipper. This is a fitter exponent of His life, who, though Lord of the Universe, was here a meek and lowly man. His praise is best set forth in the living epistles, which everywhere His true disciples are.

THE MISSION FREE READING ROOM AT MUDNAPILLY.

Reference was made in Dr. Scudder's article to the establishment of Free Reading Rooms. The one here shown, was erected by the efforts of the Rev. Jacob Chamberlain, M. D., of the Arcot Mission, early in 1870. One principal object in building it, was to get a hold upon the educated natives; those who had received some English education, and who held themselves aloof from the throng who assembled to listen to street preaching.

We copy Dr. Chamberlain's account of its opening, from the *Church Missionary Intelligencer*, of London:

DR. CHAMBERLAIN'S NARRATIVE.

"It had seemed to me that the establishment of a Free Reading Room where English and other secular newspapers and periodicals, and books of history, travels and poetry, could be made use of to draw in the educated classes, and get them under Gospel influence, would be one of the best agencies that could be used in a place like this; and I determined, several years ago, to establish such a reading room, but I could get no place in the town to open it in. I could neither buy nor rent a suitable place.

Early this year, I learned that an unoccupied bit of land at the corner of two streets, and just opposite the post-office, a site which I had long coveted, but which had been involved in

MISSION FREE READING ROOM AT MUDNAPILLY.

a law suit of several years' standing, had now, by decree of the court, been ordered to be sold. It was a chance not to be lost, but I had no money to purchase it."

GOING ON IN FAITH.

"Our Mission in its crippled state for funds, could not furnish me any, and I was just completing the building of our Telugu church and school-house, for which I had to raise all the money here. This was but just paid for, and I had not a rupee to use in buying a site, or when obtained, erecting on it a suitable building; but, after thinking and dreaming and praying over it a few days, I decided to go on at once, and trust in the Lord, whose work it was, to bring me through.

"Several times, since coming here, I have been in great straits for funds, for the completion of some project which I had undertaken; and each time the Lord has rebuked my lack of faith, by sending contibutions, unexpected and unsolicited, so that I have, in each case, come triumphantly through. So, without a rupee in hand, I determined to secure the land, and build upon it at once.

"The day after the completion of the purchase, I had workmen digging for the foundation, and in three months, it was completed and opened to the public.

THE BUILDING.

"It is a neat building with a terraced roof. built so that, though the town were to burn down round it, it could suffer no material harm. The room is nearly square, and in the side fronting towards the post-office, is a wide double door, and on the side opening on the other street, two wide windows. There is a broad verandah on each of these sides, and on lecture evenings, I have the door and windows thrown wide open, and seats arranged in the verandahs as well, so that the speaker can be heard by all, and seen by nearly all who are seated there.

THE ROOM.

"The room is matted with grass mats, and in the centre is a writing table, with ink, pens, and materials always ready. Arranged along one side are narrow tables with the newspapers, gazettes and magazines on them, together with a copy of the Bible, in each of the seven languages, more or less read here. At the further end are two glass-door book-cases, the one filled with books for reading, including works on history, travels, researches, poetry, morals, etc., most of them being in English; but including all I could find of an improving nature, in Telugu, Tamil, and Canarese, with a few in Hindustani, Mahratti, and Sanscrit. They are free to all to take and read when they please.

"The other book-case is filled with the Scriptures, tracts, school-books and Christian literature, in the various languages, for sale. Also, a supply of stationery and requisites for schools.

"The Reading Room is opened daily, excepting Sundays, at 2 P. M., and kept open till 9 P. M. On Wednesday evening of each week, a Bible lecture is given in Telugu. It is but a half-hour in length. Five minutes before the time appointed for the lecture, our native helpers go there, and sing some of their beautiful Christian songs, to native melodies."

"I always find the building and verandah both filled when I get there.

"I read selected passages from the Telugu Bible, and lecture from it, closing with a short prayer for the divine blessing.

"At the opening of the Room, the principal gentlemen of the neighborhood were invited to be present, and they attended, with many English gentlemen, who had given liberal pecuniary aid during its erection. Addresses were made in English and Telugu. I urged the people to come to the feet of Him who is the Author and Giver of spiritual life ; even Him who is revealed in the Christian Scriptures.

"Not less than ninety a day avail themselves of the privileges of the reading room. Some come to look at the Madras daily papers, others to read historical works, others to consult dictionaries, atlases, and books of reference ; and many after finishing the work for which they come, quietly take up and read a copy of the Bible, and often purchase Scripture or portions of Scripture, in their own language or in English, to take home and examine at their leisure.

"Scarcely a day passes without tracts or Scripture being sold.

"At one of my Wednesday evening lectures, a Brahmin, one of the best educated in the place, arose and politely asked permission to speak. I assented, not knowing what he wished to say, and he gave this welcome and unexpected testimony :

A BRAHMIN ON THE BIBLE.

"'Behold that mango tree on yonder roadside! Its fruit is approaching to ripeness. Bears it that fruit for itself or for its own profit? From the moment the first ripe fruits turn their yellow sides towards the morning sun until the last mango is pelted off, it is assailed with showers of sticks and stones from boys and men, and every passer by, until it stands bereft of leaves, with branches knocked off, bleeding from many a broken twig ; and piles of stone underneath, and clubs and sticks lodged in its boughs, are the only trophies of its joyous crop of fruit. Is it discouraged? Does it cease to bear fruit? Does it say, 'If I am barren, no one will pelt me, and I shall live in peace?' Not at all. The next season the budding leaves, the beauteous flowers, the tender fruit again appear. Again it is pelted, and broken and wounded, but goes on bearing, and children's children pelt its branches and enjoy its fruit.

"That is a type of these missionaries. I have watched them well, and have seen what they are. What do they come to this country for? What tempts them to leave their parents, friends and country, and come to this, to them unhealthy, climate? Is it for gain or for profit that they come? Some of us country clerks, in government offices, receive more salary than they. Is it for the sake of an easy life? See how they work, and then tell me. No: they seek, like the mango tree, to bear fruit for the benefit of others, and this too, though treated with contumely and abuse from those they are benefitting.

"Now what is it makes them do all this for us? *It is their Bible.* I have looked into it a good deal, at one time and another, in the different languages I chance to know. It is just the same in all languages. *The Bible*—there is nothing to compare with it in all our sacred books for goodness, and purity, and holiness, and love, and for motives of action.

"Where did the English speaking people get all their intelligence, and energy, and cleverness, and power? It is their Bible that gives it to them. And now they bring it to us and say: 'This is what raised us; take it and raise yourselves!' They do not force it upon us, as the Mohammedans did with their Koran; but they bring it in love, and translate it into our languages, and lay it before us and say: 'Look at it; read it; examine it, and see if it is not good.' Of one thing I am convinced: do what we will, oppose it as we may, it is the Christian's Bible that will, sooner or later, work the regeneration of this land."

A TELUGU HYMN.

REFRAIN.

Ni charanamule Nammiti, Nammiti,
Ni padamule battiti, battiti.

I.

Dikkika nive tsakkaga rave,
Mikkili mrokkudu, mrokkudu.

II.

Aihika sukamu, narisiti nitya.
Mahaha drohini, drohini.

Translation into the same meter in English

REFRAIN.

Thy refuge would I seek, blessed Jesus, blessed Jesus;
Thy mercy-giving feet would I clasp, bless d Jesus.

I.

My only help art Thou. Wilt Thou not hear me?
For on Thee, Thee alone, Thee alone do I call.
   Refrain—Thy refuge, etc.

II.

The fleeting joys of earth have not I tasted?
Traitor I wandered far, wandered far, far from Thee.
   Refrain—Thy refuge etc.

III.

My own works, all so vile, filled with pollution,
I abhor, I renounce, Saviour, turn me not away.
   Refrain—Thy refuge, etc.

IV.

My hard and sinful will, my baser passions,
Pluck them out, drive them hence ; free me Lord, deliver me.
Refrain—Thy refuge, etc.

V.

My nature so corrupt, canst thou not change it ?
Ease my pain, oh my God! save me Lord, save me now.
Refrain—Thy refuge, etc.

The picture of the Reading Room shows the thatched roof and verandah, with the group of people gathered there, and even the children looking at it will see how different this Oriental scene is, from any idea they may have of a similar place in our own land. And now, that they and their parents may know in what sort of houses our missionaries in India live, we insert a picture of Dr. Chamberlain's residence while at Mudnapilly. It is a long, low building, its rooms very small. The columns supporting its roof, like those of the Free Reading Room, are of stone untouched by tools, and split into shape by means of fire. The trees which appear, are cocoanut and mango. Over the doorway of the house, you observe the luxuriant Rangoon creeper, whose blossoms, white when they first open, become pink, then crimson and finally purple before they fade and fall.

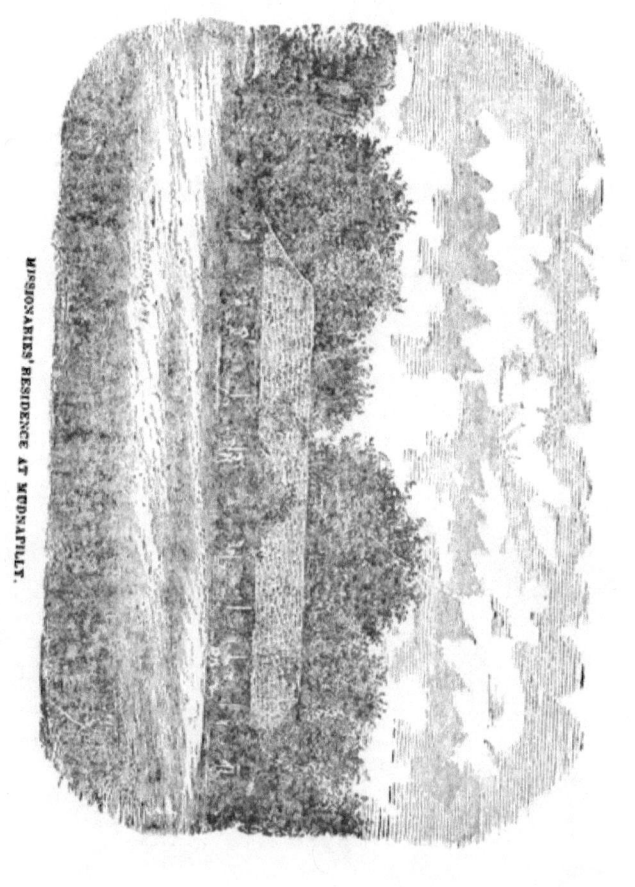

MISSIONARIES' RESIDENCE AT MUDNAPILLY.

BORNEO.

THE BORNEO MISSION.

BY

Rev. Wm. H. Steele, D. D.

At the arrival of Rev. Wm. H. Steele Sept. 16, 1842, in the roadstead of Java's chief city, Batavia, the history of those who had preceded him was this.

Of those sent out in 1836, Revs. Elihu Doty and William Youngblood were on the west coast of Borneo, and Revs. Jacob Ennis and Elbert Nevius had returned to this country in 1840 and 1842, respectively.

Of the party sent out in 1838, both members, Revs. Frederick B. Thomson and Wm. J. Pohlman were in Borneo.

Of the two who sailed from Boston, in November, 1840, Rev. Wm. T. Van Doren had returned to America, and Rev. Isaac P. Stryker had died on board an America vessel, *en route* from Batavia to Singapore, only a few days after embarking in health and gladness. The beloved Isaac was buried in the beautiful cemetery on the Morning Side of Government Hill, and the American visitor will find, at the spot where he

BORNEO.

lies, with his feet to the foe, a becoming obelisk of white marble, sent from the land of his birth, and suitably inscribed by a few of the Rutgers "Class of '37," who had known him but to love him.

All, except Stryker and the writer of this sketch, of the brethren aforenamed, were married, when commissioned by the American Board, at the nomination of our own Foreign Mission Board, as the custom then was. Our separate organization dates from the Synod of 1857.

Thus, in the seventh year of our attempt at Gospel work for Netherlands India, five ordained laborers were upon the soil of that dominion, at various points. The records are copious, during the lustrum from 1836 to 1841, touching the endeavors, the appeals, the Governmental thwartings or evasions, the journeyings, the hopings against hope. Did our missionaries ask permission to begin in Sumatra, the shades of Lyman and Munson were invoked to deter them from even prospecting the territory of that island. There were difficulties about Bali too, and American missionaries in Java could not be thought of. There were already a few Zendelings from Holland, in country places, for whom the state-paid city pastors cherished a courteously lofty scorn. Our Church had selected this heathen field, beneath the colonial sway of Holland, in trust that our name as the Reformed Protestant "Dutch," would meet with an exceptional favor. But the truth was obvious, and came out early, that this nominally Christian Government had no exceptions to make. It shrank from a pure and aggressive Gospel-work in any of its territory, remembering the beginnings in British India, and fearing trouble from its many Mohammedan stipendiaries and richly-pensioned Rajahs. They trembled that the truths of history and a sound political economy always, and necessarily, follow the enjoyment of the established Word and ordinances of the only true God, and Jesus Christ, His Divine Son.

Much had been learned, in a disheartening experience, by the fourth year, but our Church had put her hand to the plough. And when, finally, our brethren were accorded a permission to settle themselves in Borneo, the continental home of untold mineral and vegetable wealth, they accepted the ungracious boon. Traditions of cannibalism were rife, and procured ready credence in a population sparse and given to tribal feuds of blood. With the courage of all the despair that faith can know, they went.

Omitting diffuse details, we now have the position in September, 1842, in this form. Four, of the five, ordained missionaries are on the island of their compulsory selection; and the last comer is required, by Government regulations, to spend a year on Java, under vigilant, but unmeddlesome, surveillance.

To this unmarried man, in the early months of his stay, and when he had just fought himself free from summons to military duty, with low-flung Dutch, degenerate through vice, with barefooted natives of various races, and a few Africans, esteemed very choice for their endurance of the torrid clime, came a letter of importunate advice. David Abeel was on the China coast, the empire was about to open, he knew the hamper of the Borneo case, and was enthusiastic for the land of Sinim. His counsel was a torrent of affectionate urgency, for reasons personal and ministerial, that I should instantly abandon thought or plan for "that hopeless field on Borneo," take the first vessel towards China, write to the Board that I *had done so*, and they would, beyond all question, thank me for having done what the greatly changed phases warranted. The senior bachelor was clearly in earnest!

The reply to this ardent challenge was prompt, and required no study. The tempting had its allurements, but it was not an open question. The junior had volunteered on this forlorn hope intelligently; knew its past sore trials to the brethren who awaited his coming; its sure suffering of body, soul and spirit for his own future; *but* he should feel himself clothed with dishonor, as with a garment, could he even give the proposal an hour of dalliance. So spoke a young heart's faith in God and a co-operative church, in fullest unison with the dues of personal honor and covenant. He believed then, as now, that when we vow at communion seasons, that all we are and have is Christ's, the household of faith should illustrate in its life that it meant its words, and would never eat them.

Of the four members of the Mission on Borneo, Doty and Pohlman had given chief attention to the Chinese language, while Thomson and Youngblood aimed exclusively at work among the Malayan population. The former two were surrounded, at the seaboard station Pontianak, by many thousands of Chinese colonists, while the chief service at the interior post must be sought by itineracy among the Dyak villages. Those at Karangan were at a distance, against the current of the Landak River, of four to five days from their brethren below, and were largely dependent upon Pontianak, for supplies and for any connection of their "Forest Home" with the outer world.

Of course, the cry of "China Open" was not heard with listless ear by two of these Borneo four, as 1843 was gathering its scroll-record to the sky. In their views as a Mission, there was a divergence of opinion as to field of labor by a tie, and the young brother on Java would bring a casting vote. At his arrival, late in 1843, a Mission council was held at the upper station. The two who wished to go at once to China were of the same county, and one of them a townsman, with the Albany recruit, and all his personal sentiments would have gladly obliged them. Earnest and kind discussion issued in a vote of three to two, in December, 1843, that one should go immediately to China, and the other remain for labor among our myriad Chinese, for a period not to exceed one year. Meantime, we would send, and did send, most clamant entreaty for relief by other new men. With glad devoutness we regarded the issue settled, regretting much that *one* should go. March brought a re-opening, on personal wish alone. And the candor of history requires it said that the member of the Mission who had given most intensity of feeling and written thought, to opposing the departure of both; who deprecated the policy of *either* brother's leaving the large field among our Chinese colonists, but had reluctantly yielded, in part, to not unnatural longings of old associates; and the order of signatures to our appeal should show that untiring Thomson was he —now reversed his vote. Both were to go, at option. Both went, in April. And the lethal blow was dealt Now was fulfilled the saying of the Mohammedan that we wealthy zealots had come to encounter a "pro tem," privation and labor, whereby to lay up a store of merit for good works, and then withdraw; seemingly fulfilled, and they could caution the Dyak not to put stigma upon the religion of his Mohammedan rulers by sending his children to boarding-school with us, who would, ere long, go thence, and leave them, unsupported, to the rancor of the dignitaries. " While the white man is here, it is well; but he surely will not remain in this wildwood of poverty and barbarism; and when he shall finally depart, Dyak neighbor, *prenez garde!*"

Was it not easy for human nature to be impressed by this? And was it not fatal, humanly speaking, to furnish scope and point for such neighborly warning?

In the providence of God, within a few days of each other, not many weeks after setting foot in China, the wives of the brethren of the Pontianak post, so recently given up, were called away by death; and Brother Doty, who had long been an invalid from asthma, took all the motherless children to America.

Crippled as the Mission now was, much earnest endeavor signalized the following years, and its record is on high. No opposition was ever offered; we were respected, in person and work, and received honor, though little of formal thanks, for frequent medical aid. The Sabbath received external honor on our premises, for our sakes; and every wayfarer, knowing the Lord's day by the absence of all garden-labor, was ready to be catechumen or hearer, by the hour. And then, that the narrator may be entirely honest, the Dyak would, perhaps, resume his pole or net, and "go a fishing." Nevertheless, the missionary must not see him doing it. A Dyak was ashamed of detection in a lie, because he desired our good opinion and avoided theft because he believed we would intuitively know the guilty one by some medicine-man process. It would have been difficult, too, to utilize a white man's articles, in a region so nude of anything extra. Whatever the why or wherefore, we were never robbed of clothing, money nor utensils. At their villages, or by the wayside, we were well received and listened to. One fraud I do remember, and must not conceal. The usual wrapping of a corpse, was the bark of large forest trees; but in the march of civilization, joy came, one day, to the Swiss lady-member of our band. A Dyak woman came to announce the decease of her mother, and would be gratified, could she wrap her parent's remains in "Lowell Drill," which she knew us to possess. Verdure seemed to be springing upon our spiritual field, and verdancy on our side hailed it. The cloth was given, in liberal measure; and a brother who "wanted to know, you know," found, on the morrow, there had been no death! Could we have had the itineracy of our first five men, or other fit five, no one can say that we might not have been privileged to report success. We were bound, as a condition precedent, to furnish indications of permanence, and these were never presented.

If from the three buildings at "Forest Home," which, though spacious, cost but little money to build or maintain, we could have been sending, in effective and alternating succession, two or three clever, devoted and sagacious men, "wise as serpents and harmless as doves," hope would have had her fair place to stand. Our Church might have escaped the shame and crime of saying, under a Borneo sky, "there is none other name under Heaven, given among men, whereby we must be saved," and then ceasing to proclaim it. We were not driven out; we neither decayed, nor died out fully. The call for reinforcement was made by burning words, and at length by personal appeal of survivor ready to resume; but Missions that could show success were appealing in vain for new men, and our beloved Kalamantan was given over to the indolent Malay and the Dyak who was idle, because of no outlet for his industry. There were adverse political influences, such as irregular and arbitrary taxation, and the like, and a broad margin for improvement, in every respect. But God's word and messenger go to heathendom, expecting to find many obstacles to social and civic development, and to see them vanish with a widening acceptance of the only Saviour's truth.

To complete the history, Mrs. Thomson's death was followed by her husband's departure for America, by way of Europe, where he proposed to leave his youngest daughter with her grandparents in Switzerland, and thence to go to New Jersey with his first-born daughter, a native of Dutchess County, N. Y. His daughter, "Eliza DeWitt," lies buried at Karangan; his own grave is in the shadow of the Alps; the eldest child is the estimable wife of a valued dominie among us.

The Youngblood family, having buried children at Pontianak, left Borneo on the errand of health-seeking for the head, and after a year of little gain, returned, to take early departure for America at the opening of 1849.

With them, left our mission, for immediate marriage at Singapore, with view to the charge of a large Mission-school at Penang, a young lady from England, who had, at Mrs. Thomson's request, been sent to reside in her family by the same Walthamstowe association, which had originally sent herself to Batavia as a teacher. This energetic and cheerful girl came to us in May, 1844, began teaching next morning, through a vocabulary of phrases; and made her mark at Penang, and subsequently in upper China, as Mrs. Bausum, as I am informed, and verily believe.

I will not further enlarge. In the American Missionary Memorial, (Harper & Brothers, 1853,) is a very fair wood-cut from a drawing made by the gifted wife of a pastor at Upper Red Hook, in 1851, which feebly depicts the beautiful site of our long-abandoned Mission. To me it arouses full sympathy with every honest toiler, in whose throat swells the gulp of the wronged. We had acres upon acres of tropical plant and fruit, laid out by cheap labor, under white men's taste. No title in fee simple, but ground cleared and cultivated *ad libitum*. As we improved the site, the ruler smiled and the ruled were pleased.

The latter received his ten cents per diem, while the former scented his own reversionary advantage, when the lethal wound of March, 1844, should have done its work. All our outlay in embellishment could be neutralized by the quiet Malayan observation: "They want it in pleasing style, so long as they remain."

The mode of our itinerating, and the services in three languages at our home, &c., &c., are they not all of record, in journals written or printed in the long ago? The series, in many numbers of the *Christian Intelligencer*, of 1850, "by an

Antipode," is full of information; and No. 7 graphically describes the Mission premises, without at all approaching justice to the facts.

At the end of November, 1849, the last who went and the latest to return, came home, to struggle and to stay. Then there was money, but men were wanting. Now, men can be refused, because commissariat and transportation are defective. The remedy is simple, but frame and heart are breaking in Asia, meanwhile. The Woman's Board will be glad to have warrant for believing that there are, to-day, women in the Antipodal Island, who are singing, to child or grandchild, the hymnal melodies we taught them, and that the burden of their song is the remembered language of the truth those hymns contained. How much of the then perfectly committed little catechism of Brown may be retained, is matter for prayerful doubt.

The valuable commercial products of Borneo must give it a historic future. Gutta percha, dye woods, choicest timber for the tropics, coal, tin, antimony, diamonds and gold were already known in our Mission's brief era. Ambition of Governments, the greed of wealth, or other instrumentality of Providence will drive the pirate from her coasts, and tame the wild hordes of her salubrious hill country, at no far-away day. With the introduction of industry, under fair and stable rule for all classes and conditions, the time must come for God's word to enter and remain and conquer. And I devoutly believe that our Woman's Board will actively live to see that end.

MISCELLANEA.

The articles of food were venison, fresh fish, the eggs and

flesh of our own numerous poultry, wood-pigeons and the excellent meat of the game wild hog. Salted provisions could be imported, with our flour, from America; and canned salmon or meats from Britain, were known to be procurable, should the spirit of luxury ever arise.

Of vegetables, we had the sweet potato, yams, cucumbers, Indian corn, and the omnipresent rice. Fruits were in luscious variety at our own premises, and thousands of pineapples came from the plants that lined our spacious garden-paths. The Dyaks could have lived amid plantain-groves and sugar-cane, but would not have their hearts made hot by the effrontery of Malay traders or footpads who helped themselves to the first fruits of any such case.

Still fiercer were the ravages of some kingling's retinue from Landak, the royal seat of enthroned pauperism and beggarly gaud. If they brought a symbol only, it warranted plunder as their master's own presence would.

We had no animals of burden, or of prey. A bear that was harmless, and the orang utan, (the "ourang outang" of boyhood's geography,) that anger might make formidable, were the sights, beyond the myriad of monkeys. Serpents, neither few nor small, and some of them dealing swift death, there were; though seldom seen, and no injury was ever suffered from them, in treading the forest paths. There were no roads, no horses; and the cow would yield, on abundant grass, but few pints of milk. Our milk we obtained from goats we kept.

Journeying between our Mission posts was on a water-route, with Dyak oarsmen, who had been brought up to small boats and large-bladed, lazy paddle. Choosing once, a season when the river channel was flush, and the moon was full, I swept down the crooked Landak river with three such rowers, one hundred and twenty miles in sixteen hours. Here we met the partial power of flood-tide from the sea, and my tired men were suffered to go three or four miles an hour. Free lunch of rice and curry, biscuit, coffee and cucumbers, with approving smile at their exertions, achieved a peerless result, beyond any that reproof from a frequently halting smoker could have wrought. A Dyak, like other men, works the better, for seeing that his employer is pleased, and is willing to say so.

Here, I may say, that two of the Mission had titles, derived from their stature and youth; the third being sufficiently distinguished, in that he was not either of those. Surnames are little used among themselves, and a parent is known as the father or mother of the first boy, if there be one, if not, then of the first daughter. Old heads of families may employ a single personal name. The word for father is Mā; for mother, No. The two titled teachers were Tuan Tiñggi and Tuan Aŭgut.

The rate of interest among the natives was illustrative of lack of capital and want of confidence, and was five per cent. a month. Unwritten exaction of labor from the debtors was unspeakably worse, as we knew in detail. That money was borrowed in the Christian west, at five per cent. for a twelve-month, found credence; only because we, the perfect standards of veracity, had said such was the fact.

One relieving fact should, in justice to the Governor General of Netherlands, India, be added: Emboldened by his affability to Dr. Medhurst and himself, during a call they made upon him at Batavia, Mr. Steele went to his country-palace at Buitenzorg, forty miles out among the hills, and asked a waiving of the rule requiring a year's stay on Java. The Governor "fought off," in very good English, to draw out the audacious applicant; but, on being reminded that supreme discretion was *his*, to order or refuse permission, he withdrew his playful remark, that "he would see what he could do." He asked that the plea should be sent up to him in Dutch; the paper was prepared and translated and mailed; and the marvel occurred of rapidity as well as graciousness, that four days brought the option of departure at first convenience; seven months of the year had elapsed.

Subsequently, the official who had harassed our brethren in Borneo, was transformed into a gentlemanly friend, who would seek to do a favor. There had been misunderstandings in matters of etiquette, at the Resident's office; and from small beginnings, ominous restrictions grew. The visit of Dr. Isaac Ferris to the Hague, in 1841, was probably productive of advices from the Home authorities, to the advantage of the Mission. Arbitrary restrictions and withdrawal of the usual franking privilege for correspondence were abandoned, and large expense and annoyance thus avoided. The Dyack saw the Dutch magnate's silver-laced cap handsomely lifted, when he and the "Ulu" missionary met, and he treasured the incident for mention among the villages near home.

Mention should be made of the death of the first Mrs. Thomson, at Batavia, in 1839, to complete the necrology of the Mission. Thus we have our dead at Karangan and Pontianak, infants; the second Mrs. Thompson, at Pontianak; his first wife at Batavia, and Stryker at Singapore.

It may illustrate the rapacity of heathenism, to state what occurred at my sending for a Chinese Master-Mason, to arrange for placing in a Cemetery at Batavia, the monument sent out in my care by Nicholas Wyckoff, Esq., for the grave of his daughter. It was in complete readiness for erection, in three sections of marble; and was to be conveyed three miles, from the Custom House to the burial-place, and jointed upon a platform prepared for it long previously. His first demand, one hundred and twenty rupees, was instantly declined. On the morrow, with the same facts, he proposed seventy-five; but the confounding of "sacredness" (suggested by Dr. Medhurst as a palliation) with "*auri-sacra fames*," was too offensive for a new-comer. He was utterly rejected, and an equally competent builder, also a Chinaman, did the work most acceptably for twenty rupees. "*Ex pede Herculem.*"

The harvest-dance of the Dyacks had quite as much of horrid suggestiveness as of bodily grace, and followed hard after the threshing. And, as perhaps but few of my readers have been present at this scene, I may say that the threshing of the *padi* (rice in the husk) is done by the twirled feet of men and women, who grasp a rattan line suspended parallel with the floor-matting, and six feet above it. Arrack is occasionally imbibed, by the threshing wrigglers. The dance proper is at evening, by the light of cocoanut oil, from vessels that are the Dyack's own; and only the extremes of life, 1st and 7th of Shakespeare's "stages," fail to take part.

It is not unknown that this race scalps below the chin, and

that a Dyack goes for little at his majority, who cannot show a head that is anatomically, other than his own. These heads are preserved, in two senses; and on these festive occasions, the male dancer carries his victim's mummied summit, as one of our belles doth her kerchief. At my first on-looking, (yea, verily, and the *last*) a careful note was made of my bearing and expression, by some whom I had taught and preached to. Politeness forbade an entirely stolid presence, and I addressed some remark to an adjacent native, which elicited the loud inquiry from a boozy middle-aged dancer: "What does he say?" For a few seconds the conceded rudeness made silence audible; the questioned one was still, but, in another moment, the false and brutish courage of another Arrakian, in and on the line, laughingly brazened out the invented reply; "*Dosa, ujora*," i.e., "It is sin, he says." Awkward flush and silence and shifting of the feet ensued, then respectful questionings and approach by smiling and panting men; and, as it was no place to preach, and not wholly the place to stay, I left and carried away good wishes. A very little of *that*, is enough.

When relatives are seriously ill, Dyacks make vows to the great spirit Jubata, payable on recovery. The big vow of all, is the largest procurable of swine for a village feast. As the only acceptable offering to the occult Power is the odor, and the flesh goes into prompt and neighborly consumption, great interest is felt in the recovery of the sick, if there has been devoutness enough to make a vow. A Dyack pays his vows, and the neighbors as "deeply lament" the loss of his mother-in-law, as would a London *Times* "obituary," for an extra crown. Our dwellings were floored with planks, but the outer walls and partitions were of the bark of the large forest-trees about us. Oblong slabs were flattened by steaming, and when carpentered in a neat, firm style, and made brilliant with lime, their appearance against a background of verdure, was to our eyes pleasant. From the edges of the surrounding verandah, each house was perhaps 70 by 50 feet, and exercise could easily be had on that long circuit, when heat or storm was against outgoing. The central reception hall was wider than either room abreast of it, and its modest furnishing was calmly pleasant by the light of the astral evening lamp. Here, as we read or talked, was not seldom heard the whistle of a deer, startled by suddenly seeing the light from the glazed window that was new to him. Many, however, of our windows had lattice-work and no glass, for saving's sake. Matting covered the room-floors, and the ceilings of bamboo stem looked best on the upper side in the unused attic, which was bounded, far above, by the sloping steeps of thatch. Matting was laid upon these ceiling canes, but a lizard, or scorpion, or centipede could and did slip through. No fire was ever needed for comfort, and the culinary department had its own large building, rods in the rear.

Our station-services of the Lord's day, were three in number. Those in Dyack and Malay were held at nine and three P. M., in the rear building seen at the apex of the triangle; and our own service, in English, at the Mission-homes alternately, at eleven o'clock. Our monthly concert was usefully held on "the first Monday," invariably, according to original covenant, and the Hymn Books almost opened of their own motion, at the fittest choice.

Scripture translations were made and printed, and a small Hymn Book; but the readers, were nearly all in the future. Offers there were of discipleship, but time might have proven them of "rice and curry" type. They were chiefly of the cripple family.

When the outbreak of war in Bali, broke up the plan of the Governor General, to visit and examine somewhat, our inland region,—bright hopes were dashed. He was intending to go up the Saugan river by steamer, and would have passed within thirty miles south of Karangan. To intercept and join him, for interviews with Malayan Rajah and Dyack Chiefs, would have been useful, and by God's favor, acceptable. Schemes and schedules of taxation, fixing a scale with impassable maximum, would have been an untold blessing and incitement to labor. Chinese gold-digging needed only protection from the too frequent robbery or murder of the successful adventurer. And the first personal coming of Holland's supreme colonial Chief, would have been an electric boon to every worthy interest. But the outbreak in Bali called for all Dutch vessels, forbade the absence of the Governor-General, and added to the darkness of the clouds, by contrast with the rifts that had been opening. Humanly speaking, the end had come; for the West had no heartening hope to write—no re-enforcing men to send.

Usually the intervals in receiving correspondence were one hundred days—once or oftener, eight months—and the crowning achievement was fourteen months, by the highly successful neglect of our British bankers and agents at Singapore. "Man proposes, and God disposes." The Lord reigneth, the God and Father of our **Lord Jesus Christ**. For a Dyak burial, a grave of six feet by two was dug, to the depth of six feet; and from the bottom a lateral excavation was run so far under the bank, that the earth, in refilling, should not fall upon the bark-wrapped body. When it could be avoided, a corpse was not kept over night; and I have seen an infant borne to God's acre, within two hours from its death. Superstition was dense and universal, and in only one case did I ever receive invitation or permission to be present, for prayer or remark. In that instance, the usual ululations, at the close, from all present, were subdued and brief.

The incantations over those in peril by disease or casualty were a sad side-light upon what man may come to,—" having no hope, and without God in the world." A wound would be overlaid with leaves, until it became certain the blood *would* flow, and then they would report to us an almost exanimate subject. Providentially, we had uniform success; and this was necessary to our reputation, even when their own priestly physician had, avowedly, abandoned hope. Alarm was, always, signally marked, when the white man ordered a wound uncovered of every leaf, to the lowest, before he could begin to heal.

The climate of Borneo was never oppressive in-doors, though we were on the equator. Eighty-eight degrees was about our highest record in the house; while the same thermometer might register one hundred and forty degrees in the garden, between us and the crystal stream at the foot of the knoll. A coverlid and blanket were the demand of every night. A walk of twenty miles, mainly through the towering forest, need not exhaust you; and a long evening-service was rendered after it, when the bath, and the solitary meal had been attended to, between. In allusion to these scenes of the past, how joy and sadness blend in the memory of one who had sturdy Dyak friends! Names, faces, voices come up in their personal distinctiveness. God bless the survivors!

CHINA.

PORCELAIN TOWER.

THE AMOY MISSION

BY THE
REV. WM. RANKIN DURYEA, D.D.

THE land of China has excited, for centuries, the highest interest among Christian nations. Its situation, its immense population, the organization of its government, and its long preservation, arrest the thought of every student. Its knowledge of the different branches of science, and its development in the useful arts, humble our Western pride. The use of the mariner's compass, of gunpowder, of the thread of the silkworm, was common in China long before Christian nations had learned their value. Travellers through "Cathay," in the Middle Ages, brought back reports which were deemed almost fabulous, of the wealth, intelligence and order which prevailed. There was the great wall on the Northern border, thirteen hundred miles in length, and thirty feet in height, on whose top six horsemen could ride abreast. There were the number-

CHINESE CLASSICS ENGRAVED ON THE TABLETS OF STONE, IN CONFUCIAN TEMPLE, IN PEKING.

less "pagodas," or heathen temples, the most famous being that of Nanking, which was faced with porcelain of various tints, and rose to a height of two hundred and sixty-one feet, and consisted of nine stories. Each story was ornamented according to Chinese taste, with lanterns, pictures, images and pithy proverbs. Each story had a landing place, where was a window from which an agreeable and extensive view could be taken of the city, the river and the distant country. The numerous bells jingled in every passing breeze, and on festival nights, all the lanterns were lighted.

This pagoda, after standing sixteen centuries, was destroyed by the rebels in 1858. It was built in the middle of the third century, by the reigning Emperor, as a monument to his mother's memory; but it was also a temple of idolatry, filled from base to top with idol gods.

There was the majestic river, the Yang-tse-kiang—flowing for three thousand miles, and crowded with the traffic of scores and hundreds of cities. Within these swarming marts of business, rose costly homes amid the lower buildings and bazaars, while stately palaces were filled with princely officials, whose pride manifested itself in pretensions far above those of the haughtiest courts of Europe. Modern travel has confirmed the truth of many of the narratives which were once received as fanciful. China is, indeed, a land filled with a wonderful civilization; but a civilization which seemes to have reached its limit centuries ago, and from that date to be unprogressive. Thus fossilized, it strikes the mind with astonishment. We look forward, for instance, to intelligence in all our rulers, as greatly to be desired; for centuries literary eminence has been in China the only path to official position. Below the princely order, every ruler of the land must pass an examination of his attainments in knowledge, the "five classics," the "four sacred books," and Chinese history, giving the subjects. Great halls in Peking, the Northern capital, receive the students from universities and schools, who submit themselves to these tests year by year. This intelligence has undoubtedly made the Government strong and enduring, but it has not saved it from becoming corrupt and cruel almost beyond expression. The accompanying picture gives an accurate representation of the interior of a Confucian temple in Peking. In the matter of religion, China is in the deepest darkness. Its teachers have never developed the people in love to God and fellow men. Indifference to all that is spiritual, seems a national characteristic. Long before Jesus came to earth, Confucius and Lao-tse left systems of morality, which have been studied by millions of the higher classes. Their doctrines, after the lapse of twenty-five hundred years, are seen as producing nothing in the life of their followers which is really noble and pure. The Buddhist religion is followed by the masses of the Empire; a religion which is a round of forms, and which holds out the promise of annihilation as its last reward.

WORSHIP OF ANCESTORS.

The one thing to which all are devoted, is the worship of ancestors. In every home are found tablets in which the spirit of the dead is supposed to linger. Before these there is a constant adoration. Chinese people, whether Buddhists, Taoists, or followers of Confucius, are united in this super-

stition. Offerings of money, food and clothing are continually renewed before the votive shrine of their dead. The poor content themselves with small tablets, placed in some recess of the house, and bearing the names of the dead; but the wealthy pride themselves, on such an ornate and graceful Ancestral Hall, as we see in the illustration.

"The general belief is, that the unseen world is very much like this, only that things are spiritualized. The departed spirits are supposed to need food and clothing and money, just as when they resided in earthly bodies, and pious living friends, consider it a sacred duty to provide for their wants. Real food is placed for a time before the tablets, and when the spirits are thought to have consumed the spiritual part, the material part is eaten by the household. Clothing and money are symbolized by paper, which is devoutly burnt, the fire conveying it to those for whom it is intended. The Chinese think that if they forget or neglect these rites, their departed relatives will be very angry, and bring dire calamities upon them; and their belief in this is ingrained and inwoven with the whole fabric of their lives."

These tablets are the last things which the heathenism of China will yield. The people will turn from Confucius, will leave their temples, will sometimes profess Christianity,—but the real test of the convert's truthfulness, usually comes when the "ancestral tablet" is doomed to destruction.

INTRODUCTION OF PROTESTANT CHRISTIANITY.

In the sixth and seventh centuries, Nestorian missionaries are said to have penetrated the bounds of the empire. In the sixteenth century, devoted Jesuits secured a foothold for a time; but the Romish mixture of political, religious and priestly pretensions, could gain no permanent hold. At last the Empire seemed sealed against all Christianity, and even foreign trade was prohibited. In 1836, the Reformed Dutch Church in America established a mission in Borneo. Some of our missionaries employed much of their time in preaching to the Chinese, who were found thronging all the ports of the great islands adjacent to their populous native land. In 1840, a war broke forth between Great Britain and China, which changed the whole aspect of affairs. The war originated in the selfishness and sinfulness of English traders endeavoring to force a baneful traffic in opium, upon the unwilling Chinese. But wicked as was the war, God turned it to His praise. When it ceased, treaties were made, by which five ports were opened for the free entry of Christian nations. The disciples of Christ hailed the flinging back of the long barred gates, and instantly made preparations for an advance. Among those ports of ingress stood the city of Amoy.

SITUATION OF AMOY.

He who studies the map of China is usually led to mark the great island of Formosa, which lies along the Chinese coast, somewhat like Madagascar, near south-eastern Africa. Formosa is separated from the mainland, by straits, which average seventy-five miles in width, and across those straits lies the city of Amoy. As a trading port and harbor, it had been often coveted by Europeans, and near it one of the foreign "factories" had been established from early in the eighteenth century.

The city is built on a hilly island, at the mouth of a river, and the ground it occupies is closely filled by a population of two hundred thousand souls.

Near it are other islands, on the nearest of which, called Kolongsoo, much more favorable places for foreign residences are found than in Amoy. About thirty-five miles up the river, lies the city of Chiang-chin, and just north of Amoy is found Tung-an, the capital of a Chinese district. Between Chiang-chin and Amoy, Chioh-bey lies, a city with sixty thousand people. In fact, the district of forty-five miles around Amoy is computed to contain nearly three millions of inhabitants, thus supporting a population, perhaps, equal to that of the State of New York, from Lake Ontario to the Hudson.

ORIGIN OF THE MISSION.

Our Mission originated in the wisdom and counsel of one man, whose name will long be tenderly preserved in the hearts of those who love Christ's kingdom, and who is embalmed in the records of the Reformed Church, as one of her best beloved children.

The following extract from a letter of the late Mrs. T. C. Doremus, discloses the interest felt at the time in the mission of Dr. Abeel, to Amoy:—

NEW YORK, November 25, 1876.

Dear Friend:—I am very much obliged to the ladies, and you, for sending me the certificate of life membership to the Board of Missions. Will you thank them? Dr. David Abeel was the first missionary to China, 1829, invited by the generosity of Mr. Olyphant, of the firm of Talbot, Olyphant & Co., a passage out in one of their ships, and support for a year. Dr. Bridgeman accompanied him. I was on board of the ship to bid them good-bye. At the end of the year, the Dutch Board assumed

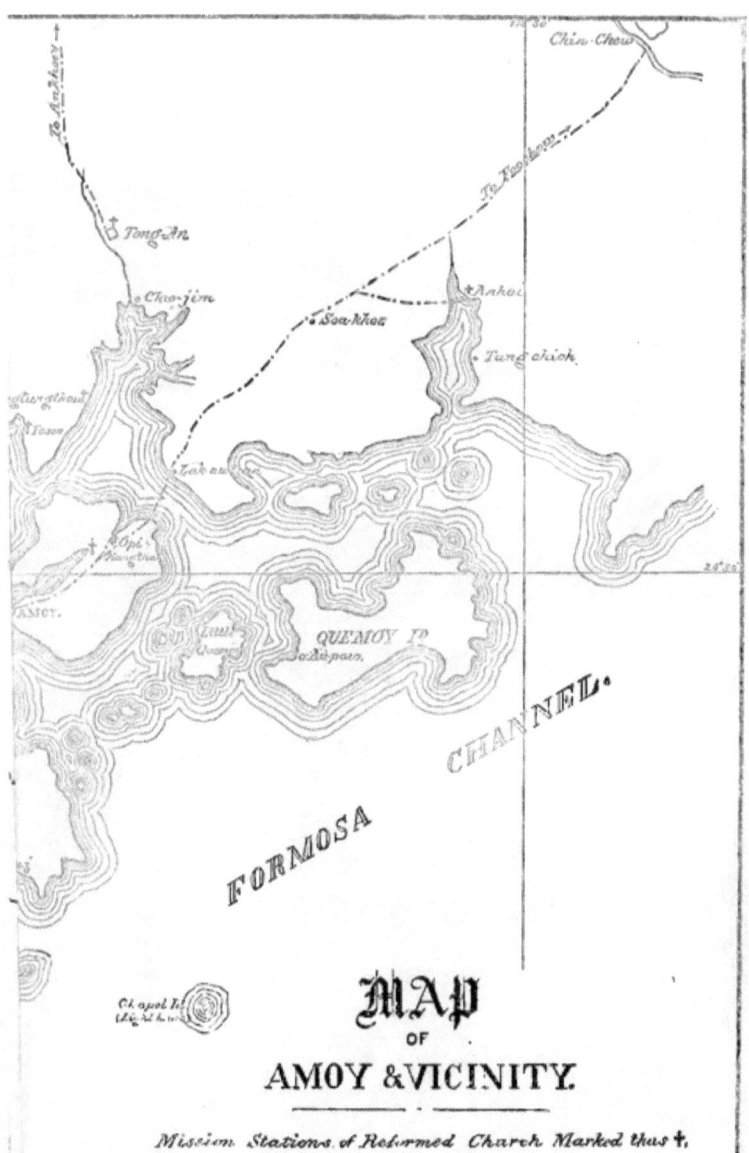

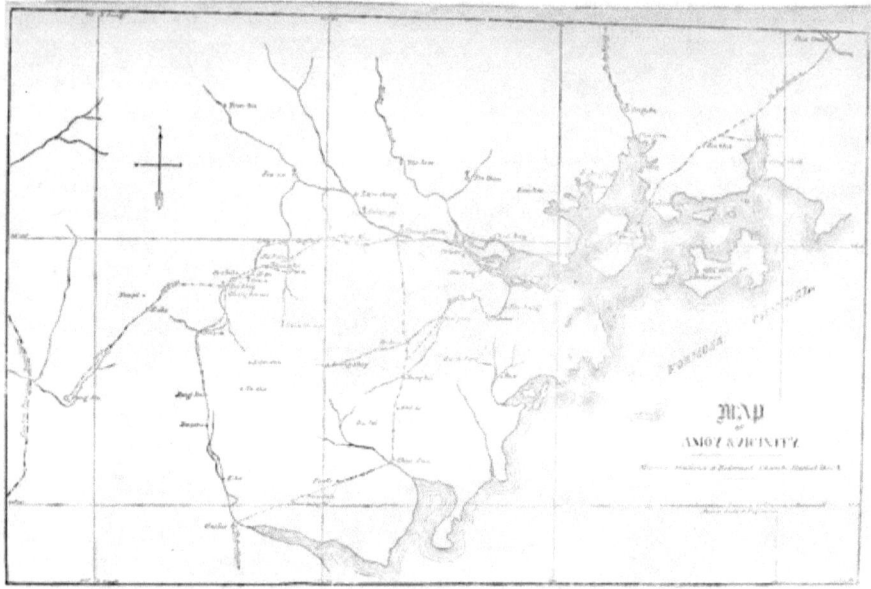

the charge of Dr. Abeel; the American Board of Dr. Bridgeman. At that time, when the Chinese teacher was instructing them, he kept the door locked, when the officers came to see what the foreigners were doing. The teacher put the books in a box, and material for making shoes on its top, before unlocking the door, as he feared he might loose his head, if he taught foreigners Chinese. In 1834, Dr. Abeel was in delicate health; the physicians recommended a voyage to his native land. There were no American ships in port; a kind English captain invited him to go in his ship to London; while there he was the guest of Mr. Suter. Dr. Abeel founded the "Society for Promoting the Female Education of the East," to send ladies to teach the women of India and China. He brought me the programme, and a meeting was called in the parlors of Dr. Matthews, in the South Dutch Church, then Garden, now Exchange, street. The meeting for final arrangement, was at the house of Mrs. Bethune, Dr. Bethune's mother. Dr. Abeel opened the meeting, and then remarked that he had a message for them: at that time, the Dutch was auxillary to the American Board. "The secretary, Dr. Rufus Anderson, wished the ladies to defer." "What!" said Mrs. Bethune, "are the American Board afraid the ladies will get ahead of them?" Some were for going on; others, out of respect to Dr. Anderson, were willing to wait; and Dr. Abeel, with tears rolling down his face, exclaimed: "What is to become of the souls of those who are ignorant of the offers of mercy and the Bible?" That English society invited us to Calcutta, the Woman's Union Missionary Society. In twelve years, 10,000 of the high caste have been taught in Calcutta, besides the lower caste.

Mrs. T. C. Doremus.

To Secretary of Woman's Board.

Burning with missionary zeal, David Abeel went out to China in 1829, intending to labor as a chaplain among seamen. Soon after his arrival at his post, he was transferred to the American Board of Foreign Missions, and under directions from home, he made a survey of the field for missionary efforts in eastern Asia. After a visit to Europe and the United States, he returned to the east, and was laboring in Borneo when the British treaty opened the gates of the Celestial Empire. He sailed in 1841, from Borneo for China, and with Bishop Boone, of the American Episcopal Church, he located himself on Kolongsoo in 1842. Instantly, he began to press the claims of Amoy upon the denomination to which he was most closely attached. His appeals were so earnest, that at last our General Synod approved of the transfer of two more missionaries from Borneo, the Rev. Elihu Doty and the Rev. William J. Pohlman. These brethren joined the pioneer in 1844. Six months after their arrival, David Abeel returned, in failing health, to America, and died at Albany in 1846, at the age of forty-two years. Had he no other monument, the living stones which have been built into the temple of Christ in Amoy, would perpetuate his memory more grandly than St. Paul's of London tells the value of the great architect whose dust lies mouldering beneath its dome.

PROGRESS OF THE MISSION.

In 1847, the Rev. John V. N. Talmage joined the little band, and in 1848 a church, for the converts, was built—the first church for native Christians which was erected in China after Protestant missions were there established. In 1850, Dr. James Young, a physician, under the direction of the English Presbyterian Church, came to Amoy, and was closely associated with our own missionaries. The devoted William C. Burns joined Dr. Young in 1851. He came from his native Scotland, filled with the same zeal which the Holy Spirit had so wonderfully blessed by revival after revival in the churches to which Mr. Burns had ministered. Soon after his arrival, a remarkable outpouring of God's grace occurred in Amoy and the neighborhood. Churches were organized, in which, a spirit of consecration prevailed, and new points were taken for greater effort. From that day to this, the missionaries of the two churches have worked in loving harmony, and the grand result is seen in a Chinese Classis or Presbytery which is managed by the representatives of the native churches. So remarkable was the early progress of the Christian work in Amoy, that, in 1853, the *Missionary Herald* referred to it as "far more successful than any mission in China." It has never lost its ground. In 1854, there was an accession of over fifty members; and, on the year following, seventy-five persons were received into the native church. A school for girls was started at an early day, though under heavy discouragements; and two prayer meetings, for women, were sustained by the converts, under the guidance of the faithful wives of our missionaries.

In January, 1849, the second of the "first three," the Rev. William J. Pohlman, perished by shipwreck as he was returning from Hong-Kong. The Rev. Elihu Doty was spared to labor fifteen years in his chosen field, dying on ship-board in 1864, when only a day or two separated him from the native land to which he was hastening. The Rev. Dr. Talmage has already passed thirty years of constant service among the Chinese. May God long spare his useful and consecrated life, and permit His servant to behold yet larger blessings, before the final summons from toil to rest is given.

We need not give the whole list of those who, since 1847, have sought to labor for the Master in distant Amoy. Twenty-five godly men and women have, at various times, been sent forth by our Board of Foreign Missions, including in this number, the names of David Abeel and his associates.* Nine of these have been compelled to give up the work on account of their health, and have returned, to remain in their native land. Eleven, out of the twenty-five, have died while in the harness; sometimes, at the very beginning of their career, stricken mysteriously down. Especially do we recall the Rev. John E. Watkins and his wife, who, sailing from New York in 1861, were never heard from after the vessel had gained the open sea. The treasure-house of God is wide, and in earth or sea, we know He guards His saints, and watches over their precious dust. But though the workmen in the field we consider have thus been subject to change, and have often been called away, God has carried on the work to a higher and higher plane.

PRESENT STATE OF THE MISSION.—1877.

Of our own missionaries, there are found on the ground, to-day, the Rev. Dr. Talmage and his wife, their daughter, Miss Mary E. Talmage, and the Rev. Leonard W. Kip and his wife. The Rev. Daniel W. Rapelje, who began his labors in 1859, is now in this country regaining his strength after years of service. Miss Helen M. Van Doren is also at home, but hoping soon with renewed health to return. This little band, blessed abundantly in the past, is appealing earnestly for re-enforcement. Dr. Talmage began his labors in 1847, Rapelje in 1859, and Kip in 1860. Surely such toilers have a right to be heard, as they ask for new associates from home.

---

* The figures are as nearly exact as I can make them, but there may be slight mistakes.—W. R. D.

THE AMOY MISSION.

NATIVE CHURCHES.

The "Tai-hoe" or Classis of Amoy, has now fifteen native Churches connected with it. In these are found *twelve hundred and fifty communicants*. To be a Christian in China, involves trials and difficulties we can scarcely imagine. For instance, we may refer to the well-known diminutive

FEET OF CHINESE LADIES.

"Parents in Christian lands are made happy in watching the natural growth and development of their children.

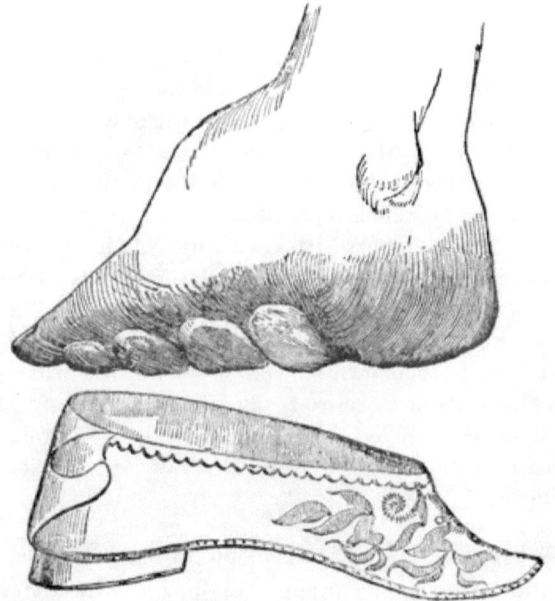

Parents in China, on the other hand, would be greatly mortified and distressed should the feet of their daughters

grow to their natural size. A Christian mother supplies her child with shoes that will fit the feet. A Chinese mother binds and bandages the foot of her child that it may fit the shoe.

The shoe pattern, in the picture given, is supposed to be made of red silk, and to be handsomely embroidered.

The Chinese, especially the richer classes, have for many centuries been in the habit of compressing the feet of their females by the use of tight bandages. The shape of the foot thus becomes very much as seen in the picture. All the toes, except the great one, are bent under the sole, and the bandages never being permanently removed, the foot remains very nearly the size it was when they were first applied. The upper part of the foot grows out of shape and proportion, and, except to the Chinese themselves, becomes very unsightly. Of course such a distorted foot makes the gait of a Chinese lady very awkward. She sways her arms to and fro, as if walking on her heels, and is usually aided by the shoulder of an attendant, or an umbrella carried as a walking-stick. But the Chinese ladies do very little walking. It is supposed by some that the practice of binding the feet was originally imposed by the men to keep the women at home. Whether this be so or not, Chinese ladies are very seldom seen in the streets, or even in their own houses; when a gentleman enters, custom obliges them to retire to an inner apartment. They enjoy few blessings of social life, and the sphere of woman in China, as in all heathen countries, is a very inferior and degraded one."

This barbarous usage is given up by our converts, who allow the little feet of the infant daughter to grow naturally. Shocking as it seems to us, the Chinese mother has been taught that the compressed feet will add to her child's rank in the community, and secure to her immunity from degrading labors. So many Chinese shoes have been brought to this country, that we only need refer to the custom as one of the practical things with which Christianity has to deal. In our churches at Amoy, a society pledged to oppose the custom has already been formed.

CONTRIBUTIONS.

Two of the churches support their own pastors entirely, and the benevolent contributions of the native Christians amount to sixteen hundred and sixty-four dollars. Our missionaries exercise only a general superintendence over the churches, and have all the work they can do in providing for vacant churches, instructing native students for the ministry, and pushing out preaching stations. To these last places, being the outposts of the field, they have to travel constantly; and for this purpose they employ their "Gospel Boat," as communication is mainly by the rivers flowing toward the harbor of Amoy. The residences of the missionaries are on Kolongsoo. The girls' school and churches are in the city of Amoy. It is much to be desired that the school, now having thirty-seven scholars, should be located on Kolongsoo, as being a far healthier position, and exposing the wives and daughters of our missionaries to less danger—since the ferriage between the island and Amoy is of primitive description. A good building, like that built for the education of girls in India, or the one recently raised in Japan, is becoming a necessity in our Chinese field.

Such, in a brief space, is the history of the Amoy Mission. But its real history what pen of earth can write? The secret sacrifices, the mental struggles, the persecutions, the temptations, the peace given to the soul, the glory granted to those who have triumphed over death, none but God knows these things. But what we can see, and can mark of progress, should give us the highest satisfaction. It should do more. It should prompt every Christian to *prayer* that God would send forth laborers to these fields "already white to the harvest," and to a *consecration* which leads to larger gifts for the prosecution of this blessed work. The "land of Sinim" belongs to Jesus Christ. To hasten the day when the Saviour we love shall be owned through all its broad extent, is a work to which God calls every Christian in our own favored country. God grant that every one who reads this sketch of faithful mission labor, may be stimulated to a deeper interest in the progress of the Redeemer's Kingdom on those distant heathen shores.

WOMAN IN CHINA.

BY

MISS HELEN M. VAN DOREN.

Woman in China has been persistently degraded and oppressed. As a child, she is, and has always been, regarded as an unwelcome incumbrance. During her early girlhood she has been immured as a prisoner. In her married life, she has been a victim and a slave. It is only in her old age that she has been regarded with honor and esteem. Could women in Christian lands understand the absolute vacuity of existence, which life means to even the most favored of their sisters in the flowery land, they would not shirk the responsibility of sending them something better. That labor among these women is abundantly repaid in success, is evidenced by the testimony of our missionaries. They have been face to face with the souls who sit in the house of bondage. They have seen those but lately redeemed from heathenism, willing to endure persecution, rather than abandon their faith. They have witnessed the awakening of intellect, the quickening of affections, and the growth of gentle graces, the fruits of the spirit, so that before their eyes, the desert has blossomed as the rose.

THE WORK IN AMOY.

Let us look at the work begun at Amoy, one of the ports of China, in which, some of us have been permitted to labor.

The more direct work there, was commenced about ten years ago, by the ladies of the Mission,* meeting with the Chinese women from week to week; forming them into classes for Bible instruction, praying with them, teaching them to read, and encouraging them in the Christian life; and sometimes, perhaps, being able to suggest to them in what way they might govern their children—in which essential, they are quite as deficient as in the knowledge of books.

This work, though carried on amid many discouragements, has proved successful. Many having learned to read the New Testament, and some colloquial books, are much more attentive to the preaching of the Word, and better able to understand and retain the truth. What they have thus gained, has not been for each one alone. The doctrine is often made known through them to others, to one of their own family, or it may be to a friend or neighbor; in this way, some, we trust, have been led to a knowledge of the true God.

This much has been accomplished, in the city churches. But what shall we say of the women, at the country stations? Living, as many of them do, a long distance from the chapel, they find it very difficult, with their small bound feet, to walk to and from the service; besides, one or more young children must always accompany the mothers, so that they can seldom give their undivided attention to the preaching, even should they desire to do so.

Then, again, although the preacher may strive to present the truth very clearly and simply, probably they will not for any length of time, remember what they hear. I have heard

---

* Mrs. Talmage and Mrs. Kip.

the preacher, in the early part of the service, ask these women questions on Scripture truths; and when asked again, during the same service, not one in ten could answer a single question, though the answers had been many times repeated to them. They have never been taught to *think* on any subject. Does it seem strange, then, that on hearing *any* new doctrine, for the first time during their lives, they fail to remember just from having it told them? Ah! if they could read, how different it would be. Then, instead of hearing the Gospel only on the Sabbath, they could daily search the Scriptures for themselves. Not until they are able to do this, can we look for progress on the part of these neglected and ignorant women.

THE YOUNG LADIES' EFFORT.

A work on their behalf was begun two years ago, by the young ladies of the Mission,[*] who went out to spend a few days, or a week, at a time, at the different out-stations, hoping to teach many of these women to read. Of course, they met discouragements—these were expected; still, the beginning of a good work was then made. It was the more hopeful, as many of the children entered heartily into the plan and became diligent pupils.

The great hope of the Church, is in the education and conversion of the children. Although the Chinese think their daughters are not worth educating, we are of a quite different opinion.

---

[*] Miss Helen M. Van Doren, Miss Kittie M. Talmage and Miss Mary E. Talmage.

GIRLS' SCHOOL IN AMOY.

We are fully aware how much depends on their being educated, and taught the Christian religion. For this purpose a school for girls, was opened in Amoy, seven years ago. Here, have been educated many of the wives of our helpers and teachers. The Bible has been made the great text book of the school. In addition to this, however, a number of other studies have been successfully introduced. They have been taught geography, arithmetic, reading, writing and composition, and have made good progress in each branch. Besides this, instruction has been given in sewing and in domestic work. It has been our earnest desire, that all the girls who come under our care, shall be thoroughly fitted for all household duties, and shall obtain the knowledge they will so greatly need in homes of their own. Very few have left this school, without having professed their faith in Christ. Thus we have great reason for gratitude to our Heavenly Father, and for encouragement in our work.

Here, in Amoy, we feel that a work is begun and going forward, which will be of untold benefit, for years to come, in the churches, and indeed, in all that region; a work well worthy of faithful effort. Shall not the workers in this field have the kind counsel and earnest prayers of all who remain at home? The work *is* great, but let us have faith that it *will* be accomplished; when many shall thirst for the hearing of the words of the Lord, and when this great kingdom, now under the dominion of sin, shall be given to Christ, for His inheritance. Can we hesitate to go forward, when we have the arm of God to strengthen us? Is there anything too hard for the Lord? Let us cease not, then, to pray that the labors of these sent to teach may be blessed, and that those who are taught, may themselves be made meet for the Master's use.

AN EXAMINATION AT AMOY.

We appropriately follow Miss Van Doren's statement, by a detailed account of one of the annual examinations, dated June 19, 1876:—

"Another year of the girls' school was completed yesterday. The closing exercises were very interesting. The pupils with some of the parents, and a few visitors, assembled at half-past nine, in the recitation room of the school. The pastor of the First Church took charge on the occasion. The older girls, after an exercise in reading, repeated the Psalms, which they had committed to memory during the year. They had finished and reviewed the first thirty. These were selected from the many Bible lessons of the year, as giving a fair idea of what they had done. Then followed the examination in geography; the recitations from the text-books were well given, after which, oceans, seas, rivers, towns, etc., were pointed out, from the outline maps, with great accuracy. Many of the lessons were repeated, first by one pupil alone, then by the class in concert.

"The examination in arithmetic was the last one in colloquial; the answers given, the repetition of the table of weights and measures, and the work of the older girls at the blackboard, were all most satisfactory. As this study has been by far the most difficult to teach, it was a real pleasure to hear the ready explanations, and the application of the rules in each division of the study; and more than all, it clearly proves that Chinese girls *can* be taught to think for themselves, if sufficient care and training is given them.

"The pastor, Choa, then took charge of the remaining examinations, which included all the lessons prepared in the character during the year. A class of young ladies have just finished Genesis; this being their first attempt in reading the Old Testament Scriptures; as they are more difficult, their attention before this, has been given entirely to the New Testament. After this, came the recitation of other classes, and finally all, down to the youngest children, had passed the ordeal of a public examination.

A PUPIL TEACHER.

"The oldest pupil has now so far advanced in the study of the character, that she has been promoted; and will, herself, have charge of this department, during the coming year. We are thus able to dismiss the teacher we had previously employed, and are much pleased to see this young lady in a position of so much usefulness. It is, indeed, a step forward.

CONVERSION OF SCHOLARS—MARRIAGE OF SAME.

"We had, last year, thirty pupils; and have this year, had but twenty-two. During the six years' existence of the school, fifty-seven pupils have, at different times, been in attendance. Sixteen of this number have been received into the Church. These all have an opportunity of imparting the knowledge they have gained, to the many ignorant around them. Eight of the pupils have been married since the school began, and six of these were church members. All have married Christians. This is very important, for each Christian household thus begun, is a light shining in a dark place.

"Some parents seem happy, and are grateful in sending their daughters; but many, still cling to the old idea, that girls are not worth educating. Only slowly, can the notions of ages of superstition be swept aside. But every educated woman will be a fact, preaching more loudly than many sermons, for the elevation of her sex. We try to carry forward instruction in domestic matters, side by side with tuition in books. The girls take turns in cooking, and in the performance of all household duties. This arrangement enables us to do without servants, and what is far more important, gives the pupils the knowledge they will need in their own homes.

INQUIRY MEETING.

"An inquiry meeting is held every week, in the Church, near the school. The girls attend regularly, and we have reason to feel that it has been the means of great good.

BOARDERS AND DAY PUPILS.

"It is not considered proper, for a Chinese girl to walk about in public, after she has attained the age of twelve. All our larger girls, who come from the four churches in Amoy, as well as from the adjoining country, board with us. The little ones are allowed to go back and forth through the streets. It should not be forgotten that this is

THE ONLY SCHOOL

for girls in a large region, inhabited by not less than ten millions of souls.

THE MATRON.

"The matron is the widow of pastor Lô, whose name is here given. She superintends the household affairs, and assists in teaching the younger children.

THE INSTRUCTION IN CHINESE.

"My teacher, Liông-to, spent for some time four afternoons in the week instructing the girls in reading and writing the Chinese character.

BIBLE STUDY.

"Though they have desired to read Christian books, it has been thought best to make the Bible the important study of the school. Besides the study of the character, instruction is given in the Romanized colloquial. In this they prepare

PASTOR LÔ, OF FIRST CHURCH, AMOY.

Bible lessons also, and are taught geography, arithmetic, reading and writing. The larger girls are reading 'Pilgrim's Progress,' and enjoy it very much. They have committed to memory all the parables of our Saviour, and when school closed, they were learning the miracles. They also write an analysis of one sermon on Sunday. A class of eight little girls are learning the 'Sermon on the Mount.' The pupils commit to memory very readily, and it is a pleasure to hear them recite.

DIFFICULTY OF TEACHING CHINESE GIRLS TO THINK.

" We find it very difficult to teach Chinese girls to think. As this is something quite new to them, great patience is required in teaching arithmetic, especially to beginners. For thousands of years, the mind of woman in China has been a blank page; her conversation has consisted of the most frivolous gossip. It is not wonderful that intellectual discipline is not easy, all at once.

INSTRUCTION IN SEWING.

" The matron, on each Wednesday afternoon, instructs the girls in cutting and making their dresses. Many Chinese women are quite incapable of making their own clothes. We particularly desire that all who attend school shall be thoroughly taught in this department. On Saturday, the morning is spent in putting the house in order and recreation, and the afternoon is devoted to sewing."

THE TESTIMONY OF THE PERSECUTED.

Possibly there are many in this Christian land who never remember what it costs a heathen to give up the religion of his childhood, and embrace Christ. The amount of suffering both physical and mental, which some of our Chinese converts have been forced to endure, reminds us of passages which we have read in the history of the church of God, in all periods when its members have had to combat error and superstition, even to the death. But we have nothing in our own experience with which to compare it.

Dr. Talmage, in 1874, wrote an account of the persecution of a woman, who had dared to become a believer. She was seized and placed in a sort of stocks, a punishment described by the Chinese, as "sleeping in two rooms." The body is placed in one apartment, and the feet are passed through a hole near the bottom of the wall, into the next room, where they are secured. Sometimes, to make the position more uncomfortable, one foot only is put through the aperture, and this was the case in the present instance. The efforts of native Christians, through the judicial courts, effected her release from this torture, but not until they had baffled severe difficulties.

Two years later, Mrs. Talmage, in a letter from Amoy, related the story of another Christian Chinese woman. A little girl of nine, she had been given away for marriage, as is common among the Chinese, her mother knowing nothing of the Christian religion. Later, the mother learned the truth; and yearned with maternal affection to have her daughter forsake idolatry, and come with her to the cross. Whenever she found an opportunity, she taught her and urged her to accept salvation through the Saviour. She at first, manifested strong opposition, but finally understood—yielded, and was baptized, when in her nineteenth year.

The family of her husband were bitterly resentful, at this change in her convictions; and her own friends, therefore endeavored to redeem her, before the marriage was consummated, by the payment of a sum of money, but this was refused. Her husband and his relatives treated her with great severity. The former whipped her every day. Her bridal attire was taken from her, and she was not allowed a room she could call her own, and was obliged to sleep wherever she could find a place. This persecution, continued in the determination to make her renounce Christ, she endured until she was twenty-three years old, when her brother took her away by stealth.

For some years, she remained with her mother, attending church regularly, and learning more fully the doctrines of the Gospel. Then, she yielded to the persuasions of her husband, and trusting to his promises that she should enjoy her faith unmolested, returned to his home. The promises were soon broken; her life was far from comfortable; she was not permitted to pray or read, and necessary articles of clothing were denied her. Her son, in his fifteenth year, was threatened with severe chastisement, if he followed in his mother's way. The mother is now in her forty-third year.

Not long since, she attended one of the woman's prayer-meetings. She spoke of her trials, and seemed almost in despair. "How is it?" she said, "I have been praying and praying all these years, and yet there is no answer." Mrs. Talmage encouraged her still to pray, and to trust, telling her that in God's time, her prayers would be heard. Surely those who read these pages, will add their petitions, that this poor, loyal heart, on the far away shore of Amoy, may be comforted at last; and that the grace of the Holy Spirit may reach the husband, and all his family, and lift them from their darkness, and bring them to a knowledge of the truth as it is in Christ.

A MISSIONARY JOURNEY.

Pastor Jap, of the Second Church, in Amoy, whose picture is here given, made, in June, 1876, a trip into the country north of Tong-an, for the purpose of obtaining a place for a chapel, at Poa-tan-chi, *i. e.*, the market-village of Poa-tan. The place has been secured, and the chapel opened. A preacher

PASTOR JAP, OF SECOND CHURCH, AMOY.

is now stationed there, with one of the members of the Tong-an Church, as chapel-keeper, and assistant teacher. Dr. Talmage afterward visited the region, and thus described his journey:

POA-TAN.

"Poa-tan is in the district of Aukoe, the next district north of Tong-an, about twenty-five miles from the city of Tong-an.

The road from Tong-an city, for some miles, passes through a fertile valley, along the banks of a beautiful stream. We left Amoy, in our boat, on Friday, at 11 A. M., landed at Tesoa, and thence proceeded by road over the hills to our chapel at Tong-an, where we spent the night.

"On Saturday morning, at seven, we left the chapel, and two hours after, began to ascend the first mountain, arriving at the highest point of the pass, about 2,000 feet above the level of the sea, a little after noon. Here, we rested. Descending, we passed through another beautiful valley, and climbed another mountain, arriving at its top at three in the afternoon. From this point the descent is continual, first very steep, then gradual, along the banks of a beautiful stream, until Poa-tan and far beyond. We arrived at Poa-tan chapel at six, having spent eleven hours on the journey, sitting in uncomfortable chairs, where the ground was not too rough, and walking over the steeper ascents and descents.

SCENERY.

The scenery along the route was sometimes exquisite for beauty, and sometimes impressive for wildness and grandeur. Perhaps the wildness and grandeur predominated. But the loveliness of some of the gorges, both sides lined with terraces far up the mountain steeps, sometimes to the very top of the gorge, covered with growing crops, and with the exquisite green of the rice, must be seen to be appreciated.

ROUGHNESS OF THE ROAD.

"This road, like most of the roads in China, even on the level ground, is seldom wide enough, and never, for any great distance, smooth enough for carts or wagons; and the steeper parts are always ascended and descended by steps. It is a great thoroughfare. We met sedan-chairs, with their passengers, many pack-mules, which are never seen at Amoy, and many coolies with their heavy burdens. The goods coming down to the sea-board market—were chiefly iron, coarse porcelain, paper and charcoal.

THE MISSIONARY STATION.

"Poa-tan is an important village, or rather cluster of villages, on the banks of a small river, in the midst of an extensive, fertile and populous valley. This makes it an eligible missionary station, where the Gospel may be preached to great multitudes. At the chapel on Sunday, the audiences, wholly composed of men, were large—morning, afternoon, and evening. Between services, I went out, and in various places, addressed women as well as men. The people everywhere seemed friendly. Their interest was doubtless prompted by curiosity, for, as yet, we had no converts here. Much of our preaching is like sowing seed by the wayside, or among thorns, and yet we trust that some will be found to take root, spring up, and bring forth fruit.

WHAT WE NEED.

"We need for this, your funds, to furnish the people with the Word of God; and your prayers, that the Word may be accompanied by the Spirit's power.

HOT SPRINGS—TEA-FIELDS.

"Near our chapel, are hot springs, impregnated with sulphur. There are also tea-fields in the neighborhood. All along the way are, here and there, places where preaching-stations might profitably be established, had we the men and means. Oh, how many such places there are in this land of China! Who will come to take possession of them in the name of the Lord?

"We journeyed back, on Tuesday, met our 'Gospel-boat' just before dark, at Chioh-jine, a few miles below Toayan City, and having a strong south-east wind, two hours and a half more, brought us home—tired and thankful, and deeply filled with the importance of great enlargement in our operations if we would evangelize China."

A TOLL BRIDGE.

Accustomed, as we are, to swift modern modes of travel, and to the triumphs of engineering skill, it is not easy for us to understand how rude and primitive are some of the features of life, in oriental countries. Perhaps we have never thought very much about it, and we do not, therefore, consider, as we ought, the privations to which our missionaries willingly submit, nor do we remember that because of some of these difficulties, the work of their hands progresses slowly. Dr. Talmage tells about the first toll-bridge he crossed in China, in these words:

"A narrow causeway was raised for a few feet into the edge of the river, then a single long plank was stretched from this to some natural rocks farther in the stream; another plank reached from this to a few large stones which had been placed there as a kind of abutment, and therefrom still another extended to the opposite shore. This is not a very costly or elegant structure, but the fare corresponds; being only two cash for one person, so that the bridge may be crossed five times for one cent."

CHEAPNESS OF LABOR.

To illustrate the cheapness of labor in China, and the consequent toil required of the masses, to obtain a mere living, it is stated that iron is carried from the mines, mostly on mens' shoulders, though pack-mules are used to some extent, many miles overland to Tong-an, and then is brought by boat to Amoy; yet it is there sold for about the price which pig-iron commands in New York.

A FIRST-CLASS HOTEL.

Dr. Talmage, writing from Amoy, in the fall of 1876, gave a graphic description of the resting-place, at which he stopped on the journey to Poa-tan. He said:

"I can only guess at its dimensions. Its side walls being joint walls of the adjoining houses, can have no windows, and probably would have none, if they were not joint walls. Its floor is a few inches higher than the street, close on which it stands. Its height on the eaves, on the street, is seven or eight feet. The front room, some fifteen or twenty feet, occupies the whole width of the house, is a little deeper than it is wide; and serves for office, parlor, dining-room, kitchen and bedroom. A dozen of us slept in it, the night we staid there. Having the ground for its floor, no whitened walls, and no ceiling; it needs neither washing nor scrubbing. Immediately behind this room are a few feet of open court, or part of the house, without a roof; and two other bedrooms of the same character as the front room, only, both together, much less than half its size, and more dirty. For the accommodation of the entire party, the whole charge was twenty-seven cents, enough to pay the rent of the establishment for some weeks. This house was a fair sample of all the houses of the village. We selected it to pass the night in, because it was reported to be the best and cleanest inn on the route."

BEAUTY OF CHINESE VILLAGES.

Many of these villages are enchanting in the distance.

TALK IN A CHINESE CITY.

The lovely grassy knolls, delightsome brooks, magnificent shade trees, and fruitful fields, with mountains rising gloriously in the background, combine to make them most attractive. But once look into the houses, and scan their immediate surroundings, and the poetry vanishes. Usually it vanishes even before that, for the sights and smells which greet you at the entrance of the village, take it all away. You can often smell a village, some time before you get to it. Yet the people who reside amid such filth, regard themselves complacently, as the only civilized race on the globe; and think of Europeans and Americans, as barbarians. I was gravely asked, by an old woman, at the inn: "Do you, in your country, have the family arrangement? Do men have their own wives? Do you acknowledge such relations as parents and grand-parents?" I answered, "Yes." With pleased surprise she turned to the bystanders, and said: "*Why, they do!*"

A WALK IN A CHINESE CITY.

A Chinese city is not in the least like London or Paris, or New York or Philadelphia. Some years ago, foreigners were rigidly excluded from all the populous towns of the Flowery Land; but now many of the seaports are open, and travellers walk through them without molestation.

Walls are built round the towns, and we enter by gates; but even outside the gates are streets of closely-packed houses and shops.

NO HIGH HOUSES IN CHINA.

You find in China no high houses, no broad streets, no horses. You see indeed some high roofs and tall towers, but these belong to pagodas or temples, and the people are forbidden to raise their houses very high, lest they should overshadow the idol temples. Few houses have more than one story. They look like big toys, for they have often fancifully carved roofs with curved corners. Some of the roofs are painted in bright colors, bells are sometimes hung from the corners; and at times, the figure of a dragon is seen, who the inhabitants think will protect them from evil spirits and bad influences. You will find no glass in the windows, but instead, very thin paper, or small panes made of thin oyster-shell.

HOW BURDENS ARE CARRIED.

"How are burdens carried, when there are no horses and few broad streets?"

Well, you see a river runs by the town, and canals have been made in different directions. The rivers are as busy and crowded as roads. Thousands of people live on river-boats, and vessels of different sizes, row up and down the water, laden with passengers and cargo. If you do not wish to travel by the river, and prefer not to walk, you can get into a sedan chair or palanquin. There will be no difficulty in finding some one to carry you.

Hundreds of coolies do the work of horses in every town. They carry not only passengers, but chests of tea, bales of silk, and all sorts of cargo, making quite as much noise as cart and carriage wheels, while they rush about with their burdens, crying, "Ah ho! Ah ho!" from morning till night. The cry seems to help them, as sailors say their call, "Pull ahoy," does half their work. The coolie's work is very hard, and he is worn out after a few years of labor.

HOW THE PEOPLE DRESS.

The coolies, and most of the men you meet, are dressed in dark blue cotton, the color universally worn by the poorer classes. Their dress, their hair, their eyes, their faces, seem all precisely alike. In town or country, you seldom see a Chinaman who has not coarse black hair, and small black eyes. The richer and higher ranks of people, wear costly and bright colored clothing of embroidered silk, satin and furs. The long tail of hair is an indispensable ornament for the men; only the coolies, who find it in the way, twist it into a knot at the back of their heads. Very few women, and those only of the poorest, walk in the streets.

CARRYING FANS, AND FLYING KITES.

Everybody is provided with a fan. A Chinese soldier would stop fighting to fan himself, and a laborer, taking a rest, uses his as gracefully as the lady of leisure. It does duty also, in place of a hat; and is held over the head, to protect it from the sun. Grown up people, and grave, elderly gentlemen, too, are often seen amusing themselves with kites, which flutter in the air like birds.

BRIGHT-COLORED SIGNS.

By the sides of the shops hang gaily colored boards, bearing mottoes, advertisements and fanciful names. Sometimes a whole street is devoted to one article; as combs or copper-kettles. Tinkers, barbers, cobblers, smiths, carvers, portrait painters and tailors, are selling and making their wares, and crying out their praises to every passer-by.

HOW CHINESE LADIES LIVE.

The married lady is expected to rise early, and see that tea is prepared for her husband; and that hot water is awaiting his convenience, when he desires to take his morning bath. She must also pay equal attention to her mother-in-law; for China is the Paradise of old women,—and while her husband's mother lives, his wife is a very secondary personage indeed. The ladies go about *en dishabille* in the early portion of the day, shouting out vehement orders to their servants, and confusion reigns.

The elaborate toilet of the lady of rank, is the great business of the day. In this, is there not something in common with too many votaries of fashion in better instructed conditions? Aimless and frivolous, wherever she be, who lives mainly to adorn her person and display her dress, she is not greatly elevated above her Chinese sister. Each fashionable woman in China has one or two maids, and a slave-girl to wait on them. The latter makes it her first care to trim and light the pipe of her mistress.

ADJUNCTS OF THE TOILET.

The dressing of the lady's hair occupies from one to two hours. A white paste is next applied to her neck and face, a rose powder to eyelids and cheeks, and a red dye to the finger nails, and she is then attired for the day.

A CHINESE BOUDOIR.

OCCUPATIONS OF CHINESE WOMEN.

Many ladies devote much time to gossiping, smoking and gambling; in which latter vice, they follow the example set them by the men. They always play for money, and when they have no visitors of their own rank to play with, they do not hesitate to engage in games with the servants. Numbers of ladies, however, are skilled in embroidery; and shoes, purses, handkerchiefs and robes pass through their cunning fingers. Before marriage, they occupy their time in preparations for the wedding—a sad wedding, one would imagine, when often the bridegroom is a stranger, whom they have never seen, and for whom they cannot care. Here and there, a woman is found, who has learned to read, and her accomplishment is in real demand. She can while away the tedious hours, by reading tales and plays, to her less fortunate friends, who are willing, often, to pay for the pleasure she bestows.

God speed the time when the blessed change, which the coming of His kingdom ever brings, shall dawn, not only, but go on to the grandeur of noon, in the land of Sinim.

JAPAN.

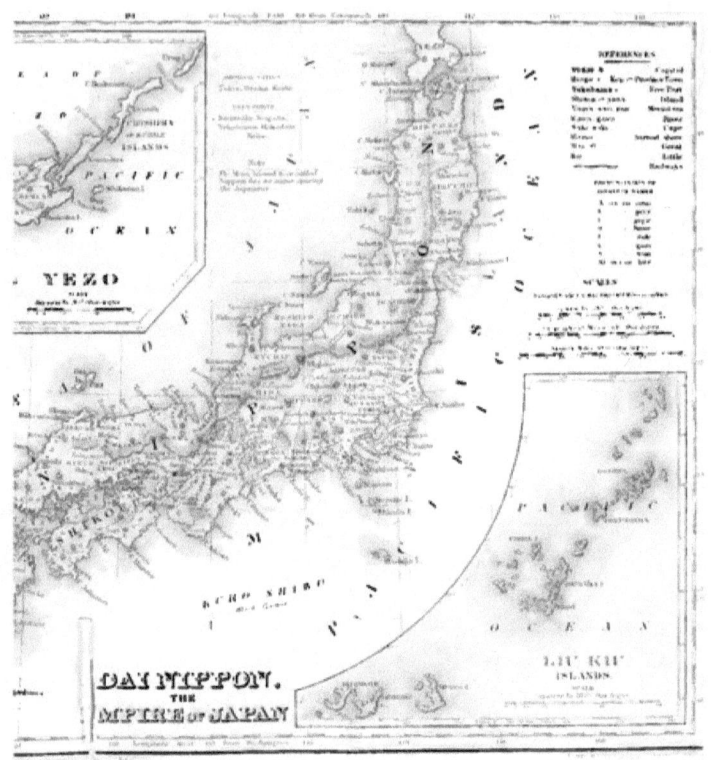

THE LAND OF THE RISING SUN,

BY THE

REV. WILLIAM E. GRIFFIS,

(Late Professor in the Imperial College of Tōkiō, Japan, author of "The Mikado's Empire."

FIFTEEN days by steam westward from our California borders in the Pacific Ocean, lies the archipelago of Japan. This Empire embraces a cluster of four large and eight small islands, surrounded by nearly four thousand islets, equal in area to the six New England states, with New York and Pennsylvania added on; or, roundly, 150,000 square miles of territory. In these islands dwell nearly 35,000,000 people.

Of the many beautiful and poetic names* of the country, two, Nippon and Japan, are most common. Nihon or Nippon, (meaning sun, root of light, day-spring or rising sun) is that used by the natives. Often they prefix the term Dai, meaning great. Thus, Dai Nippon means Great Japan. "Japan" is the European corruption of the Chinese name Jipun, or Zipan,

---

* In pronouncing Japanese names, the European sounds are used; thus : a is sounded as *a* in father ; e is sounded as *e* in prey ; i is sounded as *i* in pique ; o is sounded as *o* in bore ; u is sounded as *u* in tune ; ai is sounded as *i* in bite ; ei is sounded as *ei* in feign ; g is always hard, and s always sharp. Long vowels are marked with a bar, as o in Tō-kiō ; short vowels with a circumflex accent as u in rokû (six).

which Marco Polo first heard when in China, and introduced into Europe, whence our word Japan.

The name "Rising Sun," may have been given to the country over which the Chinese saw the sun rise from out the Eastern ocean; or, as is most probable, by the natives of the western provinces of Japan. Japan, thus coming to our ideas through Chinese and European literature, was, within the memory of most of us, in standard geographies and old methods of travel, called an oriental country—the Far East.

Americans, however, are not bound to so call or wrongly consider it. The extension of our national boundaries to the Pacific shores, have made the Japanese our nearest neighbors, and Japan lies due West of us. Five thousand miles toward the setting sun, as the steamer plows, out of the blue waves of the Tai-hei-kai, (Pacific ocean, or Sea of Great Peace) rise the perennially green bluffs and snow-crowned mountains of the Mikado's Empire.

God might have made a more beautiful land, but the writer feels sure that He never did. Nature throughout the Japanese chain, from the Arctic Kuriles to the tropical Liu Kiu, has with unstinted luxuriance, bearded the hills with timber, robed the valleys and plains with verdure and fertile soil, stored the bowels of the earth with mineral wealth, and so adapted air, moisture, temperature, mountain, sky and sea, as to yield the maximum of beauty. Nor is she a niggard in providing for the needs of man. The surface of the land is one constant succession of mountains and valleys, with only occasionally few plains. The general type of the landscape is that of varied picturesqueness, rarely of sublimity and grand-our. The climate is excellent, and with only local exceptions, conducive to general health, and manual and mental labor through as many months as are given us in our own clime.*

DIFFERENCE BETWEEN THE JAPANESE AND THE CHINESE.

The inhabitants of the Japanese archipelago are quite a different people from the Chinese, with whom persons of defective reading and powers of observation often hopelessly confound them. The two languages are almost entirely different. No Japanese can understand a Chinaman when he talks, and the two tongues are as distinct as English and Italian, or Russian and French. The Japanese do not wear "pigtails," they do not smoke opium, they do not bind the feet of their women, they do not go abroad to other countries as coolies, washmen, &c. Their dress and manners, temperament, character, disposition, government, history and many other things, are peculiar, and in many points different from their neighbors. In the use of written Chinese characters, in superstition, idolatry, polygamy, debased morals, architecture, medicine, human nature and Asiatic ideas generally, Chinese and Japanese are greatly alike.

In temperament, the Japanese are more quick, lively, mercurial than the Chinese. They are less stolid, perhaps less solid; less conservative, perhaps more fickle than the Chinese. Personally, and as friends, companions and neighbors, they are far more agreeable. They answer more closely to our

---

* For detailed information and statistics regarding the soil, climate population, productions, finance, national resources, &c., &c., of Japan see appendix to "The Mikado's Empire," New York, Harper & Brothers.

ideas of human nature. They are more like ourselves. They are much more imitative than the Chinese. They copy after us easily, and as imitation is the sincerest form of flattery, and as our vanity is greatly flattered by the Japanese changing their ways for ours, we are apt to think them far better people than the Chinese. Their general docility, politeness, amiability and sunny disposition are apt to fascinate the new-comer; and not only to disarm all prejudices, but also to lead some good souls to think that the "trail of the serpent" is less marked in Japan than in other lands. A residence of a few years makes the glamor fall from the eyes, and most old residents are pretty decided in their opinions that human nature in Japan is, as everywhere else, tough and obdurate. The underlying moral corruption, like the noisome culverts and sewers that gurgle and fester under the stately city edifices, is as foul, as horrible; and as needy of moral cleansing by Divine power, as in India or China, or the heathen slums of New York.

ORIGIN AND HISTORY.

The origin and history of the Japanese people are subjects of profound interest and fascinating inquiry. I can but sketch them here. The popular idea of the natives, is that their history begins at 660 B. C., when Jimmu, the first emperor or mikado began to reign; but his claims to be considered a historic personage, cannot stand the test of critical investigation. The Japanese had, most probably, no writing or literature prior to the sixth century after Christ, from which time they began to record their history. Before that epoch there is a large mass of tradition, myth and fable, in which are doubtless embedded many facts. Whether the analysis and scrutiny of scholars shall ever be able to construct a clear and certain history of the few centuries before the fifth or sixth of our era, remains an open question. My own opinion of the origin of the present mixed Japanese people, is as follows: First, that in ancient times, many centuries before Christ, the Japanese archipelago was uninhabited, or, if so, but sparsely. Second, that later, shipwrecked men, the waifs and strays from the Malay archipelago, the Liu-Kiu islands, Formosa, Southern China, etc., began to settle and increase in the South, in Kiushiu. From the North, originally from Tartary and Siberia, decending southward, came the Ainos, or black-haired savages, who still inhabit Yezo and the Kuriles. So that up to and even after the Christian era, the archipelago was thinly peopled by these races of fishermen and hunters. Third, at various times and places, a race of superior people and conquerors landed in Japan, and began to occupy and subdue the land for themselves, beginning from the South and West, and gradually conquering eastward and northward. Early in the sixth century, when the written and certain history begins, we find one tribe paramount in the central provinces—Yamato, not far from Kiōto. This city since the ninth century has been the residence of the Japanese mikados.

Who these conquerors were, and whence they came, is now tolerably certain. The proofs of language—that potent solvent of so many ethnologic problems, nearly demonstrate that they came over from the plains of Manchuria, and down through Corea, crossing the Sea of Japan and Gulf of Tartary, and so reached Japan. Thus, the progenitors of the Japanese were not Chinese, but Tartars—an allied branch, or wandering tribe from that great Scythian stock of people so often referred to in Scripture, to whom even the apostle Paul confessed himself a debtor. These hardy horsemen and warriors, it will be remembered, from the highland plains of the far Orient, thrice burst into Europe in conquering hordes, once in the fourth century under Attila the Hun, before Rome; once in the thirteenth century under Genghis Khan, whose Empire stretched unbroken from Corea to Poland, (some say he was a Japanese) and again in the early part of the seventeenth century, when they decended South, conquered China, compelled the Chinese to shave their fore-scalps, and adopt the hated Tartar "pigtail"—braid of hair, of which the Chinese are now so proud. Thus, has a badge of servitude become a symbol of obstinate pride!

RELIGION.

In these early times in Japan, originated and was developed the indigenous religion or cultus of Japan, called Shintō, (or "Sintooism,") which is still the official, or "state," Church of Japan. Shintō is a Chinese word, meaning, "Way or doctrine of the gods," (Shin, god; and to, way or doctrine; literally theology.) Its pure Japanese, and most ancient name, is Kami-no-michi, or the religion of the Kami gods. Up to the seventh century of our era, this was the dominant and only religion.

After Buddhism entered from India, via: China and

Corea, Shintō was corrupted or overlaid, and preserved pure only in a few places, and by a few scholars, especially at the

SHINTO OFFICIAL COLLECTING OFFERINGS.

Mikado's court in Kioto. For Shintō is essentially secular, patriotic and political. Its "priests" are rather officials. They often wear the two swords, the high cap, denoting rank, and wear their hair cut short. In the little cut, is a representation of a Shintō official collecting offerings.

About a century ago, the study of its sacred books was revived, and in 1868, on the restoration of the Mikado to full power, and the overthrow of the "Tycoon," Shintō took a new lease of life, and an attempt was made to Shintōize all Japan—an attempt which ended in a vast failure. In some parts, however, the Shintō propaganda has been successful. One strong hold upon the people's mind, is its patriotic character, even to its theories of creation. According to Shintō—which is an ancient form of the modern evolutionistic theories—"anciently the heavens and earth were not separated. All the elements floated together in chaos, like an addled egg. After motion in the mass began, the gross and heavy cohered and became like a yolk, the lighter parts sublimed and formed the aerial heavens. The earth was not yet. Finally, a thing like a rush sprouted from the warm mud, rose, grew and became a self-animate being, called the "Honorable August First-appearing Being."

Three other gods sprouted up in like manner, and after a succession of sexless beings, the first "gods," male and female, appeared. Then began the creation of Japan, with its mountains, rivers, seas, and the inhabitants, arts, sciences, etc., etc. One of the most popular of these deities is Toshitokŭ, the patron of longevity; to whom all Japanese, who desire length of days, pray. He courses through the air on a stork, which is also the symbol of long life.

TOSHITOKU, THE GOD OF LONG LIFE.

From these gods, in unbroken line, have descended the Mikados of Japan, and his nobles. The people also, are the children of the gods; and many a Japanese loves to call his beautiful country, "The Land of the Gods," or "The Divine Country." The Mikado often addresses his subjects, as the representative vice-gerent of the gods that made Heaven and earth. To a radical Shintō devotee, no other country or people can be compared for a moment to Japan; for other countries were made by the hardening of the foam and mud of the sea, and their people are the first imperfect works of the gods, on whom they tried their unskilled hands, and cast away as inferior. The Japanese are their perfect work. Ordinary Japanese, however, never think in this fashion. The Shintō Bible is called the Kojiki, (Book of Ancient Traditions,) with a sort of supplement and commentary; though a distinct work, called the Nihongi, (Annals of Japan.) To summarize, Shintō seems to be the same as the ancient Chinese and Tartar religion, before Confucius formulated it. Its essence is the worship of deified heroes and ancestors, and the fear and reverence for the spirits of the dead. It has no moral code, no formulated doctrines, no dogmas, except those which are rooted in the ideas of government and patriotism. Yet it acknowledges a sense of sin, and the need of pardon and propitiation.

In the accompanying cut is a fair representation of a popular Shintō-festival, or matsuri. On a headland by the seashore, are gathered, before sunrise, a party of people of all ages and sexes, to greet the rising sun; which, in Shintō mythology, is Amaterasŭ, the Heaven-Illuminating Diety. Between two tall poles of bamboo, which retain their feathery fronds, is stretched a straw rope, with pendant strips of white paper. Similar festoons hang round the tables of offering, and stuck on splints, mark off a square place; inside which sit, on mats of rice straw, the three Shintō priests, in flowing white robes and long folded trails, with hair cut (not with top-knots) as in our style, and with black lacquered caps. The tables are made of pure hinoki (sun-wood tree—sacred to the sun-goddess.) Wands of the same timber, with pendant strips of paper are seen, leaning against the first table; these are called the gohei. On these strips (called the spirit-substitute,) the invisible presence of the gods and goddesses is supposed to dwell. All around hang lanterns of pure white translucent paper, or gaily inscribed with characters—texts of the Kojiki, etc. The people sit, some sqat, on the ground, some on settees or on tables. The men may be known by their shorn pates and top-knots; the women by their luxuriant coiffures. Leading down from the front, is a stone staircase to the sea-shore. On the right, is a massive permanent stone lantern, now lighted. The worship will consist of offerings of fruits, fish and various cooked foods to the gods, prayers from the Kojiki, with superstitious rites, symbolical dances, and perhaps the scene will wind up by all hands becoming the worse for saké (or rice-beer.) The Japanese mix religion and jollity strangely together. On the right is a booth or temporary restaurant, and people are chatting, smoking and drinking, while the waiters are busily engaged in bustling about to supply more refreshments. Three half-naked boys are pressing near, and a merchant's errand-boy, with his bundle tied round his shoulder, according to Japanese custom, is looking on.

SHINTŌ SHRINES.

All over the country are scattered the Shintō miyas (shrines). These are smaller than the Buddhist temples and much plainer, even to austerity. They are built of hinoki wood, usually two in number, an inner and an outer shrine, and are (at least ought to be) thatched with straw, as in the one on the left in the cut. The end rafters usually project and cross, like a saw-buck. Underneath the eaves, and also under the gateway, hang the twisted rope of rice-straw or white paper strips. Notice also the upright gohei wand and notched strips. At the base of the steps is seen one of the "Heavenly dogs," of which stone sculpture there is usually a pair at each temple. Of the gateways or torii, there are often a series of from two to twenty or a hundred. They are made of wood, often of whole tree-trunks; and ought not to be painted, gilded or metal-covered, though they are sometimes so adorned. In some instances they are massive monoliths The path to the shrines is of flat stones. Inside there are properly no idols, though often there are images of heroes and gods. The mirror and gohei are proper symbols. In the picture, on

A SHINTO MATSURI, OR FESTIVAL AND WORSHIP.

the right, is a two-sworded gentleman, a lady and daughter; in the left foreground are two women listening to a pilgrim devotee called a "Rokubu," who travels over the country visiting famous shrines. He rings a bell held in his hand as he goes along, and begs his way by exhibiting an idol and shrine which he carries on his back in the long box strapped over his shoulder. In both Shintō and Buddhism, the temples are usually surrounded by tall trees of venerable girth and dense foliage. The object is for shade, to inspire reverential awe, and for catching or warding off the sparks of impending conflagrations,—which in this country of wooden dwellings are especially frequent, devastating and dangerous. In Tōkiō fires occur every day. In 1872 and in 1877, over five thousand houses were burned down at a single fire. The writer has seen twenty thousand people made temporarily homeless in the space of five hours. In the case of secluded villages suddenly annihilated and distant from help, the case is often one of grievous suffering.

INTERNAL STRIFES.

To return to history. In the seventh century, the tribe of Yamato with the mikado at its head, began the conquest of the lands north, south and east. With its career of victory, and under the stimulating effect of Chinese letters, arts and literature, were formed in Kioto grades of nobles and noble families, especially the Fujiwara, Taira and Minamoto—names still renowned in Japan. The Fujiwara became the civil officials. The political system was founded on the centralization system of China. The distant tribes were gradually

SHINTŌ MIYA, OR SHRINE.

brought under obedience to the administration of the mikado from the capitol. The Minamoto family produced in succession many great generals, whose victories secured all eastern and northern Japan, and made the mikado's brocade banner gleam even to Yezo among the Ainos. The Taira family were victorious in the South and West, and gradually in time of peace became paramount in authority at Kioto. Kiyomori, the famous Taira leader was made Prime Minister, his daughter by marrying the mikado became empress, while most of the high offices of government were filled by men of the Taira name. Pride and jealousy of the rival noble families gradually led to deadly feud; and Kiyomori being victorious and supreme plotted to exterminate the Minamo family, root and branch. Murder, assassination and exile became for years the order of the time. Yoritomo, assisted by a son of the mikado from his place of exile, called out the old adherents of the white flag of the Minamotos and made Kamakura, twelve miles from Yokohama his capitol, and the Japanese War of the Roses began. He marched up to and around Yedo, then a village. A severe campaign followed; many battles were fought, a very heavy one being near Hiōgo (Kobè). Kioto was captured, and the Taira fled to the town of Shimonoséki (of "indemnity" fame). Nobles and servitors, palace ladies, children and all, fled from the avenging Minamoto's. Among the fugitives was the infant mikado, only eight years old, in the arms of his mother. Driven from castle to castle, and finally to their boats, a great naval conflict took place A. D., 1184, in which, after hours of bloody slaughter, the Taira were nearly annihilated. It is said that 1200 junks were engaged in the battle. Only a remnant escaped to the far mountains, living alone in poverty and exile. Their hiding-place and the descendants of the refugees were not discovered until 1872—while the writer was in Japan. It was like finding the "Ten Lost Tribes."

Henceforth, from 1194, the history of Japan flows on in two streams. The Mikado and his court dwell in Kioto, but most of the real governing power of the country is in the hands of the Shōgun (general) who long afterwards, in 1853, was called "Tycoon." The Shōgun had his capital at Kamakura, where a large city sprang up, and to which wealth, power and gayety flowed. Here Yoritomo, the head of the Minamoto family, enlarged the temple of Hachiman, (or Ojin, the god of war,) which his ancestors had erected in 1063. In 1195, Yoritomo having visited the colossal image and temple of Great Buddha at Nara, (near Kioto,) "conceived the idea of erecting an image of the Eternal Buddha in Eastern Japan."

THE DEVOTION OF ITANO.

It was chiefly, however, by the efforts and begging of his serving maid, Itano, that a great gilded wooden image was erected near Kamakura. Through many years, from youth to wrinkled age, this woman toiled, rearing cotton, and selling herbs, and begging subscriptions, until at last her heart's desire was realized. In her old age, the elements having ruined the wooden image, the same Itano, by her zeal and labors, and a public subscription under the patronage of the Shōgun, secured the erection, about the year 1258, of the colossal bronze image of Great Buddha, near Kamakura, which still remains, though the surrounding shrines and temples were swept away by a tidal wave, in the year 1495. This image, the largest, finest and costliest in Japan, is visited by almost all tourists stopping at Yokohama. A lithographic picture of it is printed on the certificates of life-membership to the Missionary Societies of the Reformed Church. It is a mighty monument of the energy of a woman in heathenism. Perhaps thinking Christian women may see in it, a mute, but eloquent, appeal to equal energy and zeal in Christian missionary labor.

BUDDHISM AND A NOTED BUDDHIST TEMPLE.

The thirteenth and fourteenth centuries were marked by the erection of colossal Buddhas, pagodas, temples, lanterns and other objects of Buddhist art, and for the zeal and activity of the propagation of Buddhism.

Buddhism started as a simple atheistic humanitarian doctrine in India, five centuries before Christ. Its course of propagation divided into two streams, the northern and southern. The latter rolled through Ceylon, Siam, Burmah, Cochin, China, Cambodia, and into some parts of the Malay, Archipelago. The Northern flowed into North India, China, Thibet, Tartary, Corea, Manchuria and Japan. Buddhism is much richer in doctrine, cultus, worship, discipline and all the characteristics of a religion, properly so called, than Shintō. To compare them is to think of a Japanese rice-sack, and a gorgeously embroidered daimios' robe. The worship is intensely ritualistic. The cut represents a scene in the old temple in the eastern suburbs of Tōkiō, called "Go Hiyaku Rakan," or the "Temple of the Five Hundred Disciples" of Buddha, who propagated his doctrines. The structure is now old and tumbling to ruin, but it was once a place resorted to from all over the empire.

The high ceiled room is hung with huge, long cylindrical paper lanterns, incribed with texts from the Buddhist classics. The square pillars are likewise engraved. The grand high altar is encased with a wire screen, lest by accident, the gilded images of Buddha or his saints should be injured by the offerings of cash, thrown forward continually by the people, and from the crowd in the rear, who cannot get up close to the railing. The handfuls of the round "cash" of lead or copper coins, perforated with central square holes; are wrapped in twisted paper and thrown forward under the incense stand, scattering on the floor. On the altar are standing lanterns on four legs, while on either side, stuck on their spikes, are dozens of the vegetable wax paper-wicked candles, peculiar to the country, blazing and smoking. With the clouds of incense and carbonous smoke of the candles, the air is heavy. The chief priest, a great portly bonze, is shaven-headed, like all his fellow-bonzes, and is robed in crape and brocade canonical robes of gorgeous colors. He will pray and make genuflections, while the two accompanying bonzes chant or read the service. The second person in the procession, a boy, and evidently the son of some noble family, is to enter the priesthood by-and-by. At present he is under age. Therefore, he can eat whatever food he wishes, and is not confined to the rigid rice and vegetable diet of the full-blown bonzes. He also retains his dress, with its wide trowsers, girdle, long sleeves, and "butterfly" style of hair. He is assigned a place of honor, and holds the censer. When of age he will shave his head, don priestly robes and be a bonze.

WORSHIP AND OFFERINGS AT THE BUDDHIST TEMPLE OF THE FIVE HUNDRED DISCIPLES AT TOKIO.

Note that on the right, behind the columns, sits a man who is vigorously beating the great drum. His stick is half raised in air. See his mate behind the fire and smoke of the candles, also belaboring his drum. It is to be hoped they keep good time, which is more than can be said of some musicians at the temple festivals, where the din and noise are almost deafening.

Let us glance at the people. Notice that even while the worship is going on, there is the priest's servant peddling candles; chaffering and pressing the sale, even while the service proceeds. He holds three in his hand, and has more to sell in a box. He is dressed in wide-shouldered robes of ceremony, called *kami-shimo*. Perhaps he is telling that man that he must buy more candles to burn in behalf of his child or parent, who is suffering in purgatory, for a purgatory breeds clerical peddling as surely as decay breeds worms. In many a Buddhist temple there hangs an alms-box, inscribed "For the benefit of the hungry devils," *i. e.* for the souls suffering in Buddhist's purgatory.

The first man on the left is a laborer, who has his handkerchief or "hand-wiper" knotted over his head. The second is probably a merchant, well-to-do. His hands are held palm to palm in prayer, and thus the candle-peddler has approached him. The next is a mother with her child strapped on her back, with his chubby pink feet dangling out. See her hands palm to palm—for the Japanese never clasp the hands together—with her rosary of beads in them. The rosary is Buddhist, and was so before it was Romanist. Next come two men, then a well-dressed young lady also praying; next a small boy anxious to climb up and get a good look over the railing, helped by his sister.

Let us have another look at the picture. On the left, below the big lantern, are the memorial or ancestral tablets, with fresh flowers and offerings of saké, rice, &c. The Japanese do not worship ancestors to anything like the extent of the Chinese. They practice ancestral sacrifices, however, and here we have specimens. Perhaps those in the picture are in memory of deceased priests of special reputation for sanctity.

A word about the Buddhist missionary conquest of Japan. It was not made in a day. It took nearly a millenium to Buddhaise all Japan. It was not until the sixteenth century that the whole work was completed. It is also equally certain that for one hundred years Buddhaism has been waning in Japan, and is now in its last slow but sure stage of decay. The heart and mind of Japan are casting off its tenets and superstitions, and waiting for something better. Of the innumerable superstitions born of corrupt Buddhism, I have not space or time to speak. Many of them are revolting and abominable. Many of the so-called holy places in the country parts, are notorious as being the pest spots of gambling and prostitution. The sin of gambling, though rare in some provinces is rife in others; and I have seen poor wretches who had gambled away their last rag, sit shivering in winter, while ice and snow covered the ground.

CHARACTER OF THE BUDDHIST PRIESTS.

The Buddhist priests are in many cases, noble and honorable men according to their lights. They are, as a class, the bitter enemies of progress, education, civilization and reform A shockingly large per centage of them are ignorant, stupid and lazy. Their moral status is that painted in the troubadours' songs in Europe, of the thirteenth century Though Buddhism is not to be held directly responsible for the vices against law and society, it does not undertake to purify society and elevate the public morals above a Chinese standard.

Japan delights to call herself the "Land of Great Peace;" but the very joy in the name is a token and proof of the fierce unrest, the awful slaughter and the woes unnumbered of centuries of civil war, anarchy and blood. In other lands, men's ambitions, lusts and passions find vent in conquest, foreign or border war; those of the Japanese, as in Mexico, by fighting each other. Between the usurping "Tycoon's" following and the lawful but effeminate mikado, war raged for centuries. Between Kioto and Kamakura vibrated the pendulum of slaughter. From the twelfth to the seventeenth centuries, with an occasional lull, Japan was a land of blood and intestine feud.

INVASION OF THE MONGOLS AND THEIR DESTINATION.

The Minamoto family became extinct by assassination in 1217, when a line of pretended guardians of the various baby Shōguns, ruled one hundred and thirty-three years at Kamakura; their keepers being of the Hōjō family, some of whom were good men, others wicked and insolently oppressive. During their rule at Kamakura, the Mongol Tartars under Kublai Khan, in 1281 sent a vast Armada to invade Japan. The tempest and typhoon (which all readers of missionary reports from Japan read of, as causing damage to doors, shutters, roofs, &c., with much vexatious expense) in the air and from the sky, with Japanese skill and valor, wrought the deliverance of the Japanese and the complete destruction of the Mongols. Japan has never since been invaded by a foreign army.

VISIT OF MARCO POLO.

It was during the reign of Kublai Khan in China, that Marco Polo, a Venetian, and an officer under the great Khan's government, lived in China as governor of one of the provinces. Polo, on his return to Europe, wrote his celebrated book, in which he describes Japan, (Zipangu) and thus Europeans for the first time heard of this far off empire.

JAPANESE PIRATES.

After the Hōjō family were overthrown by the great captain Nitta, (whose tomb stands near Fukui) the Ashikaga family governed the country in the name of the Mikado, partly at Kamakura, partly at Kiōto. The period of their rule is one marked by great turbulence, clan fights, and battles on land; while Japanese pirates ravaged the coasts of China and Corea. So great was the terror they inspired that (as missionaries in China have informed me,) Chinese mothers still frighten their children by the question, "Hush! Do you think the Japanese are coming?" I have even heard of Chinese peasants in anger calling another, opprobriously, "you're a Japanese."

THE FEUDAL SYSTEM.

Under the misrule of Ashikaga, the unity of the empire was greatly broken, and the country split up into petty principalities, and Japan became feudalized as in mediæval Europe. The poor people placed themselves under the care and protection of the castle lords (dukes or daimiōs) while the soldiers held their land, paying rent in military service. The social condition of the people was low and wretched in the extreme. The pagan religions had sunk to their lowest ebb. Shintō, the  native religion, had degenerated into myths and shadows, or was overlaid by Buddhism, which at this time was externally a gorgeous ritual system, with but little power to regulate the moral life.

At this time Vasco da Gama was circumnavigating the globe, and finding a water-path to the eastern lands. Mexico and Peru were being conquered, and soon Europeans were to land upon the soil of Japan. Japanese boats and junks are unpainted. The sight of a "black ship," *i. e.* a painted ship, was soon to become familiar to the sea-coast dwellers of Japan.

A native book called the "Chronicles of Nagasaki" states that in 1530 a "black ship" touched at Funai, off Bungo, (see map,) and the crew landed. The master presented to Munéakira, the duke or daimiō of the principality, two fire-arms and other gifts. In 1543, 1544, 1549, are noted other arrivals of the white strangers in black ships, who were called "Nam ban," ("men from the south,") referring to the quarter whence they came. All were Portuguese, for at this time Portugal ruled the eastern seas.

ENTRANCE OF CHRISTIANITY.

Into one of these ships a Satsuma man named Anjiro, who had killed a man in a brawl, took refuge and sailed away to the Malay islands. He was to come back again as the first native Christian.

Christianity came first to Japan in Romish garb. Europe was then quaking with the throes of the Reformation. Luther had already nailed his theses on the church door at Wittemberg. Loyola, struck down by a cannon ball, and made a cripple for life, had planned out, on his convalescent bed, the Jesuit order, which sent out its mightiest apostle, Xavier, who in noble labor and indomitable zeal, labored as a missionary in India. Thence he went to Malacca, where he met Anjiro, whom he took, with two other natives of Japan, to India, and had them instructed in the Jesuit Seminary at Goa.

In 1549, Xavier, with his Japanese pupils, and two fellow-priests, landed at Kagoshima in Satsuma. The story of Roman Christianity in Japan has been often told.* At first prodigious success rewarded the laborers, but wicked means were used to secure good ends; and disaster, ruin, blood and persecution marked the end of Romanism in these islands. The means taken to spread the truths of Christianity, were not by translating the Scriptures, but by a plentiful use of procession and ritual crosses, pictures and symbols. Specimens of the native made crucifix and "Man of Sorrows," copied from those actually used two centuries ago, are given on the following page.

Commerce flourished while the missionaries labored, and in 1568, the daimiō of the province of Omura, granted a concession of land to certain Portuguese merchants to settle, at a little fishing village called Nagasaki (Long Cape.) In 1568 he

---

* See "The Mikado's Empire," page 247–263, and Dixon's "Japan."

built a church for them, and gradually a flourishing city arose. This port is the nearest to China, India and Europe.

Thus far the Spaniards and Portuguese enjoyed a monopoly of trade in the east, by which Lisbon became one of the

richest cities in Europe. In 1598 the germ of the Dutch East India Company was formed. After a long voyage, full of disasters, four or five Dutch sailors—the survivors of a large fleet—with their English pilot, Will Adams, arrived in Japan. Others followed, and the island of Hirado was set apart for trading with Dutchmen.

RELATIONS OF HOLLANDERS TO JAPAN.

After the expulsion of all other foreigners from Japan, the Hollanders, and they only, were allowed to reside on the little fan-shaped artificial island of Déshima, fronting the city of Nagasaki. Here, from 1535 to 1860, a company of a dozen Holland traders, lived under galling restrictions. Once a year a ship was allowed to come to Nagasaki, to exchange Japanese productions for the commodities of Europe, which latter were disposed of at public auction. The incoming ship was always compelled to stop at a certain island outside the city, and the Hollanders busied themselves in burying all evidence that they were Christians. "All the Bibles and prayer-books," writes Dr. Thunberg, an eye-witness aboard, "belonging to the sailors,

"THE TARPEIAN ROCK OF JAPAN:" THE ISLAND OF PAPPENBERG, IN NAGASAKI HARBOR.
(NOW USED AS A PIC-NIC RESORT.)

were collected and put into a chest, which was nailed down. This chest was afterwards left under the care of the Japanese, till the time of our departure, when every one received his book again."

The cut illustrates the place of anchorage. The precipitous sides of the island rise boldly from the water, and until recently, bristled with cannon to repel all foreign vessels. Firs crown the summit, under whose shade roystering pic-nic parties now hilariously enjoy themselves. On the left is seen a junk with its fluted sails made of strips of matting or canvas laced together. Fishermen's huts line the base of the rocks, down which the native Christian were once hurled. On the

A HOLLANDER, ON DESHIMA, LOOKING FOR THE ARRIVAL OF A SHIP.

right the tasseled prow of an officials' "cabin-boat" is seen with the rowers, and pennants, stamped with the crest and blazon of the daimiō, whose retainers man the boat. The Dutch gave the rocky isle the name by which it is generally known, "Pappenberg" or the "Papists' Island." It is in full view of the city of Nagasaki. In the next cut it appears in the distance between the circling hills which make Nagasaki one of the most safely land-locked harbors on the globe.

The next cut is reduced from a picture by the noted English artist, Mr. Wirgman, still resident in Japan. Mr. Wirgman represents a merchant prisoner—a fat Dutchman, long pipe in hand and mouth, longingly awaiting the arrival of the ship from Batavia and Europe. He paces the garden, laid out in Japanese style by native florists, with its pond of triple-tailed gold-fish, mimic mounds, rockery and dwarf trees.

On this historic isle of Déshima, now, 1877, stands a Protestant Christian church. The edifice erected by our Reformed Church stands in the city proper, while the mission house and residence built of stone, occupy a commanding site on the hill-sides overlooking the city, the population of which is about 30,000 souls.

Profound peace reigned in Japan from 1637 until 1862, during which time the only nations having intercourse with the Japanese were the Chinese and Dutch. Déshima was the loop-hole through which this hermit nation might look out on the world. So profound was the isolation, so deep the national sleep, that we might call Japan the Thornrose among nations. In our day, in the little town of South Kingston, in Rhode Island, was born the chivalrous prince, who was to scale the walls of the castle, and, with a kiss, wake the maiden to life and beauty. That prince was Matthew Calbraith Perry, brother of our Lake Erie Oliver.

TREATY OF 1854.

On the 7th of May, 1853, Perry steamed up the Bay of

Yedo, with his fleet of American steamers, and delivering a letter to properly accredited-officials, sailed away, to return the following spring. With consummate tact, patience, firmness and perseverance, he succeeded in making a treaty of friendship in 1854. The imposing ceremonies attendant upon the exchange of documents and presents took place at Yokohama, on the 8th of March, 1854. On this very spot, forever historic as the scene of the triumph of American genius, diplomatic skill and bloodless victory, now stands the first native Christian (Protestant) Church in Japan—a stately edifice erected by the Reformed Church in America.

THE FIRST AMERICAN MISSIONARIES.

The Perry treaty, however, was one only of friendship. In 1858, a new treaty was made, in which trade and residence were secured to Americans. Under this last treaty—not under the first—were missionaries permitted to settle in Japan. The credit of this fresh triumph of peace and skill belongs to our countryman, Hon. Townsend Harris.

Among the first missionaries appointed and sent out by the Reformed Church, were the Rev. S. R. Brown, D. D., and the Rev. G. F. Verbeck, the former to Yokohama, the latter to Nagasaki.

The date of arrival of all our missionaries is as follows: Rev. S. R. Brown, D. D., at Yokohama, Nov. 1, 1859; Rev. G. F. Verbeck, D. D., at Nagasaki, Nov. 7, 1859; Rev. Jas. H. Ballagh and wife, Yokohama, fall of 1861; Rev. Henry Stout and wife, Nagasaki, March, 1869; Miss Mary E. Kidder, now Mrs. Miller, Yokohama, Sept. 1869; Miss Mary E. Witbeck, Yokohama, Nov. 1874; Rev. James L. Amerman and wife, Yokohama, July, 1876.

Yokohama soon became a thriving centre of trade, and from a fishing village of a few hundred souls, in a marsh, bloomed into a city. At the present time, it has a population of about fifteen hundred foreigners, an equal number of Chinese, and about sixty thousand Japanese, including the surrounding villages. In the cut, reduced from a photograph, the view is from "the bluff," or range of hills which girdle the port, and on one of the most commanding of which, the Ferris Seminary for girls, is erected. The houses of natives and foreign residents are heavily roofed with tiles, and constructed of a frame of timber plastered on the outside. The banks and larger "hongs" (business houses,) are of stone. The canal, crossed by a wooden and an iron bridge, divides the native town of Homoko, on the side towards the bluff, from the foreign settlement. The bay is full of ships, junks and steamers of the American, French, English and Japanese lines. War ships of many nationalities, float their flags and drop their anchors. Across the bay, rise and swell the blue mountains of Kadzusa; and on the left, across the arm of the bay, is the town of Kanagawa and the Tōkaidō, or great high road of the empire, from Kioto to Tōkiō. Note at the bottom of the cut, the top of a *torii* or gateway, leading to a Shintō shrine at the top of the bluff. Many of the roofs are quadrangular, but the large two-sided roof, on the right, is that of the English church. The native Christian church (Reformed) is near the water at the foot of the street leading from the bridge on the left. Yokohama is the chief focus of the missionary operations of

VIEW OF THE CITY OF YOKOHAMA, FROM THE BLUFF.

the Reformed Church. Here are located the Rev. Messrs. Brown, Ballagh, Miller and Amerman, with their wives and families. Here also is the church, the Theological Class of young men, and the Ferris Seminary for girls. Rev. G. F. and Mrs. Verbeck are in Tōkiō, the capital, which is twenty miles from Yokohama. Uyéda is a city about sixty mile north-west of Tōkiō, in which is also a Christian church, gathered mainly through the efforts of Rev. E. R. Miller. In the extreme north of the main island, in the city of Hirosaki, is also a Christian church, organized by the Rev. Mr. Wolff, formerly of the Reformed Church Mission. Nagasaki is in the extreme south of the island of Kiushin. Yokohama has often been called the "New York of Japan," and is the centre of the new life of the nation.

NAGASAKI.

Nagasaki is also a focus of interest, the port nearest to China and India, and commercially the centre of the great island of Kiushiu, whose nine provinces contain a population of nearly five millions. The city is surrounded by green hills on every side, and is noted for its beautiful scenery. The dwellings composing the town, nestle among the glades and valleys in very picturesque style. In the engraving, on the "bund" or river front, are the government buildings and consulates. On the left, and in the rear, on the hill-slopes, are the native houses, and the mission buildings of the Reformed Church. The latter partly concealed by the trees and foliage. It is, however, on a very beautiful, commanding and convenient site for work and comfort.

GOVERNMENT BUILDINGS AT NAGASAKI. MISSION HOUSE ON THE HILL.

On first reaching the country, the missionaries began the study of the language. They found the people friendly, but bitterly opposed to Christianity. Even now, in 1877, foreigners are not yet allowed to travel farther than twenty-five miles from the treaty-ports, nor to live outside the foreign settlement or "concession." In special cases, however, by obtaining a passport, travel is allowed in the interior. In all their walks they could see the blasphemous anti-Christian edicts of the Government, hung up alongside those which forbade murder, theft, treason, adultery, etc. The accompanying cut represents the great kosatsŭ (edict-boards) at Nihon-Bashi (Bridge of Japan,) which, since 1624 and until 1873, stood before the daily sight of the millions that visited or lived in the bustling capital.

From a heavy base of masonry rises a massive frame of timber, roofed with tiles and carved gables; under these, inscribed wooden tablets hang. On the right is the copper-topped end post of the Nihon bridge, whence distances were reckoned to all parts of the empire. Beneath are the boats and canal, houses and fire-proof storehouses. In the distance are the castle walls and towers, the groves of "Maple Mountain" (Momiji Yama,) in the centre, the range of the Hakoné mountains, and the glorious white throne of Fuji yama—the crown of Japan's natural glories. On the same board with the edicts against murder, arson and robbery is that against the religion of Jesus Christ, or rather that of Rome.

No. 1 against Christianity, reads as follows:

"The Evil sect called Christian (*Ki-ro-shi-tan*) is strictly

NIHON BASHI IN TŌKIŌ. THE KŌSATSU, THE CASTLE, AND MOUNT FUJI IN THE DISTANCE. (FROM A DRAWING BY NANROKU OZAWA.)

prohibited. Suspicious persons should be reported to the proper officers, and rewards will be given.

By order of
THE GREAT COUNCIL OF THE GOVERNMENT." *

The writer, who went out to Japan, under appointment of the daimiō of Echizen, to organize schools upon the American principle, and to teach, landed in Japan, December 29th, 1870. There were then not ten Protestant Christians known to be in Japan, nor was there a vestige of an organized native church. Earnest missionary labor was, however, being performed in the way of teaching, Bible study and translation of the Scriptures.

Gradually the rigidity of the native laws against Christianity relaxed, and after numerous seizures and banishment of native "Christians" (Romanists), and a few native Protestant Christians, the organizations were not disturbed, and the missionaries were left to preach and teach freely in their own houses and churches. The first Christian church (Protestant) in Japan was organized with eleven members by the Rev. James Ballagh in Yokohama, March 10th, 1872. This church has steadily grown in membership, until it now numbers one hundred and forty-five communicants. The edifice in which the native Christians worship was erected by the Reformed church, at an expense of $6,000, and seats about four hundred and fifty persons. The accompanying cut

---

* Six years ago, when our missionaries, Mrs Pruyn, Miss Crosby, and Mrs. Pierson went to Yokohama, it was placarded in the streets, "Whoever reads the Bible their heads shall come off." I saw one of those boards at Dr. Clark's house in Albany. The Committee of the Dutch Board met and passed a resolution that the church should be called "The Christian Church," not to make it objectionable to any.—*Extract from letter of Mrs. T. C. Doremus, Nov. 25, 1876.*—COMPILER.

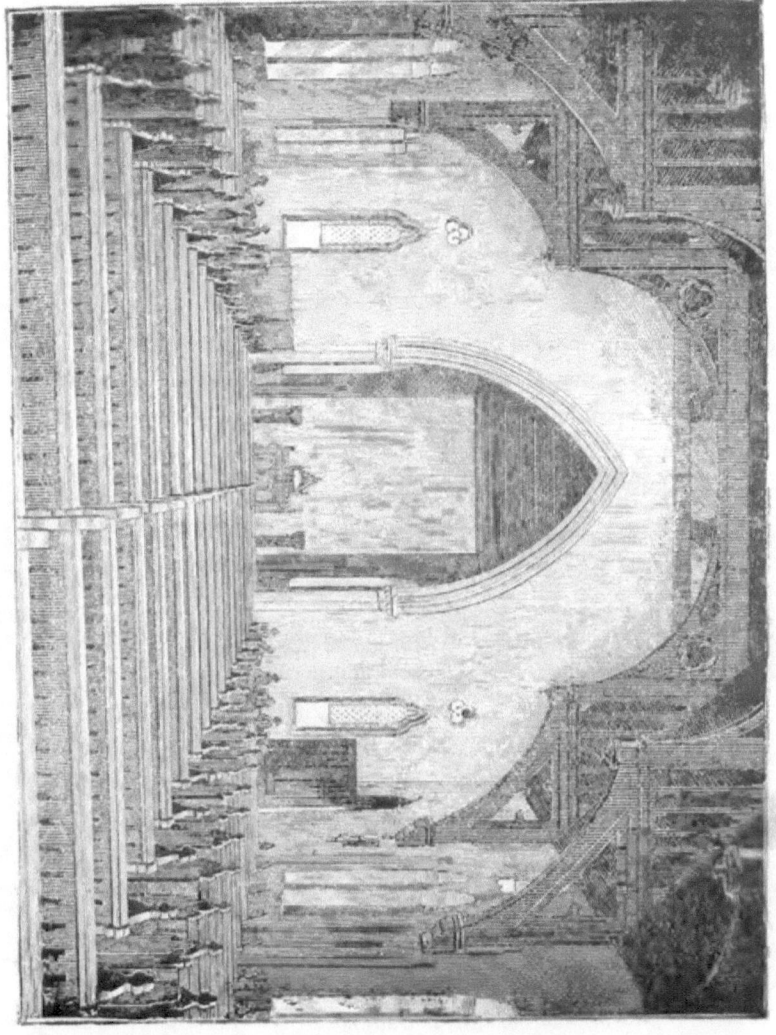

INTERIOR OF THE NATIVE CHRISTIAN CHURCH, AT YOKOHAMA.

represents the interior of the building. The stained glass windows are a contribution made some years ago by the Christianized natives of the Sandwich Islands. The communion service is the gift of Miss Van Schaick, of Albany; and the bell, which rings out an invitation to God's house each Sabbath, was presented by Garret Kowenhoven, Newtown, L. I.

BENEFICENT RESULTS.

To the careful observer there is no surer evidence of the victories of our Master's religion in Japan than in the salutary leavening influence in home and social life. How many an idol shelf has been taken down, and the idols used to heat the bath fire, or split into kindling wood! How many a Japanese Demetrius has lost his occupation and exchanged it for a better! How many a house purged of concubinage and bigamy made into a Christian home, ordered by one wife! How many a mouth and life purged of gross uncleanness! The two great ceremonies of life, marriage and burial, have been sanctified and purified. Christian Japanese now lead their brides to Christian altars; and the last low whispers of the dying are burdened with the name of Christ. The Christian dead are laid in Christian graves, in the name of Him who has plucked the sting from death and robbed the grave of victory.

IDOL CARVER.

A JAPANESE WEDDING.

The cut represents a Japanese wedding, an interesting ceremony, but thoroughly pagan and godless. On the walls are hung the characteristic pictures of Hotei, the jolly god of fun and children; Toshitokŭ, the fat and long-headed god of wisdom; and Ebisu, the god of daily food, having his fish, line, jar and cap. Handsome screens adorn and divide the room. On the left are the shelves and cuddy-holes for holding bric-a-brac. The recess in which the pictures hang is found in every Japanese house. It here contains a stand with a perfumed stick set upright, smoldering its tiny wreath of sweet odor. In the centre is another stand with rock and storks, symbolizing endurance and longevity. In front of the *tokonoma* (recess), on the clean, matting-covered floor, sits the husband in ceremonial dress (kami-shimo) of hempen cloth or brocade. The bride kneels, six feet distant, arrayed in a handsome silk dress, with long sleeves trailing to the ground, white cap of floss silk, etc. Between them, on a stand of hinoki wood, is the ever-enduring pine tree, under which may be seen the old couple of Takasago—a fabled terrestial paradise. The old man holds a rake, and the old woman a broom, to rake together and sweep up happiness and connubial joys—even to the humble ones that might be gleaned along the wayside of life. A tortoise at the foot of the tree is another emblem of long life. On a smaller table, at the side, are two wagtails. The twittering birds are commemorative of the first gods, having the Izanami and Izanagi; who, on first seeing the dalliance of the two birds, invented the art of love. The two young ladies who are the bridesmaids, or, in Japanese, "butterflies," coming forward, bear two decanters of sake, which will be united with a white ribbon or cord of paper. Each will be decorated with a butterfly made of paper, one male and the other female. No priest or magistrate is present, but only

JAPANESE WEDDING CEREMONY.

the relatives of the couple to be united. No "yes" or "no" is uttered; no question of mutual love, honor or obedience is asked. On a tray overlaid in tiers are three shallow, red-lacquered wine-cups. Of these each drinks alternately three times, and the ceremony is completed. Feasting and mirth end the festivities. Such things as marriage tours are not yet known in Japan.

Undoubtedly there is much love and some honor in Japanese marriage relations, especially on the wife's part— the husband having a decidedly free foot. Yet, after all, marriage to a Japanese woman is but the transference of a passive member or chattel of one household into another; while concubinage, polygamy, and the undisputed right of a husband to be a rake and a libertine exists unchallenged. Home life in Japan can never be pure, worthy of the name, or superior, if indeed equal to the Mormon standard, while polygamy and concubinage prevail.

BURIAL USAGES.

The question of burial has been a troublesome one to the rising Christian church in Japan. The guardianship of the graves and temple yards is the last stronghold of pagan hierarchy. Almost all burial places are attached to temples and owned by the priests as consecrated ground. It is difficult at present to bury a Christian, except with Shintō or Buddhist rites. The illustration here given is representative of the home of departed dust in Japan. On the right are seen the temple-porch and columns, and in the background the corridor leading to the bonzerie.

FLORAL OFFERINGS AT JAPANESE TOMBS.

Both inhumation and cremation are practiced, the latter being the most common. In burial a round or square cask or large earthen jar is used, the body occupying a bent position, the chin on the knees; the pre-natal position being purposely chosen for symbolical intent. In cremation, only a few of the calcined bones or ashes, left after the fire, are placed in a hollow of the tomb. Friends and relatives visit the cemeteries, at stated intervals, to pray at the tombs, and sometimes to the spirit of the departed, but usually for their welfare in the other world. Fresh flowers are placed in the bamboo tubes or sockets cut into the stone. The rosary or string of prayer-beads is much used. When the hands are otherwise occupied, the strings of beads are hung over the ear. Buckets of water are at hand to scrub out the tombs and keep the inscriptions legible. The actual living name of the deceased is rarely placed upon the tomb, but instead the "homio" or "spirit," or posthumous name. Every defunct Japanese, from mikado to beggar, is known after death by another title than his living name.

OUR OPPORTUNITY.

Into, and forward with, the work of Christ in Japan, the Reformed Church may go with heartiness and cheer. Our hopes are bright; the prospects are inviting. A nation waking from the blindness of ignorance and superstition, asks for light; for a true religion; for pure homes; for a regenerated society. Nor is their desire less real and deep, though they seek to use wrong means, and attempt to quench their thirst with waters that cannot satisfy. Besides a gospel preached to the men and the masses in general, special means must be put forth to elevate and instruct the women and girls, that they be not pagan, but Christian mothers; not stolid upholders of an effete system of idol-worship and superstition, but intelligent helpers in the faith of Christ and in the ordering of Christian households. To preach the gospel is to *graft* our Master's religion in Japan, to convert the women; to sanctify the home is to *plant* it. To this noble work—a tree of God's own planting—let the Christian women of our Church go forward and through with it to the victorious end.

The writer would conclude this most imperfect sketch with the statement of two contrasted facts, which speak with an eloquence wholly their own:—

I landed on the soil of Japan December 29, 1870. There were then not ten Protestant Christians in all Japan, nor a native Christian church. There are now, in January, 1878, fifteen Christian churches, with a membership of over thirteen hundred souls.

What hath God wrought?

SCHENECTADY, N. Y. 1878.

AN EXPLANATION
REGARDING THE CHURCH AT YOKOHAMA

A mis-statement with regard to the erection of the Reformed Church at Yokohama, has been widely circulated. It is unfortunate that there are always some persons residing near missions, who are not in sympathy with them, and who take pains to sneer and cavil at what God's servants are doing. As the error in question, reflects unjustly on one of our most devoted missionaries, the Rev. J. H. Ballagh, the Executive Committee of the Woman's Board, have determined to put its correction on record, in the permanent form for which this volume gives opportunity.

DONATION OF A PLOT OF GROUND.

In an early period in the history of the Mission to Japan, the Japanese Government gave to the Reformed Church, a valuable plot of ground, centrally located, in the city of Yokohama. For this, as is customary in such cases, the Mission had to pay a large annual ground-rent.

CONTRIBUTIONS TOWARD A BUILDING FUND.

A native Church in Honolulu, Sandwich Islands, sent to the missionaries, $1,000, toward the building of a church on this spot. The Hon. Townsend Harris contributed another $1,000; and the Hon. Robert H. Pruyn added $500. T. C. Doremus, Esq., of New York, sent the stained glass windows, now in the building, and other valuable gifts. Small donations were received from other friends in Yokohama.

ERECTION OF A SCHOOL-HOUSE.

The sum now in hand, was still not enough to build such a sanctuary as it was desirable to place on this ground. Mr. Ballagh resolved, therefore, to erect, on the rear of the lot, a small edifice, to be used as a school, but which eventually might form a wing of the future Church. A portion of the money was taken for this purpose, and the remainder invested, at a fair rate of interest.

MR. BALLAGH'S VISIT TO AMERICA.

In 1868, Mr. Ballagh came to the United States, and made appeals to the churches, in behalf of the building-fund. He raised the sum of $2,373.83. The Synod's Board was, at that juncture, greatly embarrassed. It could not afford him the means to return to his work. It, therefore, authorized him to use a portion of this newly collected money to pay his expenses back, agreeing to refund it.

THE DWELLING-HOUSE.

While Mr. Ballagh was in America, the Mission in Yokohama, received, from two wealthy merchants there, a proposition, which was regarded favorably. These gentlemen wished to build a dwelling-house for their own occupation. They needed it only for a term of years. They asked permission to erect it on the lot, where the school-house already stood, assuming the entire ground-rent, and binding themselves, at the proper time, to give the house to the Mission. This proposal seemed fair, and after due formalities, the merchants built a spacious and elegant mansion, and proceeded to reside in it with their families.

But a series of calamities fell upon them. One embarked

AN EXPLANATION.

on a voyage of importance, and as his ship was never heard from, it was supposed that it had gone down in a tempest. The other suddenly died. The property reverted to the Mission much sooner than had been expected, and the beautiful house stood vacant at its disposal.

ITS OCCUPANCY BY MR. BALLAGH.

Mr. Ballagh received a yearly sum from the Board, to be used in hiring a dwelling for himself. He resolved to avail himself of the vacant house, and pay the amount of the rent into the building-fund. During three months of the year, he found an opportunity to rent it to the silk-worm merchants, who came to Yokohama to collect cocoons, and the large amount they were willing to pay, went also to the treasury, while he and his family found quarters, temporarily, wherever they could. During three months he taught in a Government school, and gave the salary he received, $559, to the same purpose.

CONCLUSION.

The Board made up the sum taken from the $3,000 mentioned, and the beautiful church, which forms the frontispiece of this volume was erected. The slander that a missionary was residing in a magnificent habitation from the surplus bricks of which he had built an insignificant church, is thus refuted. It never had any foundation.

For the facts in this explanation, we are indebted to Mrs. Mary Pruyn, who was on the ground, an eye-witness to the occurrences, and who cheerfully gives us her testimony.

THE DAUGHTERS OF THE ISLES.

THE story of what has been accomplished in the way of establishing schools for women in Japan, follows naturally after Mr. Griffis' account of the political and religious condition of the land. When the wives and mothers of this fair Eastern empire, shall have learned to sit like Mary, at the feet of Jesus, a clearer and brighter day will dawn upon its hills and vales. Our faithful missionaries who have toiled on hopefully, amid manifold discouragements, who have prayerfully done what they could, and who are now joyously gathering the first fruits of the harvest, will themselves tell the history of their years of labor. Though they say nothing concerning their own patience, gentleness and steadfast courage, these qualities are revealed as clearly as light through a transparency, in their modest narratives. First, properly comes

THE BEGINNING OF FERRIS SEMINARY.   BY MRS. MARY E. MILLER.

In the autumn of 1869, I began my work in Japan, having been led here, as I hope, by a gracious heavenly Father.

FERRIS SEMINARY, YOKOHAMA, JAPAN.

My first home in this country, was with the family of Doctor S. R. Brown, who was in the employ of the Japanese Government, at the city of Nugata, on the western coast. Here we remained until July, 1870. While here, my time was wholly given to the acquisition of the language. I had one pupil who learned a little from me, while I gained very much from her. We were entirely among the Japanese, there being no other foreign ladies in Nugata, and this greatly facilitated my opportunities for study. Our house was constantly thronged by curious natives, so that I always felt as if I were a show. After remaining here about eight months, the Government recalled Dr. Brown to Yokohama; but we were not settled in our own house until September, when I resumed my study, and also began to teach three hours each day.

FIRST PUPILS.

I had, at first, three pupils, two girls and one boy, all of whom, had already learned their A, B, C, with one of the other missionaries. She asked me to relieve her from their instruction. After much urging, a former pupil of the same lady returned from the interior, where her father had sent her, with the excuse " that she was a fool, who would learn nothing." This man was my teacher for two years, and when I came to know him better, I discovered that he, rather than his daughter, was the fool, since he spent the money which he earned in drinking saké. The girl, who has been with us ever since, is now our assistant teacher. Her name is

RIO HARADA.

She is a consistent and devoted follower of our dear Lord. For a Japanese, she was an unusually self-willed and independent girl; and till she came into the boarding school, she purposely learned as little as she could, about the Christian religion, saying she thought it would be the worse for her, if she understood and did not believe. She was one of those of whom our Lord said: "Their eyes they have closed, lest at any time, they should see with their eyes, and be converted."

Another of my first three pupils, waited and longed for the boarding school, but was finally married, and went to Tokiō to live, about a year before the house was built. She was a dear girl, and seemed very near the kingdom of heaven. I cannot but hope that she may yet enter the open door, though both her father's and father-in-law's families are very bigoted heathen. I do not intend to lose sight of her, nor has she forgotten her warm affection for me.

The third passed from earth a year and a half ago. She had not for a long time been my pupil, nor did I know of her illness till she was gone. Her relatives, who manifest some interest in the Christian religion, say that she died a Christian. She knew the way of life, and I hope to meet her at last.

REMOVAL TO ISE YAMA.

At the close of the first year of my teaching, I had six girls in my class, so I resigned the boys to a missionary lady who had just come to Japan, while I devoted myself wholly to the girls. During the second year my pupils increased to twenty-two, and in July my class was removed from the room which had been kindly lent me by the Presbyterian Mission, to a house in the native official part of the town, known as Ise Yama. This place was procured through the

KINDNESS OF THE JAPANESE GOVERNOR,

Mr. Oye, who assisted me in various ways, so that for some time the school was no expense to the Mission. Among other things, he presented me with a very pretty closed carriage, to be drawn by coolies, remarking, "that the distance was too great to walk, and he would do himself the pleasure of giving me a conveyance."

FIRST CONVERTS.

With one exception, none of my pupils had yet shown any love for Christ or His word, although they had heard the Bible every day, during the two years in which I had been teaching. They sang the Sunday-school hymns and enjoyed them, because they were new, but they seemed not to have the Spirit in their hearts. In the autumn of 1872,

HIZA OKUNO,

the daughter of Okuno, our good elder, asked for baptism; and she, with her mother and little brother, were baptized. She was quite an accomplished girl in the Japanese way, writing a beautiful hand, drawing and painting from natural objects, and playing the native guitar. She is now a fine scholar in English, and is still with us, a valuable assistant, as well as pupil, in the school. In her Christian life, she is modest, consistent and earnest, and her example is always such as becomes a follower of our Saviour.

TRIALS.

During the winter of 1872 and 1873, our school numbered more pupils than at any time before or since; but many of them came, expecting to learn English in a few months, and, of course, they were soon discouraged. In the spring several left, because they had lost faith in my promises that we should have a boarding school. This last was very hard to bear. Another trial was the failing health of the efficient helper, whom the Board had sent out in the previous November, making it impossible for her to teach in the autumn of 1873. Of course, many of the lessons which our pupils pursued, when there were two teachers, had to be given up for lack of time, when there was but one. This change was very discouraging to our ambitious pupils, and with the prospect of the promised boarding school still distant, was a severe blow to our interests.

Interrupting Mrs. Miller's narrative here, it may be well to explain why teacher and scholars were so anxious to have a boarding-school. There may be some, who will inquire, "Could not the pupils attend their classes daily, and eat and sleep at home?" In reply, we must remember that distances are great in Japan, and many of the towns and villages are scattered and straggling. People employed officially in the Government towns, would have kindred and friends in, perhaps, remote places, to whom they would send the tidings of the new opportunities for female instruction. Yet young girls who wished to avail themselves of these advantages, could not do so, for lack of a home while pursuing their studies. Again, one great desire and aim of our missionaries was to give their pupils the idea of the Christian home, as we have it in Protestant civilized lands. They wanted to impart it, in a daily object lesson; throwing around these girls, in their tender childhood, or as they stood on the threshold of womanly maturity, the benign atmosphere of the home, which always acknowledges the care of the Father who is in heaven. Resuming Mrs. Miller's account, we hear of

THE PRESENCE OF THE HOLY SPIRIT.

In the spring of 1874, the light of the Holy Spirit again pierced the darkness, and Ko Okada asked for baptism. Like Iliza, she showed such earnest love and faith, with so clear an understanding of the step she was about to take, that she was joyfully received into the Church. Of the trial of her faith and victory through the Spirit, I must tell you. Remember ing in what subservience to man, the women of Japan have been educated, and considering how youthful and inexperienced was this sweet Christian girl, her patience and fortitude were wonderful. Serenely and undauntedly she braved persecution, joyfully bearing all suffering which came to her because she held fast to the faith.

KO'S CONFLICT.

In the August following her baptism, Ko came to me saying she wished for advice. Her father who was of the military class in feudal days, had become poor. Her brother, who took care of the family, was a civil engineer in the employ of the Government, which does not insure large pay, as it might in some other country; so that her old father and mother, younger sister, brother's wife and two children, all being dependent upon this one brother, were, as you may imagine, in very straightened circumstances. Ko worked for her board in a kind foreigner's family, and came regularly to school. One day, shortly before she came to ask my counsel, a wealthy Japanese lady, who knew Ko well, invited her father and herself to visit her. They went wondering why she wished to see them, but they soon discovered the reason. The lady said that a Japanese gentleman, who had been heir to a large daimiate in feudal times, and who was now an officer of high position in the Government, wished Ko for his wife; he had met her at this lady's house, although Ko did not remember him. Of course, the father heard this offer with pride, but in silence; and finally he replied, with many thanks, that, although so desirable, it was impossible to accept it, as he was too poor to give Ko an outfit suitable for such a position. The lady replied, that she would attend to that. As everything seemed to be arranged, they turned to Ko, expecting to see her overwhelmed with delight, the lady saying "But there is one thing, Ko; you must give up this Christian religion, and let us hear no more about it." Ko did not seem so pleased as they expected at the opportunity of changing her poverty for wealth, luxury and high position, and astonished them by quietly and modestly saying that she did not wish to be married. They could hardly believe their ears; and, partly in indignation, and partly in astonishment, said that they would give her a week to think about it.

When the father reached his home the assembled family heard of the offered fortune, and wondered more and more why Ko did not eagerly accept. Her father and brother said: "Now, tell us the true reason, and if it is a good one we will respect your wishes."

Ko said: "Because I *cannot* give up my religion." "But," they replied, "you can *say* you will give it up, and secretly cherish it." So wide is the difference between lying heathenism and our true Christian religion!

Next they appealed to her love for her parents and family, saying how much she could do for them with her wealth. When they saw it was in vain, they told her she did not care for her parents; and next, that she was crazy and they would build a prison and put her into it, take all her books away and burn them, and would disown her as a member of the family. So they persecuted her. She came to ask us what she ought to do. She said though the intended husband were to promise that she might keep her religion, she could not trust him; he would break his word as soon as they were married.

Her younger sister was taken from our school immediately, and the family continued to persecute Ko, although her mother partially relented, so that she often visited her home when her father and brother were absent.

About the middle of the following winter she asked me to go with her to visit her younger sister, who was very ill, and whom she was afraid would die. I had not met the sister since she left school, but upon Ko's assuring me that the family would be willing to see me, I accompanied her to her home. We were kindly received, and they accepted my offer to send a foreign physician. She was very ill with fever, and the doctor thought her recovery impossible. The family were so subdued by their affliction that they were quite willing to listen to prayer and religious teaching every day. The sister soon began slowly to recover, I believe, wholly in answer to earnest prayer; for every other circumstance was adverse to her restoration. The family frankly confess that they think so too; and although none of them have professed their love for Christ, they have since that time been more or less interested, and have never said anything more about Ko's marrying a heathen.

Ko is still with us, loved and admired by every one, for her sweet and earnest piety as well as for her energy of character. I sometimes call her "my right hand."

THE SUNDAY-SCHOOL.

When I came to Japan, in 1869, there was a Sunday-school, under the superintendence of the Presbyterian Mission, numbering some thirty or forty children, mostly foreigners, and belonging to the families of the Tenth English Regiment, stationed here. I found in the Sunday-school the work which I loved, and assisted the superintendent till she gave the care into my hands and went to China for rest. When she returned she did not care to resume it, so it fell into my hands, although several others assisted in teaching singing, and playing the organ, which we afterwards received.

The number of children in the town increased so that, although the Tenth Regiment soon left, taking away many children, the school still flourished, numbering about Christmas time every year upwards of eighty.

The greater part of my Japanese pupils attended, and a few other Japanese came in, making a class of about twenty, whom I taught myself after the opening exercises. Through the kindness of friends here and at home, we were enabled to get a very well-selected library, of nearly a hundred volumes, of the best Sunday-school books to be found in New York. With these, the children were greatly delighted.

Our school was conducted like most of the schools at home. We sang children's Sunday-school hymns for a half hour at the beginning, then had reading of Scripture and prayer, after which we separated into classes, I teaching the Japanese.

OUR HOME SUNDAY-SCHOOL.

In September of 1874 I concluded to withdraw my Japanese pupils from the foreign Sunday-school, and with my husband opened a school at Ise Yama, in the house where I taught during the week, hoping thereby to draw in others beside my own pupils. This Japanese Sunday-school has continued without interruption to the present time. The foreign school has always been flourishing, and is still continued. I have been thus explicit in speaking of the Sunday-school work here, because it has been reported, upon seemingly good authority, at home, that there was no Sunday-school in Japan till 1874.

A LEASE OBTAINED AND BUILDING BEGUN.

The summer and autumn of 1874 were very trying in regard to the school. Our Mission Board were unable to furnish sufficient funds to purchase a desirable lot of ground and put up a suitable building for a boarding-school, and I had used every exertion to procure a gift or lease of land from the Government of this country, in order to relieve the Board from all expense except the building.

Although the Governor of this place did what he could to help me, and also our Consul-General, yet as everything must be referred to the general Government at Tōkiō, we were a long time in obtaining the lease; and many times I was ready to give up my school in despair. A *successful* day-school seemed impossible; pupils coming and going among this moving people, as their parents went hither and thither, was not the kind of school I desired; and I came to the conclusion that I had better give up the school and unite with the Presbyterian Board, with which my husband was still connected; but, owing to circumstances which I need not recite here, my husband concluded to sever his connection with that Mission, and he sent his resignation home in October. In November, we obtained the lease of the land so long sought, and also the money from home to begin building.

MISS WITBECK'S ARRIVAL.

Miss Witbeck also arrived the same month, to be with me in the school, and the whole horizon began to brighten. During our long waiting we had matured the plan for the building, so that before the new year the ground was prepared and the timber was on the lot, with a contract signed for the completion of the building in May, 1875.

BAPTISM OF KUNI TAMANU.

In March Kuni Tamanu, one of our very bright, energetic and exceedingly intelligent pupils, asked for baptism, and was received into the church. She had come from a place about one hundred miles north of Tōkiō, and was living with us, as we were housekeeping and waiting for the boarding-school.

She had for about a year given evidence of a change of heart, but was rather younger than the others who had been baptized; so we had thought it well for her to wait. Her examination was very satisfactory, and her knowledge of the doctrines quite equal to that of well-trained girls at home, as she has a very retentive memory.

OPENING OF THE BOARDING-SCHOOL.

Our boarding-school was opened the 1st of June, 1875, by a dedicatory Japanese service. The day-school had been continued up to that time in order, if possible, to keep our few remaining pupils together. Although July was very hot, we thought it best to have two months of school before vacation. In June we had fourteen pupils, and we closed in July with nineteen. When we resumed, in September, some of our pupils did not return; but others came in, so that we closed the year, in December, with nineteen pupils—the same as in summer.

But during the next year, 1876, our numbers steadily increased, so that we closed with thirty-four pupils, thirty of whom were boarders; and it seems now as if our school were established on a firm foundation. The blessing of our dear Father in Heaven seemed *abiding* in our household all through the year.

BAPTISM OF RIO, TENYA AND SAYA.

In May, 1876, three more of our dear girls asked for baptism, and were received into the Church. One was Rio Harada.

Another was Tenya Fugiyama, who is betrothed to Mr. Segawa, a native Christian helper in Nagasaki. She was sent to us in the October previous, in order to bring her directly under Christian influences, also that she might be better fitted to be a helpmate to Mr. Segawa in his work. Almost from her coming here she seemed interested in religion, and appears now to have but one desire, and that, the salvation of her countrymen. She spends much time in prayer, and is always at the feet of Jesus. A few months since, she heard that her parents, who are in Nagasaki, were both interested in religion, so she came to my room to tell me that her prayers were answered. As she was leaving the room she looked back, as if she had something more upon her mind; and to my question as to what it was, she said, her kindred, except her parents, were far from Nagasaki, and there was no one to teach them the love of Christ. This, she longs to do herself. I am sure that every day she prays many times for them; she has already learned the mighty power of prayer. There will be many stars in the crown awaiting her.

Saya Mayeda was the third who received baptism last May. She was a day pupil for some time, at Iso Yama, when her parents lived in Yokohama; but left about three years ago, because her father was appointed to a place in the Treasury Department at Tōkiō. She returned to us last March, and in May asked for baptism, having had the full consent of her parents, who, she said, believed that the Christian religion was true. She was gladly received.

She is a superior Chinese scholar, and of a gentle and affectionate disposition naturally. She began her Christian work by going to her home and bringing back her little sister who, she said, was obstinate and spoiled, and learning nothing. We found her report quite true, and had much trouble with little Ikku at first, because she was home-sick, and determined to go home. Now she is improving, and very happy, and does not wish to stay at home, although she has been there twice on holiday visits.

THE WEEKLY PRAYER-MEETING.

For about three years, our pupils have held a weekly prayer-meeting, and since September have met with the pupils of "The Mission Home," alternately here and there on Friday afternoons for prayer. Although some of the teachers are always present, the girls take part with great freedom, reading a few texts of Scripture and commenting upon them, or leading in prayer. These meetings are both interesting and edifying.

INSTRUCTION IN THE CATECHISM.

We teach the catechism very thoroughly. Last April, I promised my class of thirteen little girls, about ten years old, a present to the one who could say the most of the catechism in Japanese, at the end of June. We examined them on the eighty questions which they had learned, and but two missed or hesitated; so that, instead of giving the two pretty books which I had selected for the two best, I was obliged to find something for eleven, so I gave them each a small copy of one of the Gospels. Last month the same class were examined, in the presence of most of our Mission, in the entire catechism, which they completed just before the new year, and not one missed a word.

BIBLE KNOWLEDGE.

Our pupils are very familiar with the Gospels and the Acts of the Apostles, and are somewhat acquainted with all the historical parts of the Bible. We are now studying the Old Testament in the morning, and the New Testament in the evening, and on Sunday evenings I spend a "delightful hour," (a name given by the children themselves,) with all the dear little girls gathered closely about me, telling them Old Testament stories.

OTHER BRANCHES TAUGHT.

As you know, beside the religious teaching, our pupils are instructed in simple sciences, in English, also in reading and writing their own language and Chinese. So that they are obliged to study very hard. On Saturday mornings they are taught to mend their clothing, after which, they do fancy work, having only a half holiday.

EXPENSE TO THE PUPILS.

From our experience of the willingness of the Japanese to receive whatever is given to them, although able to pay for it, we concluded, from the beginning, not to make ours quite a free school, but to fix a moderate price, and require its payment. We settled upon three dollars for boarders, and one dollar per month, for day scholars, in order to encourage boarders. Our pupils furnish their clothing, bedding, books and stationery,—while we give them rooms, fuel, lights, food, teaching, washing, and care for their health. The school part of our house is somewhat modified to suit the habits of the Japanese.

FURNITURE AND BEDDING.

Although the pupils use desks and chairs, like foreign children, we have the floors covered with the wadded straw mats, so that they need only wear their neat socks as in their own houses. They sit at table and use napkins and knives and forks, but eat Japanese food, such as fish, rice, eggs, etc., with the exception of beef once a week, which we consider better for their health, and milk, which we give to those who are not very strong. Their sleeping rooms also have the wadded straw mats, so that they require only the thick quilts which they use in their own homes in place of a mattress, and these are taken up, folded and laid away in a large closet in the daytime, leaving their rooms clean and neat.

DIVISION OF LABOR.

During the first year of our boarding-school, closing July, 1876, I took the care of the school as well as the housekeeping; Miss Witbeck sharing with me the teaching, and devoting herself to the study of the language. I found, however, that so much care was too great a strain upon my brain, and something must be done to relieve me, so we decided to put much more teaching upon the older girls, who were assisting us. Miss Witbeck, who since September, has had the entire care of the school room, finds them very efficient, so that I am scarcely missed, although relieved from all teaching during the week, except the morning Bible lesson and superintending the sewing on Saturdays. I still do the housekeeping, and look after the health of our flock, which is quite a work among so many. By the blessing of Providence we have been preserved from all severe illness, and for the past six months have not been obliged to call a physician.

> "The past is not so dark as once it seemed,
> For there Thy footprints now distinct I see;
> And seed in weakness sown, from death redeemed,
> Is springing up, and bearing fruit in Thee,
> Not all that hath been, Lord, henceforth shall be:
> A low, sweet, cheering strain is in mine ear,
> Thanksgiving, and the voice of melody,
> Are ushering in from Heaven a blest New Year."

THE WORK REVIEWED, EXAMINATIONS, ETC.

The missionaries have steadily kept in view the idea that they were educating the girls, to become good wives and mothers in Japan. To so teach them, that they would be dissatisfied with, and discontented in their own homes, would be no kindness. So they have been encouraged to retain their own pretty native costume, and some of their distinctive daily customs, while also they have learned some of our refinements of behavior.

The following particulars are taken from a review of the

first year's work, received from the teachers of the Girls' School at Yokohama.

COST OF BUILDING.

In regard to the school, the original proposition was to expend $5,000 on this building, but when the plans were drawn, it was found, that by adding $500 to the outlay, a much more satisfactory house could be obtained, and the addition was authorized. The building is about seventy-five feet front, and nearly forty feet deep, and will afford fine accommodation for the boarding-school and teachers. It is situated in a commanding position on the bluff, behind the city, overlooking the town and harbor. (See picture on page 241.)

OPENING OF THE SCHOOL.

When the school was opened, on the 1st of June, 1875, there were present fourteen scholars, all of whom had been day pupils with Mrs. Miller on Nogo Hill. Two little girls from Ozaka came as boarders in July, and two from Yokohama as day scholars, so that at the close of the session in July, there were eighteen pupils. The ladies would have preferred, for some reasons, to wait until the beginning of September, for the opening of the school, but knowing the peculiarities of Japanese character, they feared that by the end of three months, the scholars would be scattered, so they determined to keep the girls with them for two months, and then dismiss them for a vacation of six weeks.

Vacation over, the school was resumed on September 15th. Five pupils had left in the interim, one, a girl of fifteen only, to be married. Three, their friends promised, should return when they were older. At the end of the month, we numbered fifteen, and a few weeks later two others of our absentees returned. One of these was Rio, the dear girl who had been longest with us. She had been visiting at Yeddo, and while there had been sent to the Government Girls' School, which is under the patronage of the Empress. She was very glad to be back with us.

A REMARKABLE WOMAN.

Returning from our vacation trip into the interior, we dismissed the former Japanese teacher of the girls, and secured the services of another, a woman who had been a sort of Shintō priestess, and whom Okuno had known twenty years ago. She is very learned, and under her instruction the girls make great progress in Chinese and Japanese.

The growth of the school has been steady. Four of the older girls are employed as assistants in the care of the little ones, and in teaching them how to learn their lessons. These are paid, on the terms which have been mentioned before, $5.00 each a month, and of this $3.00 goes to their board.

Looking back over a year's work, we are filled with thankfulness, one source of which is, that our school was not very large at first. We needed experience, and even a family of fourteen may tax the powers of a novice.

OUR COOK.

Our Japanese cook has been a treasure. Upon him rests the burden of providing for the girls' table, our province being merely to give directions. We have a gardener, and five house-servants. Two and a half of the latter, if we may use the expression, we regard as belonging to the school. They have been with us from the beginning and are very faithful and diligent.

WHERE THE SCHOLARS COME FROM.

Most of our girls come from Yeddo, and Yokohama, and are the daughters of Government officials, yet we have pupils from different parts of the Empire, from Nagasaki, in the extreme south-west, from near Ozato and Kioto, the Western Capital, both of which are about the centre of the main island; from Kiushiu, at the entrance of the Inland Sea, and from Shintō Fenki, about one hundred miles north of Yeddo.

JAPANESE FOOD.

The best Japanese food, and that to which the girls are accustomed at home, is prepared for them at school. It consists of fish, rice, eggs, and all kinds of vegetables, but neither meat, bread nor milk.

BEDS AND BEDDING.

A Japanese bed consists of two heavy quilts, on one of which the person lies, while the other forms a covering. The upper one resembles their own lower garments, but is very heavy. Their pillows are little stool-like cushions, about as comfortable as an octavo book set on edge, and looking as if intended to cut the neck rather than to rest it; but then, these high neck-rests possess one advantage. They allow the young ladies to preserve their elaborate coiffures several days undisturbed. Some of the little ones have their hair more simply arranged, and they sleep more comfortably on flatter pillows, stuffed with rice-bran. They dress in the native costume, but we require them to wear a white undergarment, which can be changed when soiled. These, with their heavy white socks, we have washed in the house. It is to be hoped that among other improvements, they may be induced to wear their hair in some more sensible way, and yet the crimps and puffs of Christian young women in America, are hardly more tasteful than the fashion of the Japanese.

SCHOOL HOURS.

Our school-hours are from nine to half-past twelve in the

morning for English, opening with a singing exercise and prayer, reading the Bible in English, and explaining it in Japanese.

We have some half dozen classes, which, however, are not all entirely distinct, the girls who are together in one class, being sometimes separated in another. Our English branches at present are, first lessons in philosophy, physiology, history, botany, Quackenbos' composition, reading, spelling, writing, arithmetic, geography and conversation, all of which the girls are required to translate from the English text-books, giving double work to them as well as to their teachers.

Some of the older girls are learning to play upon the melodeon; and we hope, before very long, that they will be able to play at the Japanese church-service.

The morning study-hours are from after breakfast, which is at 7 A. M. in winter, and 6 A. M. in summer, till 8:40. To this study all the day-scholars come, some of them a mile and a half, in all weathers. Think of little girls at home, only five or six years old, coming at half-past seven of a winter's morning, in order to have time to study before school.

The evening study-hours are from tea-time, 5 P. M., till evening prayers at 6:30. After prayers, the little ones are put to bed, and the older girls stay up till 9 and 9:45. Even then, it is hard to get them to go to bed, and at play-time, they generally have to be literally driven out of doors.

Evening prayers are conducted in Japanese, and all the servants attend.

A CHRISTMAS FESTIVAL AT THE FERRIS SEMINARY, 1876.

THE parents of the pupils are not, as a rule, interested in religious things; although a few of them are church members, and a few others attend some of the religious services. Over and over have they declined invitations to come and hear the teaching, but in vain; so at this time, the ladies thought to catch them with a little parade. The week before Christmas, invitations were sent to all of them to come on the following Sunday, as that is now their leisure day, to a " Matsuri ;" or, religious festival. At the same time, Mr. Okuno, an elder in the church, and the most eloquent speaker among the native Christians, was asked to prepare an address, and also to make it appropriate to Christmas. He was glad to do so. His heart is always alive to the salvation of his people.

EVERGREENS AND BRIGHT BERRIES.

On Saturday the 23d, the ladies decorated the school-room with beautiful wreaths of green, and bright berries, with which at this season, the country abounds. Sunday, the 24th, at 3 P.M., there was assembled the school of thirty-four pupils, and about forty of the parents and friends.

The services began by singing Antioch, translated into Japanese; after which Mr. Okuno, led in prayer; then Rio, who is learning to play on the organ, played, while all sang from the hymns of the church, " Good News," and " Hark, the Herald Angels sing!" This was in English.

THE DAUGHTERS OF THE ISLES.   279

Then Okuno preached from "Glory to God in the Highest," telling the people who this God is, in a way so animated, as to fix their attention for the whole sermon. After

OKUNO.   OGAWA.
ELDERS OF THE CHURCH AT YOKOHAMA.

the sermon, we sang a pretty little original hymn by Okuno, relating the story of our Redeemer's birth.

REFRESHMENTS.

At the close of the exercises, the ladies had Japanese sponge-cake and tea passed to all the guests and pupils. It is supposed that the Japanese learned how to make sponge-cake from the Jesuits, several centuries ago.

CHRISTMAS GIFTS.

We had some little presents of books, pictures, fancy-work and dolls, which had the previous year been sent to Mrs.

Miller, but the box arriving too late for Christmas, its contents were reserved. On Saturday night, Mrs. Miller and Miss Witbeck prepared thirty-four stockings, filling the feet with oranges and candies, and putting the presents on, or in them, they laid them aside until Sunday night, when the children were all in bed. The clothes-line was put up in the school-room, and we pinned on the thirty-four stockings, with thirty-four names attached. In the morning, they enjoyed the surprise and their presents exceedingly, and had a merry time, getting to the bottom of their long stockings.

This was Christmas morning, of course. About ten o'clock, the pupils went to the Japanese church, after which we had a pleasant time with the native church-members, at the Mission House next door to the church, into which Mr. and Mrs. Amerman had just moved. In a large vacant room, the members of our Mission prepared a table, around which we sang and talked, and the Japanese ate. Thus, even in Japan, were enjoyed and remembered the blessings which came to all the world, through our loving Saviour.

The account of the school and its progress has so far been given by Mrs. Miller. Her husband now takes up the pen in an informal letter, from which we make some quotations.

SUMMER EXAMINATION OF THE GIRLS' SCHOOL AT YOKOHAMA.

BY
Rev. E. R. Miller.

I write by this mail, since our school will be closed at the end of next week, to remain so during the hot weather. We have kept on till this late day, because the heat has been so slow in coming. We shall be scattered soon; Mrs. Miller and I will go to Uyedo, where there has been a good deal of interest excited, and where they are very anxious to have some one come to teach them. Heretofore, they have had very little instruction of any kind. Two of them have been down here—one was baptized in Yeddo, and one here; and when Mr. Oshikawa passed through Uyeda, on his way to Nugata, he was persuaded to remain for a few days and instruct them. Probably Mr. Maki, one of the elders, will go with us, both on account of his health, and to assist in teaching. He is one of the young men who are studying for the ministry; we know and like him very much.

THE JAPANESE TEACHER.

A week or so ago, we had our first examination by the Japanese teacher. The English examination was held just before Christmas. Our teacher, of whom you have doubtless heard before, conducted it all in her own way, and I wish you could have seen it. Many were very much interested, who could not understand one word.

All the desks were cleared away for the visitors. The scholars were ranged on their chairs on the sides of the smaller school-room, which was thrown open into the large one, where sat the spectators. In front of the scholars, and facing the audience was a single small table and chair, at which sat each girl as she came up to read in her turn. The teacher sat with her side to the audience on a large cane arm-chair; her feet, in immense carpet slippers, resting on a foot-stool. Her dress was new for the occasion; she wore the official wide pantaloons, which in her case were made of stiff figured yellow gauze. She sat in grand state, not condescending to do anything but preserve her dignity, and fan herself. One of the oldest girls, an excellent Chinese scholar, who acted as her assistant, sat beside her, and called the names of the different scholars in order; and as they went up to recite gave them their books, and told them where to read. The younger girls read only, while the older ones, both read and explained. The text-books were generally histories in Japanese and Chinese.

SPECIMENS OF THEIR WRITING.

The walls were hung with specimens of their writing, in different styles; some the free running hand, others the square Chinese hand, and others partly a combination. The elder girls' specimens were original odes or sonnets.

MISS WITBECK'S LETTER.

Miss Witbeck thus sums up the results of the first year's work:

"Yesterday school closed with twenty-nine scholars, and now all but two are gone, leaving us somewhat lonely, and decidedly quiet. Our Japanese examination occurred on the 23d of last month, and the girls acquitted themselves in a manner which greatly delighted their friends; but of this I presume you have already heard from Mrs. Miller. Perhaps you will ask, 'What are the results of your year's work in the Ferris Seminary?' To which I would reply, that so far as I was able to judge from the two standpoints,—that of the Japanese, and that of the missionary,—the results have been beyond my expectations. Among the Japanese, the school has gained a reputation, or as they express it, has become famous; and that means much in a country where the people are so devoted to things which are popular. Already we have a number of pupils from distant provinces. Looking at our labor as work in the Master's service, we feel that He has truly been with us, blessing our weak endeavors, and answering many prayers. Three of the girls have confessed their faith, and are now members of Mr. Ballagh's church, and others have expressed the wish to be baptized; besides this, there has been a silent influence pervading the school, which has been greatly blessed to many of our girls.

Now that they have gone to their friends, they must tell some of the truths of Christianity, and thus we hope that more may be brought to Christ. One of our Christian scholars will return to her home at Nikko, for the purpose of teaching the Bible to her country-women, and I am expecting to accompany her. We start on Tuesday, and I shall probably return in a month, leaving her in Nikko."

COMPOSITIONS AND LETTERS OF THE JAPANESE GIRLS.

Nothing in our own seminaries, proves the advancement of pupils, and sets forth the degree of their culture, so manifestly as an original composition. Their progress in grammar, in spelling, and in writing, are all shown in this way; and even more clearly is displayed, their ability to express themselves with intelligence, and to make use of what they have acquired. The Japanese girls appear to have a natural gift for letter-writing, and the teachers have found it easy to induce them to exercise it. Some of the Bands have corresponded with their beneficiaries, and have received very gratifying epistles, in return for their own.

RIO'S LETTER.

Addressed to the Mission Board at Bronxville:

FERRIS SEMINARY, Yokohama.

MY DEAR FRIENDS:

I have not yet seen you, but I have heard of you from our dear teachers. I thank you, that pitying us, so far away, you have sent much money for our education in this school. From ancient times in Japan, there were no special schools for women, and they did not know anything, but during their whole lives they were slaves to the men, and did not know another right religion, and a happy way; therefore their minds being darkened, and believing in many bewildering doctrines, they served false gods, and worshipped idols. But now we are thankful that, being led by the mercy of God, we have come to this school, and through the kindness and love of these teachers, here first heard of the true and living God, who made heaven and earth and all things, and dwells in heaven. He beheld and pitied the suffering condition of mankind in sin, and sent His Son Jesus Christ, who descended to a low estate, in His deep love and pity, for which I am truly thankful, and also that Jesus Christ put His back on the cross, and His body was broken, and His blood flowed, and He suffered and was wounded to save us from suffering and sin. We are glad to believe the Gospel, and, repenting of our former sins, have been baptized, and received Jesus the Saviour, and trusting everything to Him, and with love following Him, we hope to have eternal life, and eternal glory in Heaven.

Now we are thankful to be in this Christian home, with dear teachers, friends and sisters, through the grace of God, being always blessed and happy.

And it is always our hope, with strong faith, to love each other, and the Lord Jesus, and to walk in the straight and holy way, and never to go in wondering paths. So, with peaceful and humble hearts, we hope to leave this world without fear, and to go to heaven, and meet by the side of the "pure river."

Please always remember us in your prayers, and we will remember you. Rio.

Ko Okada, whose story has already been told, has pleased her instructors, not less by her amiability of disposition, and her constancy of principle, than by the steady growth of her mind, under the influence of the school. The composition here given, was read by her, at the examination, which Mr. Miller and Miss Witbeck have described.

A JAPANESE GIRL'S COMPOSITION.

A TRIP TO SHANGHAI, BY KO OKADA.

"We left Yokohama, Saturday, September 11th, by the Tokiomaru, for Shanghai. The first day was calm, but at night the sea was rough, and I was very sick until we arrived at Kobe, where we stayed one day. Kobe is a very fine place, situated at the foot of a range of hills, and has a pretty waterfall, so I like it very much. The next place at which we stopped was Nagasaki, on a lovely bay of the same name. After leaving Nagasaki, we sailed through the Mud Sea, so called because of the color of the water, and on Saturday we entered the Yangtsekiang River, arriving at Shanghai about noon. The Tokiomaru sailed up to her dock, so we did not need little boats, because we could go directly from the steamer to land. The harbor was beautiful, and many ships were in port. The country is level. The roads are narrow and dirty, with rows of trees, of which the great part are willow, planted on both sides. The Public Gardens are more beautiful than those of Yokohama. Every evening, the foreign gentlemen and ladies, with their children, visit the garden. There are no wells, and all the people drink the water of the river. While

I was at the hotel, some Chinese ladies came to us. Their feet were as small as a child's. Whenever I went out, children followed after me, and gathered around in crowds, when I stopped at the shops, so that I did not like to walk out in the day-time. Excepting that the Chinese dress their hair in a way peculiar to themselves, their customs are much like those of the Japanese."

It is doubtful whether there are many American girls who could write a more graphic description than this of a trip to Philadelphia or Boston, and if it were required of them, to write in a foreign tongue, French, or German, or Japanese, the task would be indeed difficult. Beside the composition, Mrs. J. P. Cumming, of Yonkers, Home Corresponding Secretary of the Woman's Board, has kindly sent to this volume, a story, and three letters, written at different periods by Ko. The letters were addressed to the Yonkers Auxiliary, which has undertaken Ko's support. Of the little story Mrs. Miller wrote:

"I found this in my drawer, and remember it, as a story which Ko wrote and brought to me some time ago, for correction. I mislaid it, and it was forgotten, and I now send it without any correction."

THE STORY OF THE JELLY-FISH.

"I will tell you a little story which I heard from my friend. In ancient times, there was another world at the bottom of the ocean; no one could go there, for it was a secret place. A beautiful woman governed the nation, and all her attendants were fishes and beasts of the sea. At length she fell sick, and coming worse, day after day. All the subjects were very anxious, and talked with each other about it. Some of them said that the liver of an ape was very good medicine for that disease, therefore, they sent a tortoise to catch it; so he went to a mountain, and brought an ape on his back, which he presented him to the queen; she was glad to receive a remedy for her disease, but she was sorry that he had to be killed. She told her servants to feed it with nice food, and let him play in the garden. While he was standing alone by a pond, a jelly-fish came to him and said, 'I am very sorry for you, because you will be killed;' then ape said 'Why? I have not done anything wrong,' and the jelly-fish replied 'The queen wants your liver for her medicine.' Then the ape was very afraid, and began to contrive how he might save his life. After awhile as the rain was falling, he returned to the palace, and stood crying in the hall. At that time the tortoise came, and asked: 'Why do you cry,' and the ape answered, 'because I forgotten to bring my liver, and it is raining now, so my liver will decay; and when the subjects heard this, they were troubled, and said, 'he is good for nothing if he has no liver, and we must send him to bring it,' so that they sent him to bring it; but when he reached a mountain, the ape ran away, and the tortoise waited until evening, but it was unnecessary. The tortoise returned, and told the queen about it, and she said, 'it must have known our project, and some of my servants must have told it,' so she gathered together all her attendants and said 'All of you come here and worship the god, but whosoever did wrong, the god will punish him,' but jelly-fish would not go there, knowing his fault. So she knew who did it, and said to the jelly-fish, 'you will not remain any longer among fish.' She took off his shell. Since that time jelly-fish have no shells."

KO'S LETTERS.

The first bears date December 9th, 1875:

YOKOHAMA, Japan, Ferris Seminary.

MY DEAR FRIEND:

I hope you are well, and I thank for your kindness. I am

staying at the school, many boarding-scholars are here. We have study in English from nine till half-past twelve; we are divided into six classes; I am studying History, Geography, Arithmetic, Philosophy, Botany and Composition. Every morning we read in Acts, and teacher explains to us. In the afternoon we have Japanese reading, and writing lessons. Every Saturday we have sewing half of day. On Sunday we go to church, which is settled in Japan by the grace of God. The building is very splendid. The sevice begain at nine. When we come back to home, we all go to school, some one of the Christian young man preach to us. In the afternoon we have the Sunday school, there are three classes in which I am. One is reading Genesis in English. Many of our brethren have learned about Bible, and they go about the teaching the people earnestly, so that the Capital city, seaport, and several villages are prevailing the religion. Therefore many of our countrymen know about Jesus Christ. Four of our brethren have been elected the elders of the church, and we are about to choose a pastor.

Please pray for us, and our teachers, friends, and every school in Japan. I am thank God for your kindness. Farewell,
Yours Affectionately,
Ko Okada.

The second, written July 19th, 1876, shows progress:

My Dear Friends:

I hope you are always in good health through the grace of our Heavenly Father. I have not written to you for a long time, but I have not forgotten your kindness all the time. Our school closed the 15th of this month, so I have retired with one of my school-mates to spend the vacation, and our teachers will go to some place in the hills, to escape from the heat of the summer. Our country is progressing in civilization, for we have many curious things, that have never been used here before, such as steamboats, railroads, gas and many other things. The house where I am living now is that of the famous rich merchant in Yokohama. He seems the most civilized one of them all, for he has lighted all the house with gas, and he, wishing to educate the people well, founded a school, and on

Sundays he makes the men-servants, and maid-servants rest; yet it is not true civilization, for although it is lightened with gas, and all around it is spread great darkness, and although this rich man and his family know the name of the Saviour, they do not care at all. Whenever you kneel down to pray, please remember them.

One of the Japanese Christians went to a village called Totsuka to preach the Gospel, and the people are very glad to hear it, so that one of the old Christian men goes there every Saturday to preach. At first a few people came, but gradually the number has increased, and now almost a hundred people go there, with the women and their children. My father is living there; he goes to hear the preaching too; and he wishes me to go there, and teach the people how to sing, and I intend to go there sometimes during my vacation. I hope that my father will become a true Christian. Please pray to God for these people, and that other heathen persons may turn to the true religion. Good-by, I hope you will have a pleasant time in this vacation.

Yours Affectionately,

Ko Okada.

MR. BALLAGH'S TESTIMONY.

Mr. Ballagh's letter, dated Yohohama, July 24, 1876, contains these sentences: "There is much of interest in Japanese affairs, and in mission work, and all of an encouraging nature. The school examinations are being held, and very creditable they all have been. The Ferris Seminary examination in Japanese and Chinese studies, under their native teachers took place yesterday, and was largely attended by Japanese gentlemen and ladies, and parents of the pupils. The proficiency of the scholars in reading and translating Chinese, was something wonderful to us Europeans. Their writing, specimens of which adorned the walls, were very creditable. The performer at the organ was one of the girls, and the whole was a decided success. The English examination was held in mid-winter. The American Womans' Mission School Examination in English, was entirely satisfactory.

Interest in the Gospel increases in all directions. Two of our elders are engaged constantly in preaching, one in Yeddo, and the other at a village six or eight miles from here. Calls come from all parts of the country to visit them in the summer vacation.

MUSIC AS A STUDY.

"Several of the older girls are learning to play the organ, among them Rio, Ko, and Hiza. Their progress is rapid, and they are highly complimented by their teacher, Miss Witbeck. This accomplishment will enable them greatly to assist, in the musical part of their church services."

IMPRESSIONS OF MR. KIP.

Rev. Leonard W. Kip, of the Amoy Mission, while travelling in Japan for his health, in September, 1875, wrote concerning

NATIVE ASSEMBLIES.

"We were happy in being present at the dedication of the new Union Church at Yokohama. Services are held in in this building, both in Japanese and in English, so there is union in more senses than one. The building is more nearly like our churches at home, than those we commonly find here. The congregation by no means fills it, so there is room for growth. Several things connected with this work, are striking to one who has lived in China.

SITTING TOGETHER OF MEN AND WOMEN.

"One is, that in the native assemblies, men and women sit together, as in our churches at home. It will be a long time time before we see men and women in China sitting together in church. In these neighboring Empires, we see two extremes, the reserve of China, contrasting strongly with the free social intercourse of Japan.

"At Nagasaki too, the pretty church building is often well

filled with hearers. All that has been told of the lovely scenery of this part of the world is true, for every prospect pleases, and alas! only man is vile. Yet our missionaries are not without encouragement here. Few have been baptized, but many seem interested."

A BELL TO YOKOHAMA.

There is no sweeter sound in Christian lands, than the voice of the Sabbath bell, as it summons the worshippers to the house of prayer. When the silver tones are borne over the quiet hillsides and flowery vales of our own dear country, they seem in themselves to carry an earnest and a pledge of the protection which belongs to all who are gathered under the banner of the cross; so it is no wonder that loyal hearts have delighted to send far over the blue-rounding billows, to distant tropic shores, bells which shall summon to the sanctuary, those who were lately wending their ways to temples of idolatry. On December 16, 1875, our Board shipped a fine bell, with the frame-work necessary to mount it, to Dr. James H. Ballagh, for the native church at Yokohama. Its weight was six hundred and six pounds. It was the gift, mainly, of Garret Kouvenhoven, Esq., of Newtown, L. I. Messrs Meneely & Co., of West Troy, also dealt very generously with us, and made a handsome donation. This gift followed promptly upon the need, for in July, 1875, the building had been solemnly dedicated to the worship of God; the first Christian church ever erected in Japan.*

---

* "The Foreign Board of the Reformed Church sent seven missionaries to Japan, when it was just opened,—Dr. S. R. Brown, Mrs. Brown and daughter, Dr. and Mrs. Verbec, Dr. and Mrs. Simmons. The building for the church was delayed by the Government, and only consecrated a year ago last July; the stained windows were there thirteen years before they would allow the church to be built. April 1, 1876, the bell, sent by a gentlemen of the Dutch Church, on Long Island, was rung, and the Japanese Government proclaimed 'Religious Liberty.'"—*Extract from a letter of Mrs. T. C. Doremus to the Secretary of the Woman's Board.*

A VISIT TO UYEDA.

BY
Rev. E. R. Miller.

UYEDA is in the country of Shinsee, the highest part of Japan. It lies a little to the north or west from Yeddo, from which it is distant some 115 miles, or about three days travel. Situated some fifteen miles from the foot of Asama Yama, the great smoking volcano of Japan; it is in a basin formed by the surrounding hills, and although very cold in winter, is so shut in from wind and rain, that the heat in summer is oppressive, notwithstanding the elevation.

"Uyeda is one of the old castle towns of Japan, but like so many others, the castle has been suffered to go to ruin, till there is nothing left but a partially filled moat and the heavy gate-walls. It is a large town, but like most inland Japanese towns, is straggling; and as it is near the silk district, its principal products are raw silk, cocoons, and coarse silk woven goods.

"That however, which attracts the attention of Christians to Uyeda, is the interest in Christianity which has sprung up there, within the last year. The first interest was awakened by Mr. Suzuki, one of the church members of Yokohama. He went to Uyeda, in the summer of 1873, to visit his relations, and remained there for several weeks. He spoke to his friends and relations of the truths of the Bible, and finding among his acquaintances those who had already heard of Christianity, he explained it to them more fully. Among these friends was a

MR. INAGAKI,

who, by his teaching, was persuaded to embrace Christianity. As this man became a sort of leader of the little band of Christians, a few lines may be devoted to his history. Some years ago, while Matsulaira was in Yeddo, Mr. Inagaki went up to the capital, and entered the school of Mr. Fukusawa, and while there attended Mr. Thompson's preaching. Afterwards he was under Mr. John Ballagh's teaching, and also for about a year was at Nagasaki, where he heard Mr. Stout preach. He was not, however, brought to a conviction of the truth, till he heard Mr. Suzuki. When the latter had to leave for Yokohama, he requested Mr. Inagaki, to take his place, in teaching his sister; this charge was undertaken, and faithfully carried out. Though he is not rich, he has enough to live on, and support quite a large family, and as he has no other employment, gives his whole time and strength to preaching and teaching, as best he is able. He came down last January to be baptized, and so was examined and united with the church here.

A JAPANESE TEMPERANCE SOCIETY.

While Mr. Suzuki was in Uyeda, he told his friends of a Japanese Temperance Society, which had been started in Yokohama, and explained its objects. This so struck the minds of some, that they determined to begin one at Uyeda, and accordingly some months after Mr. Suzuki left, they founded a society with some seven members. These assembled with Mr. Inagaki three times a month, and at these meetings he explained the Bible. Some of these members had heard of Christianity through Chinese Bibles, and other books, and they all soon became intensely interested in studying its truths, and assembled every Sunday, and at other times also, for study and prayer.

WAITING FOR THE WORD.

Hoping that before long some of the missionaries would pass through the place, some of the believers resolved to meet together, and go carefully over one of the Gospels, which had been translated, marking those passages which especially needed explanation, knowing that in this way, they could gain satisfactory knowledge in a short time, from one who might even be hurriedly passing through. One of the women who had heard of these meetings, insisted upon joining them, as she said the study of the Gospels, was something which concerned her, as much as any one. This woman, Mrs. Kojuna, who is a family connection of Mr. Suzuki's sister, has given such remarkable proofs of her faith, that I may be pardoned for mentioning them in this connection.

MRS. KOJUNA.

After Mr. Suzuki left for Yokohama, Mr. Inagaki took his place, and continued to teach his sister, who finally had her eyes opened by the Spirit, to see the truth. When she became interested she spoke to her sister-in-law, who is a widow, and she in turn, spoke to her own sister, Mrs. Kojuna. Mrs. Kojuna, is the mother of a large family, and has had trouble. On some occasions, she would drink to drown her sorrows, not out of the little thimble-like cups of the Japanese, but from one large enough to produce an immediate effect, and cause her not only to forget present trials, but truth itself. Once when she went to hear Mr. Inagaki preach, she was so struck with what she considered a description of her own sin, that she wondered what kind friend had given so a vivid an account of her habits and failings to the preacher. This made her think upon her conduct, and long after, when speaking to Mr. Inagaki, of the possibility of such a person as herself joining the temperance society, he said it would certainly be right to do so, and put her name down on the spot.

JAPANESE POLITENESS.

This took her completely by surprise, as she had no intention of joining, yet with true Japanese ideas of politeness, she did not dare to say anything against it, but went home, feeling that death would be preferable to resigning her saké, since she thought that as her name was pledged it would be impossible to break her word. Before this, she had been accustomed to drink every night, and she said afterwards, that the desire to drink, came upon her very strongly for several nights, but it soon passed away, and she has never broken her pledge.

PRACTICING SELF-DENIAL.

Soon after becoming a believer, she came to Mr. Inagaki, and told him that since she had heard him speak on the text, "Whatsoever ye would that men should do to you, do ye even so to them," she had been thinking of herself, and wanted his advice. She was extravagantly fond of fish, which in Uyeda was something of a rarity, and whenever she had any, she ate it by herself, not even dividing it with her children, and if any was left over from one meal, it was carefully put away for the next. She wished to know if this was right, for if the words of Christ meant that she must give up her fish to others, she did not think she could obey them. Mr. Inagaki told her that the meaning of the words was plain enough, but that she might understand them better, if she pictured to herself what her thoughts would be, if any one should treat her as she treated her family. She saw at once the force of his reasoning, and promised to try to practice the self-denial which seemed so hard to her. In a day or two she came back, her whole face beaming with satisfaction, and declared that never in her life, had she enjoyed her fish so much, as when she had divided it with others; since that time, when she has had it, she has shared it with the whole family. Mrs. Kojima has since visited Yokohama, her object being to bring her sons under the influence of the Gospel. She willingly undertook the journey, fearing that her letters would not induce them to attend the preaching services.

Others beside this woman have given strong proof of their faith and love to our Saviour. Their neighbors bear witness, that there must be something in a religion which can change men and women who have led profligate lives, into steady industrious and loving members of the community.

Some have had persecution to bear, not from the Government, but from their own families. Such a people, as it might be supposed would be eager to hear the Gospel preached, and anxiously would they look for the time when some Missionary would come to them, so that they might receive baptism. One young girl was especially troubled when our visit was delayed beyond the time they had expected us. She was dying and was longing to be baptized. Mr. Inagaki read to her the story of the thief on the cross—the one who was to be with Christ, although unbaptized; and showed her that faith was all that on her part, was needed. She was comforted, and in a few days fell asleep, trusting in her Redeemer.

VISIT OF THE MISSIONARIES.

We had sent word that we would probably be in Uyeda on the 4th or 5th of August, and knew that Mr. Inagaki would have everything in readiness for us. But how great was our surprise and delight to meet a deputation, at a little town five miles from there, consisting of Mr. Inagaki and four young men, who had come to receive us, and who had been waiting ever since morning.

We felt at ease immediately, and were escorted to the pleasant quiet house which had been engaged for us. There we spent ten very delightful days, our comfort marred only by the intense heat. As soon as we arrived, the Christians hastened to welcome us. Mr. Maki, one of the young men who are studying for the ministry, went up with us, to help in teaching, and especially in examining candidates for baptism. This aid was invaluable.

Our preaching sermons began Sunday morning, when all the believers assembled for worship. We then arranged for daily services in the morning and afternoon. It was a very busy time of the year, being the silk season, but all were willing to make an extra effort to come. Mr. Maki had the morning service at about half-past seven o'clock, to which, however, only believers, and those who were very much interested, came. He had an average attendance of twenty persons. I took the afternoon service at five o'clock, to which, from seventy-five to one hundred people came, consisting of believers, and as well of children, and of grown people, curious to see what was going on, and to hear the foreigners preach. The interest in the meetings continued to increase all the time we were there, and some of the faces grew quite familiar from their constant attendance. On examining the candidates for baptism, I asked them what first led them to think of Christianity. Most of them replied that it was the preaching of Mr. Suzuki, or of Mr. Inagaki, while a few had been led to study it from reading the Chinese Bibles, or other books. One man, of middle age, whose son was also baptized, said that a clause in the treaty between America and Japan, executed some eleven years ago, had first called his attention to religion. Whatever may have been the clause, it served, in one instance at least, a higher purpose, than had probably entered into the minds of its makers.

IDEAS OF THE CONVERTS WITH REGARD TO PRIVATE PRAYER.

In teaching them I found that one important subject for some strange reason seemed to have been dropped from their instructions, namely, the uses and duty of private prayer. This was the more singular, as some of them had given very decided proofs of their faith. Some of them, like too many Christians at home, thought that meeting on Sunday, and joining in the prayers of the leaders, was all that was required of them. They joyfully received teachings, however, and promised to follow it. Mrs. Miller had several meetings with the women to teach them hymn-tunes; she also began a prayer-meeting among them, which they have ever since sustained.

A SUNDAY AT UYEDA.

The last Sunday we spent at Uyeda, will not soon be forgotten. I had before spoken on the subject of baptism. So Mr. Maki read the form for the admission of members to the Church, which is used at Yokohama. I then baptized the fifteen who had been previously examined. Most of them were members of the temperance society. Of this number, four were widows past middle age, one a young girl, Mr. Inagaki's sister, and ten were men, two in middle life, and the rest young. Three of the latter were teachers in the Government primary schools in the neighboring villages. One little babe, the daughter of Mr. Inagaki, was baptized, and her name was *Love*.

THE LORD'S SUPPER.

After speaking a few words in explanation of the ordinance of the Lord's supper, I administered it in that far away town, surrounded by those who were hostile or indifferent to that blessed religion we had come to teach. Most of those who had been baptized, had been waiting long to receive that sacrament, and profess before men the faith in their hearts; and they now sat with tearful eyes to receive their first communion from the hands of one whom they had known but a week, and yet whom they loved as in the service with them of a common Lord. Others there were who would have been glad to join us, but had not come forward for examination.

THE FIRST SUNDAY-SCHOOL IN UYEDA.

In the afternoon, the little church commemorated its first communion by opening a Sunday-School with six or seven pupils. On the next Sunday, the number was doubled; and it has now increased to twenty-five. The scholars are interested, and have committed to memory a great part of the Child's Catechism.

FAREWELL MEETING.

I thought to bid them good-bye that night, as we expected to start on the next morning before daylight. But they said they would come to see us once more, no matter how early it was. We hardly expected many to be there; but at three o'clock, we were awakened by the clatterings of their wooden clogs upon the stones. They waited until we had dressed and had breakfast, after which we spent a few minutes in prayer with them, and then left; some of them were moved to tears. It was like departing from home. Not many congregations are there, who would leave their beds before daylight, to say farewell to a pastor whom they had known but ten days. The thirty who had come, included some who were not then believers; but who have since avowed their love to the Saviour, though they have not as yet been baptized. We were comforted in our going, that we were able to leave as an efficient substitute as Mr. Maki. He remained at the urgent request of the people until the end of September.

Mr. Maki and Mr. Inagaki have visited several villages in the vicinity, at which regular meetings are held, and well attended.

THE WORK EVIDENTLY THAT OF THE SPIRIT.

I would not have you think that this work in Uyeda is something unprecedented. It is only an example of what is taking place in different parts of the country. It has come under our own observation, and it is a wonderful illustration of what the Holy Spirit often does in teaching men without the ordinary means of preaching. I am confident that none of those whom I baptized had ever heard a foreigner preach before I went there. There were in Uyeda, but three baptized persons, Inagaki, whom Mr. Ballagh had received in Yokohama; Sakamaki, who had gone to Yeddo in the spring, and who had been baptized by Mr. Thompson; and a blind man, baptized by Dr. Palm at Nugata.

May all those who read of these Japanese believers, have their pure minds stirred up to faith and good works, in the name of Jesus Christ, their Lord and ours.

THE FIRST BAPTISM OF CONVERTS IN JAPAN.

BY
The Rev. G. F. Verbeck, D. D.

THE history of the first baptism in Japan has never before been published. At the time, when the two men to whom it refers were baptized, any public mention or disclosure of their action would have imperilled their own lives, and the lives of their families and friends, and rendered their property liable to confiscation. While for themselves, they would have been willing to undergo death, if such witness-bearing were a necessity, they felt that they had no right to involve their kindred in a like danger. The letter, telling of their belief and their union with the church, has been lying all these years in the Mission Rooms of our church, in New York,—read by only a few.

Dr. Verbeck's narrative begins,

SOWING THE SEED.

"In several of my former letters and reports, mention was made of a company of five men being engaged in searching the Scriptures. These men lived in the capital S―― of the principality of H――, one of the most powerful as well as the most civilized of the Japanese countries, two days' journey from Yokohama. They were long since supplied by me with Bibles, books and tracts from the Chinese mission presses, principally the Presbyterian. As early as 1860, I sent some books to S—— in March; again, in May, 1861, several copies of the New Testament, and Evidences of Christianity. In the Autumn of 1862, one of these men, Ayabe, came to this place, and became a regular inquirer and diligent Bible-reader with me, and at the time I was struck with his honesty and simplicity of heart. It was the same man, who, in the troubles of the Spring of '63, came to me at night, and warned me of the danger to which I and my family were exposed, in our then distant and isolated dwelling. On the 13th of May of that year, and on account of the same disturbances, it will be remembered, we sailed for Shanghai, where we remained during the summer. A few days before our departure, however, I had the pleasure of receiving a large supply of books from the Presbyterian Mission Press at Shanghai, more than one hundred volumes of which, many of them being tracts, I forwarded to my friends at S——. On our return hither from Shanghai, October, '63, I found that my faithful pupil Ayabe, had been recalled to his home, where he had been promoted in office, and that he would not be likely soon, if ever, to return to our town. It seems that in this strange country, the higher a man rises in office, the more are his movements circumscribed, until we reach the Emperor, who is supposed hardly ever to leave his palace grounds. So it appeared as though in the providence of God, I was to be effectually separated from the men in whom so much pains had been bestowed, and on whose behalf we had pleaded so often at the Throne of Grace.

THEIR MESSENGER—A BIBLE CLASS HELD BY PROXY.

But not long afterward they sent a messenger, Motono, a young officer, and vassal servant of one of the company, him-

THE FIRST BAPTISM IN JAPAN.

self an intelligent man, and quite an English scholar. Motono's instructions were to read with me such parts of the New Testament, as they found most difficult fully to understand by themselves, to obtain such new books or tracts as I might from time to time receive, and sometimes to make inquiry on special points of doctrine. This was rather a roundabout way of holding a Bible-class, but the messenger was faithful to his trust. The result has shown that there is no restraint to the Lord, to save by many or by few," and that he can make small and apparently imperfect means do His will, and perform great things.

Matters went on thus for two years and more, my messenger disappearing and reappearing from time to time, carrying good news both ways, yet not perceptibly bringing things to the much desired issue. But my want of hopefulness was to be strikingly reproved, for on the 14th of May of this year, a messenger came to my house to say, that some high officers of the principality H——, had just arrived in town, and desired me to state day and hour for an interview. These men, to my indescribable joy and surprise, proved to be three of the interesting company of five inquirers, mentioned above. They were to visit me in two parties, so I fixed the next day at 2 P. M., for the first, and the same hour two days later, for the second interview.

THE INTERVIEW WITH THE NOBLEMEN.

Accordingly, on the afternoon of the 15th of May, my visitor presented himself with a retinue of about thirty men, consisting of a number of attendant officers, who quite filled my parlor, and of a greater number of common retainers, all two-sworded, who had to content themselves with an outside view of our premises. Among these followers were several men whom I had met and known formerly. My principal visitor proved to be no less a personage than a relative of the Prince of H———. He was a tall man, of commanding appearance, a little lame of one foot, or rather hip. He had an intelligent, but somewhat stern cast of features, like a man accustomed to deep serious thought, yet he conversed quite pleasantly. After the usual introductory compliments, the absorbing topic of the "doctrine" was entered upon, with a good deal of interest. I may say that I reasoned with him of "righteousness, temperance and judgment to come," but I could hardly bring him and his attendants to dwell on the higher topics of faith, hope and love; for my august visitor insisted on reasoning concerning the unprofitable subjects of the origin of evil in the world, the mysterious permission of the continuance of evil, the justice of God, or the apparent want of it, under various aspects, and more of the like. I was prepared for his arguments, as I have found that, on heathen ground, we are often obliged to rehandle the bones of contention of the church of old, but my principal endeavor was to get him to see and feel, the wickedness and danger of all evil; that it is infinitely more important to know how to be now and forever saved from it, than to know all about its origin, and yet be left helpless; that it is vastly more worthy of our thought, to know how we are to escape hell and gain heaven, than to find out the exact locality of either, if such a thing were possible. Yet my efforts to lead him to higher views, at the time were vain, as he constantly returned to his favorite topics, and the afternoon passed away without any immediate result for good, which the eye of man could see. We also had a satisfactory conversation on the most approved methods of education of the young, upon which he had evidently bestowed much thought, and on the whole I brought him so far, as to agree to the truth and justice of my positions, while the only way left him to express his determined dissent on the question of evil was a doubting shake of the head. He had made up his mind, I think, beforehand,

that for him the convenient season had not yet come. But we
parted as good friends. I have strong hopes that the Spirit
may yet bring savingly home to his heart, the truth which so
far had impressed only his intellect.

THE SECOND INTERVIEW.

The interview of the other parties was arranged to take
place on the 17th of May. My visitors on this occasion were

WAKASEI. THE FIRST BAPTIZED BELIEVER IN JAPAN.

WAKASA, one of the ministers of state, or governors of the
principality H———, and his younger brother, AYABE. WAKASA
was a tall man, about forty-five years of age, and looking older.
His is one of those faces that make sunshine in a shady place,
most pleasing and amiable in expression, with a very dignified
bearing. His eyes beamed love and pleasure as I met him.

He said he had long known me in his mind, had long desired to see and converse with me, and that he was very happy that now, in God's Providence, he was permitted to do so. His visit, and that of his brother, were in a manner accidental, as he had unexpectedly obtained leave from the Prince to visit a relative near this town.

At this time there were admitted to our parlor, WAKASA, AYABE, WAKASA's two sons, young men of twenty and twenty-two, respectively, and the servant, MOTONO, who had acted the part of messenger between us for four years. How different was this meeting, from that of two days before. These men, like those of Berea, in the Apostles' time, had received the Word, with all readiness of mind, and did not come to puzzle themselves or me, with unprofitable controversies, but asked several quite natural and sensible questions, to gain additional light on some points in reference, principally, to Christian characters and customs. They had been taught of the Spirit.

They showed great familiarity with their Bibles, made several, pertinent quotations, and when, during the conversation, I referred them to sacred passages, they readily identified them, and always accepted them as conclusive proofs. They were prepared to believe all that Jesus said, and to do all that He required.

It must be remembered that these men had been studying the Scriptures, and reading a great variety of religious books, with great diligence, for at least four years, having begun to do so with a favorable disposition of mind. Like perhaps most of the higher classes in this country, they had no faith in Buddhism, the religion of the common people, while at the same time, they were graciously withheld from falling into the opposite of a total atheism. Their minds were in a state of expectant transition, when, just in time, they were led to search for, and find salvation through faith in Christ.

THEIR EXPERIENCE.

Their experience had been thorough. They felt their sins to be grievous, and realized the need of a Saviour from sin, and the curse of sin. They were convinced of the inefficiency of all other systems, which thus far had come to their knowledge, and they joyfully received Christ as all sufficient for time and eternity.

THEY ASK FOR BAPTISM.

We spent a delightful afternoon, in conversing on the saving power and love of Christ, and just as I thought my friends were about to leave me, WAKASA took me by surprise, by inquiring, if I would object to baptize him and his brother AYABE, before they left town. I was surprised, because so many Japanese had, at different times, talked to me of the great peril of becoming Christians in the full sense of the word. I had expected from these men to hear something as follows: "We believe, and would like to be baptized; but we cannot think of realizing our wish, in this one particular, so long as the law of the land, hangs the inevitable sword over the heads of all who dare to change their religion; for the present, we must remain as we are, but when this cruel edict is repealed, we will come forward for baptism."

I had been thoughtless that afternoon, too, in that, while we had spoken of baptism, I had not urged them, as I should have done. So that I felt, as one who, having prayed only for a part, suddenly should receive the whole, of his ardent wishes.

I warned my visitors not to think lightly of the act, and not to entertain superstitious notions concerning its efficacy. I urged the solemn importance of the sacrament, and the great obligations which devolve on those to whom it is administered; I repeated to them the questions which, according to our form, they would have to answer with a hearty affirmative; and finally, told them to decide, as if in the presence of God, who searches the heart.

They listened attentively, and repeated their desire to be baptized, requesting only that it should be done and kept in secrecy. About this they were anxious, even asking that it should not be reported even in America, lest the news should return to Japan, and endanger their own, and their families, lives. I agreed to this, and we fixed the day for the solemn rite.

THE DAY OF PENTECOST.

The following Lord's Day, the Day of Pentecost, was chosen, the hour selected being 7 o'clock, P. M. WAKASA, whose position did not permit him to move about the streets, without a half-dozen followers, and who could not visit me, without making himself conspicuous. I did not see him again until the appointed hour on Sunday night. But AYABE came to me twice, during the intervening days, and I gave him such instructions for himself and his brother, as I thought might be useful to them.

THE BAPTISMAL CEREMONY.

At last, when the Sabbath evening came, the two candidates presented themselves, attended into the room by none but MOTONO. The retinue, consisting of eight followers, was dismissed at our door, with orders to return in an hour. I had arranged everything beforehand, to avoid unnecessary detention. The shutters were closed, the lamps lit, a white cloth spread on the centre-table, a large, cut-glass fruit dish, for want of anything better, prepared to serve as a font. Besides MOTONO, my wife was the only witness present, so that there were but five persons in the room. I began by reading Matthew 28th, then dwelt on the concluding verses, spoke of the purpose of missionary societies, and referred to the bearing of the words of Jesus, upon our present meeting. I exhorted them not to be discouraged in their peculiarly difficult situation, but rather by a life of faith, of love, and of holiness, to disarm all the criticisms of their neighbors, and even persecution itself. We then united in prayer, both in English and Japanese, proceeded with our liturgy, translating extempore, the form for baptism, and after the administration of the sacrament, concluded with prayer and thanksgiving. It was indeed a sacred hour. I deeply felt the great privilege the Lord had vouchsafed in allowing me, a weak, unworthy servant, to be instrumental in leading these dear brethren to the Saviour; and in introducing them to the church of God. After the conclusion of our happy meeting, WAKASA said, with cheerful calmness, "Now I have that which since long I have heartily wished for."

BREAD UPON THE WATERS.

Then he told us, how twelve years before, a little book, in English, had been found by some natives, floating in the bay of Nagasaki, probably lost overboard, from one of the earliest American or English ships that visited Japan, about 1854. This book fell into his hands, and he was anxious to find out what it contained, but all he could then learn about it was, that it was different from any other book, that had hitherto been brought to Japan, and that it treated of God and Jesus Christ. In fact, it was a New Testament. He did not rest, till at last he found a Chinese translation of it, five or six years ago.

Then he began diligently to read the Word, and induced four others to do the same, among them AYABE, MOTONO, and the nobleman who came to me first. Then followed the visits of AYABE and MOTONO, to this place, their attendance, and instruction, and the final sequel.

This took place May 20th, 1866.

NAGASAKI AND THE GIRLS' SCHOOL.

NAGASAKI, on the island of Kiushin, is said to possess one of the finest harbors in the world. Sir Rutherford Alcock, in his interesting work, *The Capital of the Tycoon,* speaks with enthusiasm of its beautiful land-locked bay, where, however wild the gale outside, the breeze but ruffles the water gently, and touches the waves with a white feather-edge of foam. The first aspect of the bay, recalled to his mind, the picturesque fiords of Norway, and also the loveliness of some of the Swiss lakes. The hills rise boldly from the water's verge, clothed with pine. But all along the paths as one walks for the first time, the eye is captivated by the palm and bamboo, the pomegranate and persimmon. "The gardinia and camellia flourish too, and everywhere our common ferns may be seen, and ivy covering the walls, while by the roadside the thistle is not wanting, to confound all geographical divisions into floral zones."

Rev. Henry Stout, writing of it to one of our secretaries, says:

"It seems almost as if designed by nature, as a place to which men might retire, and dream away a life of easy content. The placid harbor, except in typhoons, is scarcely stirred by a ripple. The city occupies the only spot on the shores, available for a city, and having just filled the level space seems not impatient to extend its bounds. The people have settled down into quiet going ways, and business is carried on as though time and tide would be pleased to wait."

The town of Nagasaki has a population of thirty-three thousand, and the island on which it is built, contains several millions. There are three mission-stations, and three missionary families are resident there. The fact that it was once overswept by the Romanists, has added to the difficulty of winning attention to the truth. Woman's work, has, owing to peculiar circumstances, never been fairly entered upon. Mrs. Stout, at one time, gathered a number of girls and taught them English and sewing, but so soon as it was found that she was teaching them also the religion of Jesus, her pupils were taken away. The desire of the Woman's Board, and the urgent wishes of those on the ground, alike point now to the establishment, in Nagasaki, of a School for Girls, similar to the Ferris Seminary at Yokohama. Thus, opposite each other, at a distance of eight hundred miles, would stand these two beacons, diffusing the light of truth. From their friendly flame, how many household lamps would be lighted in the Island Empire.

During our Centennial year, we sought to raise the sum of $5,000, for this object, and though we have not yet obtained the whole amount, we confidently expect to raise it soon. This sum would cover the expense of a building, and the cost of sending out and supporting two teachers for one year. The money sent to our Treasurer, for this special object, has been kept in a separate fund, and at the issuing of our Third Annual Report, April 30, 1877, it amounted to $2,578.00.

We are now endeavoring to secure teachers, who will go with glad hearts, to engage in this labor of love. We are advised to defer the beginning of our building, until the proper persons shall be found to enter on the work of instruction. Several responses are now under consideration, and ere long the desired result may be obtained.

Remembering the associations of Nagasaki with Holland, the long years during which Dutch merchants, with patient tenacity, endured exile there, for the sake of commercial interests, is it too much now, to expect that the children of the Reformed church in America, shall aid the present plan? The stubborn hostility of the people to our faith seems to be yielding. The door is open. The Rev. Henry Stout pleads earnestly the necessity of at once doing something in the cause of female education. Without abating our zeal or our liberality in other directions, let us bend our energies, toward beginning the needed Girls' School and Home here.

THE JAPANESE EMBASSY TO AMERICA

ON the establishment of diplomatic relations between Japan and the United States, Mr. Arinori Mori was sent to represent his government at Washington. He applied himself with great diligence and with a statesman's sagacity, to the study of our form of government, to the working of our institutions; the nature of our educational system; and in short, all the constituents of our national life and prosperity. The farther his observations were extended, the deeper grew his desire to have an Embassy Extraordinary sent from Japan to this country, to examine everything here worthy of their attention; and to make a report which might exert its due influence over all the factions and parties then existing in his native land. Due arrangements and preparations having been made, and a complete understanding established, the Embassy at length arrived by way of San Francisco, early in the year 1872. It is quite beside our purpose to write its history. It had in view three grand objects: To examine our Christian civilization in all its combining elements, to scrutinize industrial arts, to make note of the processes of education, and in general, learn what they might commend to the attention of the Imperial Government at home.

Circumstances brought this Embassy into close relations with many prominent and philanthropic members of the

Reformed Church. Its missionaries, Messrs Brown, Verbeck and Simmons, had been the first to enter Japan.

After the treaty secured by Mr. Townsend Harris, the Hon. Robert H. Pruyn of Albany, had been despatched as the first American Minister Plenipotentiary to Yeddo, (now styled Tōkiō), to carry its provisions into effect. Many of the young men of Japan had also been sent to this country, to be educated under the supervision of the authorities of this church. Among these were two sons of Tomomi Iwakura, the head of the Embassy Extraordinary, who were in Rutger's College, N. J., at the time when their distinguished father arrived.

Another circumstance had contributed to beget the special confidence of this embassy, not only in our Foreign Board, but in some of its most liberal supporters. During the progress of the Revolution which had raged in Japan, between the Mikado and certain powerful Daimios, it had been impossible to send funds to this country, for the expenses of the Japanese youth, who were receiving their education in various schools. The amount necessary to defray these expenses had been cheerfully and liberally advanced by certain members of the Reformed Church, and this generous conduct on their part called forth the gratitude of the Embassy, and awakened a desire to see some of the benefactors of their young countrymen. The sums advanced were repaid, but the kindness was not forgotten.

During the stay of the Embassy in New York City, every attention proper was shown it, not only by the civic authorities, but also by persons in private station. Among those who had aided the young Japanese was the late Mr. Jonathan Sturges, a Christian merchant, who rejoiced in unostentatious benevolence. His large and long acquaintance with all the institutions of the city, and his liberal courtesy enabled him to render particular service to our Japanese visitors. He conducted them to many places of interest, explained to their quick comprehension, the character of our schools of learning, art and science, and showed them our factories and bazaars. They were very specially interested in noticing the many industrial spheres open to women in our land, and expressed both amazement and pleasure, as they observed their various employments.

Mrs. Thomas C. Doremus was also unwearied in her attentions, and devoted herself with her wonted zeal and energy, to an exposition positive and practical, of the importance of female education. She accompanied Mr. Tanaki, the Japanese envoy on education, with others, to the New York Normal College, where they saw fourteen hundred young ladies preparing to become teachers to the Deaf and Dumb, and Blind Asylums, and the Bible House. They manifested acute intelligence, were interested in everything, and the fruits of their new ideas were seen when they returned home. It is impossible to tell how much the influence of this noble woman may, through this Embassy, have contributed toward the elevation and higher education of our sex in Japan.

The events to which this allusion has been made had their direct Providential bearings, on the work of Evangelization in the Empire of the Rising Sun. As year after year shall augment the power of the Gospel there, the services of those who gave a Christian greeting of the Embassy of 1872, during its visit to our continent, will continue to be vital and imperishable.

WOMEN AS MISSIONARIES.

BY

Rev. Elbert S. Porter, D. D.

THAT Christianity is divine in origin, method and purpose is proved by its fruits. To the vast systems of superstitions, which have fastened themselves, through ages of ever increasing darkness upon many millions, it opposes the purity of truth, the wisdom of God, and the sufficiency of Almighty love. Beginning at Jerusalem in apparent obscurity and weakness, it rapidly overran the Roman Empire, and planted the cross on the ruins of ancient idolatry. For its extension it was indebted neither to the power of arms, nor to the patronage of the great. At first, its chief advocates were the poor and the unlearned. "God chose the weak things of the world, to confound the mighty." The wise, the prudent and the proud contemned, but the weakness of divine grace prevailed. The distinctive force of the Christian movement displayed itself from the start, in developing the characters of individuals, through the operation of a new life from above; and next in reconstructing the domestic and social order. Woman, found in Christ her restorer. The mighty miracle of the incarnation, placed upon her head a glory, which no earthly diadem could confer. Saluted by angels, and remembered by tender affection upon the cross, Mary, the mother of our Lord, became the type of that long and illustrious line of saintly women, which, in unbroken succession, has contributed to fill earth with praise, and Heaven with rejoicing.

The Miriams and Hannahs, the Deborahs and the Ruths, of the elder dispensation,—with all their unnamed sisters, in the theocratic church,—had indeed set forth, in clear demonstration, that the religion which came from God, was the especial protector and helper of woman, as the co-partner of man, in evolving the deep and mysterious problems of human life. The expectation, that the Messiah would be born of a virgin, gave to the daughters of Israel, an assurance, that in some way the glory of womanhood would be attained, through the strong and divine Deliverer. While, indeed, our Lord did not call women into the apostolic college, nevertheless He welcomed, and by His divine benignity and grace, consecrated, the services of their faith. Nor do we find in the early church, as vivified by the Holy Ghost, any disposition to exclude women from its sacred privileges. There was neither male nor female in Christ, who came to bless and save all believing in His name. It was a woman who broke the alabaster box, and anointed the body of our Lord, with grateful anticipative faith, for its burial. The memorial of her devotion has been made a perpetual example. Devout women, proof against despair, and confident that He, in whom they had trusted, would verify His promise, took the light of the earliest dawn, to find their way to the sepulchre, and it was to one of these that Christ first announced His resurrection. Afterward, in the early struggles and conflicts of the rising church, women were closely associated with the apostles, in works of faith and love. Many of their names, fragrant and precious, are immortalized for all time in the inspired epistles.

Among the inscriptions of the catacombs, are seen, in great numbers, the records of woman's faith, patience and self-sacrifice. She shared in all the horrors of successive fiery persecutions, and often attained the ecstacy and the glory of martyrdom. Of such women the world was not worthy. They ministered to the saints; they kept unbroken vows; they taught their children to be loyal to Christ; they encouraged the timid and the temporizing, and if their names do not appear in classic annals, nevertheless they are recorded in the Lamb's Book of Life. Their quiet deeds have entered into the processes of the world's uplifting, from beneath its sorrows and its burdens.

The history of the conversion of the Gentiles is closely inwrought with the lives of pious women. It could not have been otherwise. The condition of woman at all times, in all places, and under all skies, is the index and measure of the actual civilization or degradation of mankind. No substantial progress is possible, where she is degraded, despised, or left, to wander in uncertain gloom. She is the educator of the race; the fountain of power or of weakness. Mohammedanism, Brahminism, Buddhism, Shintōism, no less than the classic Heathenism, of ancient Greece and Rome, deny to woman her proper rank and place. They divest her of natural, social, domestic and personal rights. They enslave her, and reap in return, the bitter fruits of her cruel servitude. The depression of women, the wide world round, is accompanied by the forfeiture of the sweetest affections, the most sacred joys, and the purest aims. Natural strength, which grows out of well-ordered homes, is but a varnished delusion, where woman's right to be the equal of man, is rudely, ignorantly or barbarously, withheld.

It is well to remember all this, when, considering the character and claims of missionary work. It would be pleasant, and perhaps profitable, did space allow, to trace here, in rapid outline, some of the ever illustrious services, rendered by Christian women, to the early and the later progress of the church. Their missionary zeal is eminently worthy of our imitation. Their names compose a galaxy, shining above the stars in splendor, over the long succession of Christian centuries. The Helenas, the Agneses, the Berthas of Greek, Gothic and English story, illuminated the sombre firmaments in which they shone. France had her Margaret of Navarre, and England her Countess of Huntingdon, in days of spiritual declension. When the pure and saintly Fenelon aimed to purify the religion of his countrymen, he found in the high and rapt devotion of Madam Guyon, an instructor and counselor. These, however, are but hurried glintings, drawn from a large horizon, filled with luminaries, and reveal with grand and eloquent testimony, the place and power of woman, in the diffusive system of Evangelical grace.

The modern missionary work of the Church at large, in all its branches, Papal and Protestant, has been carried forward by the immense, unwearied, and manifold exertions of pious and devout women. The history of Protestant missions has no brighter pages than those which record the daring adventures and hopeful undertakings of a multitude of women, who, as wives or helpers, or teachers or readers, have gone to the uttermost parts of the earth to instruct their heathen sisters. With the memoirs of some of these noble women, the literature of the age has been enriched, and their examples have shed a benign light, in which a multitude are walking with heroic faith. Such women as the Judsons, Ann H. and Sarah, Mrs. Catherine H. Scudder, Mrs. Winslow, Mrs. Comstock, Mrs. White, Mrs. Simpson, who perilled their lives, and lost to gain them in the high places of the field, are not dead, but yet speak to their Christian sisters in America.

Their work done in India, Africa, Asia Minor, Burmah, has been like the handful of corn on the top of the mountains, which in our day is seen to wave with the stately majesty of the cedars of Lebanon. There is, however, a goodly number of consecrated women, sustaining by their presence, their prayers, their labors and their sympathies, many foreign missions now existing on the face of the globe, and whose toils and sacrifices are like, or similar to those endured by those who have already gone up on high, to behold the gathering of the sheaves from the fields wherein they had sown with tears, the incorruptible seed of the kingdom.

It would, however, be singularly unjust in this survey of woman's work, to confine our attention exclusively to the foreign field. For over the entire domain of this imperial Republic of the West, where the interests of the future church, are, to a great degree, concentered, we may see the toils and the spoils of female faith. Not only have the advancing borders of new settlements enlisted the zeal of Christian women for the enlargement of the kingdom, but in all the more established portions of the American church, there have been, all along, honorable women not a few, who have kept alive in their respective places, the flame of the missionary spirit. They have organized assisting societies, raised money, diffused information, prepared garments and done what they could to support, encourage and sustain missionaries, at home and abroad.

To a great extent, the educational force in our country has been left to the peculiar genius and aptitudes of women. In literature, in schools and academies, in several of the arts and professions, they have been called to high, noble and arduous services. And to this we are sure is owing the special type of Christian culture which has taken possession of our entire scheme of republican civilization. Here woman has an almost unbounded field for the exertion of her best powers, and the putting forth of most salutary influence. The songs of the troubadours, the legends of knight errantry, the wild romances of feudal days, the tragic stories of dynastic intrigues have passed, and we have in their stead the heroic examples of Caroline Fry, Florence Nightingale, Miss Coutts in England and the biographies of American women, like Mrs. Isabella Graham and Mrs. Thomas C. Doremus and others who have converted the forms of Christian charity into sublime epics, wherein may be found the regnant charms of every Christian grace. The very ideas which once exalted woman as the object of sentimental idolatry, are buried beneath the floods of admiration which are now rising and gathering from every land in praise of her deeds done in charity for Christ's sake.

In that glorious church of the future which is yet to

spring and rise into transcendent power and spiritual beauty, women will share especial honors as aids and helpers in every good work. This is evident from what they are now doing, in and through the many beneficent organizations which they are conducting without weariness, for the benefit of our fallen race. There are but few active charities in our day that are not more or less dependent upon female sympathy and support. We do not find in this condition of affairs any evidence that Christianity is lacking in robust vigor. It challenges our admiration and confidence the rather, because it has a place for woman as the helpmeet of man in all the supreme concerns of human life as they are affected by the redemption that is in Christ.

There is in woman's nature that quick sympathy with suffering, that instinctive hatred of wrong, that intuitive sense of benevolence, which, when sanctified and brought under the control of the truth as it is in Jesus, qualify her for a species of service in the church which man is unable to render. She needs his aggressive energy; he needs her acute, but gentler and more patient spirit. Together, they form that co-partnership of labor, by which, through assisting grace, the whole world shall yet be made to rejoice in the advent of the long desired day.

Among recent organizations, the Woman's Board of Missions of the Reformed Church, has already justified its right to be, and has given proof of intentions to render effective aid in the great work of publishing the gospel in foreign parts. Of its particular aims or operations thus far, it is not needful that anything should be said here, inasmuch as they are stated and elucidated in official documents, easy of access. Still I cannot withhold the expression of my belief that this association of Christian women in our Reformed Church is sure to awaken a new spirit of missionary zeal among us. When auxiliaries shall have been formed, in each particular congregation, the result will be a cohesiveness of purpose which first of all is much to be desired, and in the next place a combination of effort which cannot possibly fail to increase resources for the prosecution of the work in hand. Method is power. It utilizes atoms and co-ordinates them into solid force, and impressive momentum. Auxiliary bands in our several churches, acting under and with a central Board may bring all the tithes into the store house, and prepare the way for copious blessings of spiritual favor.

When it is remembered that modern missions, are yet in their infancy, and that the world at large, within the present century, has been fairly opened to the light of the Gospel, it is impossible to conjecture how rapidly that light may be made to spread, when once the whole church, in all its parts, has been aroused to discern its opportunity and its duty. The old is ready to vanish away. Distant nations show a growing discontent with their incapable gods. They are looking to the Christian powers, for instruction and sympathy. Ethiopia is stretching forth its hands in supplication. Sinim gropes blindly toward the dawn; Hindooism wanes; Japan is waiting for the eyelids of the morning to be uplifted upon her, and all along the seats of ancient Mediterranean Empire, change and revolution, turnings and overturnings, are preparing a highway for the Lord. When the field is thus white, the reapers may enter with glad alacrity. The fullness of the time has come for large increasing, generous endeavors, to plant the standard of the Cross, on every continent and on every island. The angel flying in the midst of Heaven, with the everlasting Gospel, is sounding the charge of battle and of victory.

There is then every inducement held out before the Christian women of our connection, to join hearts and hands, prayers and labors, for the furtherance of the Gospel "in regions beyond." Enlargement will come to their own souls, thereby. They will read and speak and write of the glory of the kingdom, and to this end will gather information from all sources, concerning the mighty operations of the sceptred Messiah.

Intrinsically it is the most worthy and comprehensive work to which woman's love and woman's faith can be devoted. It has in view a supreme object. It is glorified by the most illustrious characters that shine along the troubled ways of history. It has, for its leader and director, one, who though He was rich, became poor, to pour through the channels of His sorrows, an unspeakable wealth of joy, upon a long groaning creation. It has for its propulsion, the noblest love that can swell a human heart—the constraining love of Christ. For the earnest prosecution of this work, the most piteous appeals come up from the Zenanas, the Harems, the slave herds of heathendom, from women, who can find deliverance only through the intervention of Christian helpers. Well may the happy and honored mothers, the cultivated and queenly girls of our land, with all privileges to exalt them, and all favors to crown them, bethink themselves of the claims of their wretched sisters, in lands where superstitions dire, yet lift their horrid and monstrous forms. If the giving of a cup of cold water, in the name of the Master, to one of the least of his suffering creatures, shall not fail of its reward, how much more shall they do, who, by their prayers, and alms, and sympathies, may aid in restoring lost nations to the knowledge of God? Oh, mothers and daughters of Zion! get ye up into the high mountain and behold, how the uttermost parts of the earth, are waiting for the light, which is to rise upon them in golden splendor, when the ransomed church is ready to make known to them, the unsearchable riches of the Gospel!

ARIZONA.

URING the winter of 1876–'77, an appeal was made through Mrs. E. T. Martin, of Auburn, from the agent in Arizona, for aid for the tribes of Indians in that country, who had been placed under the care of the Reformed Church, by our Government.

The appeal was promptly and liberally responded to, by nearly all of the auxiliary societies connected with the Woman's Board, and a large box of much needed goods, was forwarded to these tribes. The money given amounted to $210. The gifts consisted of woolen shawls, flannels, unbleached muslin, calico, thread, needles, illustrated Scripture cards, etc. The Pimas, Maricopas, and Papagoes, to whom the donations were sent, are peaceful and civilized, desiring schools and teachers for their children, and anxious to learn the arts of civilized life. They are calling upon us for instruction, and petition that men and women be sent to teach and direct them. The Synod's Board, for two or three years, paid $600 to Mrs. Stout, the wife of the agent, on condition that she should teach when she could.

The field is open, and we could do a great deal, had we a Mission there, and money to pay men and women to work. Till we Christianize the Indians, they must always be a trouble and a terror, but experience has demonstrated that they can become law-abiding citizens, if only they are brought to Christ.

www.ingramcontent.com/pod-product-compliance
Lightning Source LLC
Chambersburg PA
CBHW030316240426
43673CB00040B/1188